TONY RYAN

Ireland's Aviator

[illegible],
Good to finally meet you.
Hope you Enjoy the book
Regards, [illegible] Ryan

The Author

Richard Aldous holds the Eugene Meyer Chair at Bard College, New York, having previously taught for fifteen years at UCD. He is the bestselling author of numerous books, including *Great Irish Speeches*, *Reagan and Thatcher* and *The Lion and the Unicorn: Gladstone vs. Disraeli.*

TONY RYAN

Ireland's Aviator

RICHARD ALDOUS

Gill & Macmillan

Gill & Macmillan
Hume Avenue, Park West, Dublin 12
www.gillmacmillanbooks.ie

978 07171 6552 0

Index compiled by Eileen O'Neill
Typography design by Make Communication
Print origination by Carole Lynch
Printed and bound by CPI Group (UK) Ltd,
Croydon, CR0 4YY

This book is typeset in Linotype Minion and
Neue Helvetica.

The paper used in this book comes from the wood
pulp of managed forests. For every tree felled, at
least one tree is planted, thereby renewing natural
resources.

A CIP catalogue record for this book is available
from the British Library.

5 4 3 2

CONTENTS

FOREWORD

Perhaps in Tony's mind he felt like George Orwell, who said, 'Autobiography is only to be trusted when it reveals something disgraceful. A man who gives a good account of himself is probably lying, since any life when viewed from the inside is simply a series of defeats.'

Really I wish this book could have been penned by Tony, perhaps with Richard's guidance. This is particularly true because he was such a great writer of letters and an avid reader of books. He did have a couple of conversations with a publisher, but nothing was ever concluded. We also talked on his sickbed about the completion of his story, and he was particularly focused on making sure that (to use his exact language) 'some of the wankers' in his life got a special mention.

Our hope with this biography is that the story reflects the truth, humour and determination of his life, because that's the kind of guy he was. This is the story of a single-minded young man from Tipperary who went on to be one of Ireland's greatest entrepreneurs. With the significant economic crisis that faces Ireland and the rest of the world today, what we all need more than ever is a story such as Tony's to illustrate the fact that Irish people can still be world leaders in business.

I think regularly about what Tony would have done in the current crisis. What I know for certain is that it wouldn't be standing still or lamenting our mistakes. That determination never to give up is the real lesson of this story.

Declan Ryan

Chapter 1

IT'S A LONG WAY FROM TIPPERARY

Lyons Demesne, Co. Kildare, Sunday 14 October 2007

Everyone, including the man himself, had been determined that this day would not be a gloomy occasion. No expense or effort had been spared, and the weather, never the most reliable aspect of Irish life, had also more than done its bit. Under a bright autumnal sky, family, friends and admirers gathered at Tony Ryan's country estate to say farewell. The setting was magnificent and one to which Tony had given so much of the later part of his life. When he took over the house a decade earlier it was in a state of decrepitude. Now lovingly and meticulously restored, it stood once again as a masterpiece of Georgian Ireland.

On the lawn beside the formal gardens, replanted by Tony to the original design, the hundreds invited to this memorial service stood reminiscing. Childhood friends mixed with the titans of Irish business, including Tony's exact contemporaries Michael Smurfit and Tony O'Reilly, and his protégé, the telecoms billionaire Denis O'Brien.

As guests moved towards the lake for the service, there came roaring low and fast over Lyons a spectacular flypast, led by a new Boeing 737 jet aircraft flying under the flag of the airline Tony had founded in 1985 and that bore his name—Ryanair—accompanied by a Challenger jet and a restored Stearman biplane. 'Mourners were left agog,' reported the *Irish Times*, 'no doubt just as Ryan would have wanted.'

The lakeside service, held not far from the Clonaghlis graveyard at the edge of the Lyons estate where Tony had been buried, was characterised by warmth and humour. Tony's middle son, Declan, spoke movingly about his father. The eldest, Cathal, who himself would sadly pass away from rapid-onset cancer just months afterwards, perfectly imitated their father's Tipperary accent. Shane, the youngest, read one of Tony's own poems.

Among the eulogies was one from Michael O'Leary, another of Tony's protégés and by now the high-profile chief executive of Ryanair. The relationship between the two had been both close and highly combustible. Yet whatever their tussles—and they were legend—O'Leary was, says Declan Ryan, 'like family'. Perhaps the most touching signal of O'Leary's respect that day was that, for the first time in as long as anyone could remember, he was wearing a tie.

O'Leary's eulogy proclaimed Tony a 'visionary' and 'one of the great Irishmen of the twentieth century'. Here, he said, was a man who had lived up to Tony's father's often-repeated aphorism that 'it is better to wear away than rust away.'

Not that Tony was without his faults and even his failures: 'Tony Ryan wasn't perfect; he wasn't always right,' O'Leary reminded everyone. 'Tipperary is not the centre of the universe.'

It was a funny line and one that poked gentle fun at Tony's fierce and vocal pride in his native county. Yet, as O'Leary well knew, the one-liner was only half right.

Certainly part of the Tony Ryan story is the rise of a lad born in a backwater of an impoverished country that was itself on the periphery of Europe. Indeed, many would have said that Tony was a boy from nowhere; the man himself would have said that he was in fact a boy from somewhere. But, crucially, that 'somewhere' was also the junction to somewhere else.

———

Limerick Junction in Co. Tipperary may have been not much more than a small village, but it was famous throughout Ireland and beyond. It was here that the Dublin–Cork and Limerick–Waterford railway lines crossed at an angle of 90 degrees. That gave it the sense of a place from where you could quite literally go places. The station was famous everywhere, says Albert Maher in *Signalman's Memories*, as 'the most extraordinary railway junction in the world.' Its unique layout comprised a long island platform with a range of bays and intricate points and switches. Trains arriving from any direction had to run clear of the station before making all kinds of complicated 'reversings' in order to get to a platform.

The train coming from Waterford would begin this process at Keane's Points, where, on 2 February 1936, Thomas Anthony Ryan was born in the small railway cottage beside the signal box during the worst snowstorm that anyone could remember that century. With no cot in the house, he was tucked in the top drawer of a chest of drawers, which soon led to a long-standing family joke that he had been 'top drawer' from the beginning.

Tony was the first child of Martin and Elizabeth ('Lily') Ryan, who had married the previous year. The couple had met in the station restaurant in Mallow, Co. Cork, where Lily worked as a waitress. They shared a love of amateur dramatics, and in 1932 they had played alongside each other in a production of T. C. Murray's melodrama *Autumn Fire*, put on by the Railway Men's Dramatic Society of Limerick Junction. Later on, young Tony and his siblings—Catherine, Simon, Mary and Kell—would all be taught to recite by heart passages from Shakespeare, particularly Lily's favourite, *The Merchant of Venice*.

Martin Ryan was a Tipperary man from Solloghodbeg, near Limerick Junction. He was listed as being ten years old in the 1911 census, which also recorded his ability to read and write. When Tony was born, his father was a fireman on the railway, working out of Limerick Junction. He was a well-built, athletic man who played Gaelic football and hurling, winning the cup three years running for the local football team. Although he was a heavy smoker (Player's Navy Cut, because the sailor on the packet was often said to be modelled on Charles Stewart Parnell), Martin placed a strong emphasis on clean living. Sports were encouraged. There were frequent trips by train to the coast for long walks. He was a teetotaller and a member of the Pioneer Total Abstinence Association. 'The only bottle that would have been in the house contained holy water,' Simon Ryan recalled.

In photographs Martin always appeared smart and dapper. It left an impression on his children. Kell Ryan recalled that his father would only ever wear his work overalls once before putting them to be washed, which ensured that each day he left the house looking clean and pressed. It was a characteristic he passed on to his children, not least to Tony, who always took great pride in his appearance and later developed a taste for expensive handmade suits. In family photographs of the 1930s and 40s, whether informal or studio photographs for Confirmations and First Communions, the Ryans always looked well turned out. 'We may have been poor,' Simon remembered, 'but we never looked poor.'

Later, Tony would express frustration at self-made men who, like Dickens's Mr Bounderby, loudly proclaim the depth of their childhood poverty. It was never a line that interested him. When pushed on the subject, he would briskly reply, 'We were a very wealthy family even if we did not have any money.' It was an attitude typical of the 'respectable' working class. Martin was industrious and keen to get on, and his immaculately laundered overalls and the boots 'spit and polished' to a gleam signalled an attitude to life, not just personal cleanliness.

Although the Ryan household was staunchly 'Tipp', the matriarch at its centre was in fact a Cork girl. Lily's father had been the head gamekeeper in Longueville House, near Mallow. The family lived in the gate lodge until her father's early death, when they moved back into the town. Later the Ryan children would spend the summers with their grandmother in Mallow, which was handily placed on the Dublin–Cork main line and allowed the family to take advantage of the cheap rail fares that were a perk of Martin's job.

Lily remained a proud Corkwoman throughout her life. She was unafraid to stoke the traditional hurling rivalry between her home county and her new Tipp family. Simon recalled that she kept two garden gnomes at the front of the house, one painted red and white, which she called 'Christy', after the great Cork hurler Christy Ring, and another in blue and gold, called 'Mickie', after Tipperary's Mickie 'the Rattler' Byrne, who lived nearby. 'If Tipp had won, Mickie Byrne would make a point of walking past the house and slagging my mother about Christy,' Simon remembered, 'but if Tipp weren't winning, or if Cork were, he'd be sure to choose an alternative route to avoid the gnomes.'

Lily could be formidable too. Kell even recalled her hitting his father over the head with a frying pan after a prank went wrong. This strong woman also had a quick and enquiring mind. She was an enthusiastic reader, mostly of Irish biographies, and devoured the *Irish Press* each day. Her politics, like Martin's, were straight up and down Fianna Fáil: Éamon de Valera was venerated; the *Irish Independent* was not allowed in the house. Lily would speak with great bitterness about the burning of Mallow in 1920. 'If we were watching "Gone with the Wind",' Kell recalled, 'the big scene with the burning of the plantation, she'd say, "That was Mallow. You should have seen the burning of Mallow." It was typical Cork.'

Martin, on the other hand, talked little about the War of Independence. He had been involved with the North Tipperary Flying Column—Dan Breen would later attend Martin's funeral—and each year he would go to the commemoration parade on Easter Sunday. On these occasions his children would sometimes get a rare glimpse of the frustrations underneath as Martin raged at all the people marching, noting that if the Easter Rising had been as well supported in the first place there might never have been a civil war in Ireland.

In 1937, less than a year after Tony was born, Martin Ryan and his young family moved from Keane's Points to 83 Railway Cottage, a small but not unattractive single-level house beside the station. It had a scullery and three rooms, with a bellows by the fire in the front room. For young Tony the most exciting aspect of the house as he grew up was that he could climb onto the roof with his father to watch the meets at the Limerick Junction racecourse. It was the beginning of a love affair with horses that would last his entire life.

A mile and a half down the Limerick road was the local national school in Monard, where Tony began his education. Each day he would walk the three-mile round trip to the small school, which was run by two, sometimes three, teachers. A school photograph from the time shows forty-one pupils. Most of them look cheerful if not well off. Of the twelve children whose feet are visible, seven are not wearing shoes. Many of the children's parents, like Martin, would have worked on the railway. All told, Tony and his classmates were typical and unremarkable for working-class children growing up in rural Ireland in the 1940s.

The first big upheaval in Tony's life came in 1944–5, when the Ryan family 'emigrated' to the cathedral town of Thurles—hallowed throughout Ireland as the birthplace of the GAA. In many ways the move was a step down for the Ryans. The nice cottage in Limerick Junction was replaced with extremely cramped accommodation in an upstairs room at 45 Butler Avenue, with only a curtain to divide the children from the parents at night. The Ryans would remain here for five years—a struggle for two adults and five growing children. 'It was tiny, absolutely tiny,' Kell remembered. Martin applied to be rehoused by the council but was turned down. Tony later said that watching his father tell his mother the bad news was a heartbreaking moment—perhaps his first introduction to the harshness of life without influence or privilege. 'Tony always said it was this incident that drove his hunger,' his son Declan recalls.

For all the difficulties, the move from Limerick Junction was an important lesson for Tony in another way, even if he could not have articulated it at the time. He might have asked why his father had uprooted the family from the pleasant surroundings of their cottage for the inadequate accommodation in Butler Avenue. The answer was as simple as it was instructive: pure ambition. The reason for the move was that Martin had been promoted from fireman to engine driver on the railway. That move 'up' may in other ways have been a step down for the family; but for Martin Ryan it was the fulfilment of an aspiration that he had held all his life. And it was one that gave Tony a real pride that his father was now 'someone'. For in 1940s Ireland few small boys were not attracted to the glamour and thrill of the life of the engine driver.

Years afterwards Tony would reflect on the excitement he felt travelling on the footplate of a train beside his father:

> They stoked the gaping furnace with the poor wartime anthracite to build up the steam pressure and I was soon enveloped in that delicious childhood cocoon of excitement and terror, the red roaring furnace and the clattering steel and hissing steam and belching smoke coming to confirm my conditioned image of hell. But my father was there with his easy balance and [authority] and hell only could threaten. On the short journey to Goold's Cross the men put the driver's cap on my head and pointed out landmarks and the farms of friends and talked about horses and hurlers. They even fried the traditional engine-driver's breakfast on the long steel shovel, but I was not going to be distracted. I was a train driver. I was going to be one for ever. My grandfather was one. My uncle was a Station Master at Bruree. My family was on the railway. Trains were in my blood. Nothing would change.

That sense of direction, the confidence that in all likelihood he would end up on the railways himself, may explain why Tony as a boy did not seem particularly restless or ambitious. There are no stories of audacious moneymaking schemes or bold plans for the future. At Thurles Christian Brothers' School he was a hard-working but quiet student. His mother later described him as 'purposeful', coming home in the evening and disappearing upstairs first to do his homework, then to head out to the field to play sports.

Returning to his school in 1990, when he donated a computer room, Tony would praise the Christian Brothers above all for teaching him, as his father had, about the need for a good work ethic in life. 'They demonstrated time and again that each of us, with encouragement and good example, can attain higher goals than we believed,' he told his successor pupils. 'I feel a deep sense of gratitude to the men who dedicated their careers to me and my generation.'

In 1950 Martin's risk in bringing everyone to Thurles finally paid off, when the Ryans moved to a smart new terraced council house at 10 Bohernamona Road (where the rival gnomes took up sentry outside). They were living in a more spacious house with front and back gardens and neat little steps on the path leading up to the front door. Tony, as the eldest, finally got his own bed.

The move marked the beginning of a happy period in the family's life. The children were settled at their schools, the girls going to the Presentation Convent. First Communions and Confirmations were made at Thurles Cathedral. Although no-one was too religious or had any special vocations or devotions, the boys joined the confraternity, and the girls were in the Legion of Mary.

Tony was also an enthusiastic scout, which gave him his 'first experience of leadership and the right kind of discipline'. He 'adored' the camping and long route marches as well as the 'thrill' of becoming a patrol leader.

There was sporting success too, with Tony winning a county minor football medal with Thurles Sarsfield, although, in true Tipp fashion, he always preferred hurling. His friend Margaret Downes remembered how at parties he always 'had a transistor to his ear listening to the match and oblivious to what was going on around him.' Years later pilots in Tony's employ would get used to the request made in far-flung places to find out the hurling score.

School holidays in Ireland were long—from the end of May to the beginning of September—so over the summer months Tony and his brothers brought some extra money into the house by 'footing the turf' for Bord na Móna. Early each morning a truck would pick the boys up in Thurles to take them to the bog. There they would board a narrow-gauge 'bog train' that would transport them three or four miles out. A foreman would give each a 'spread' to cut—payment was by the spread, however long it took. 'It was brilliant craic,' remembered Simon, 'five or six days' work would mean a guy taking home around three pounds, ten shillings a week—good money in those days.' But they had to work for it. 'This was literally backbreaking work,' Kell recalled. 'I mean you were stooped down all the time, getting things off the ground, back up again. Nobody had gloves. The wind would be blowing, or sometimes you'd get sunstroke.' Tony would later reflect that, for all the ups and downs of life in business, 'I always thought it was a better job than cutting turf in the bog—now that's real work.'

It was also during the years at 10 Bohernamona Road that one of the deepest and most important chapters opened in Tony's life. In his Intermediate Cert year, aged sixteen, he began to notice the attractive girl who passed the house each morning on her way to school. Eventually he got to chatting to her, and they clicked. Five years later these childhood sweethearts married. Mairéad was literally 'the girl around the corner', living in Mitchel Street, from where she could see the tower of St Patrick's Cathedral. Although her name was also Ryan, they were not related. 'I always used to smile when I was a child,' Tony and Mairéad's son Declan later recalled, 'because my grandfather [Mairéad's father] and my grandmother [Tony's mother] always used to call each other Mr Ryan and Mrs Ryan. I'd get a kick out of that.'

The Ryans of Mitchel Street were builders and, as such, better off than their namesakes in Bohernamona Road. 'I'd say there was an element that she was a little bit above Tony,' Declan recalls, 'which actually got right up his nose, but there was always respect for them.' Later on, Tony's father-in-law would help him build a family home on the outskirts of Cork, at the Blackrock Castle end, high up on the hill, with beautiful views.

In 1954 Tony took his Leaving Cert and finished at Thurles CBS. There never seems to have been any expectation that he would move on to university. Even had he wanted to continue his education it would have meant winning a scholarship, most likely to University College, Cork. Although he was hard-working and bright, Tony was never exceptional academically. As a temporary measure he took a job in the sugar factory for that autumn's sugarbeet campaign.

Working in the sugar factory was never what Tony Ryan wanted to do with his life. It was travel that was in his blood, although by the 1950s he had changed his mode of transport. If the boy had wanted to be a train driver like his father, the man was attracted to aircraft as a newer, even more dramatic way of getting around.

'He had ambitions to join the Air Corps,' Kell recalled, 'but there was some problem with colour and his eyesight.' It was a blow to Tony's ambitions, but he was not to be deterred. He was advised that his colour-blindness, which was not severe, would not necessarily stop him becoming a commercial pilot. Yet, even more so than going to university, training to become a pilot was an expensive business. Most of the pilots in Aer Lingus were already highly experienced and had trained in Britain or the United States. So when Tony saw an advertisement for a traffic assistant, the lowest rung on the ladder in Aer Lingus, he took the chance that it might some day lead to an opportunity to learn to fly. Instead, it was the first step on a journey that would see him transform the world of commercial aviation.

To join the national airline in the 1950s brought with it a measure of social respectability. Both Tony's parents were proud to see him 'getting on'. But only a few short months after he had begun working at Shannon Airport, tragedy struck the Ryan household and changed everything. In the spring of 1955 Martin was uncharacteristically taken ill, with what looked like the flu. He was an extremely active man, rarely missing a day of work in his life, so he was anxious to get back to his engine. On 30 April he struggled into work, where he was again taken ill. His supervisor would not let him on the train and told him to have a cup of tea and go home. Under protest Martin agreed. Getting up on his bike and pedalling off, he suffered a massive heart attack outside Thurles station and died. Martin Ryan was fifty-four years of age.

Martin's early death brought immediate hardship to 10 Bohernamona Road. Lily now had to bring up a young family, including Kell, who was just ten, on a small CIE pension. In order to make ends meet, the family made the heart-wrenching but all too common decision to send the eldest girl, Catherine (Rena), to live with an aunt in the United States. From there she would send back money to help keep the rest of the family. Tony also had new responsibilities, as the head of the family. Each weekend he made the fifty-mile train journey from Shannon to Thurles to see his mother, always giving her money from his pay packet and bringing Urney chocolates as a treat for Saturday night.

His father's death left its mark on Tony in other ways. No doubt Martin's heavy smoking was a contributory factor in his death, but just as important were the long days and the exhausting work he had undertaken all his life. Tony concluded that his father had worked himself to death. 'The long hours he worked had a very significant influence on me,' he later recalled. 'When people say to me, toadying, "You work very hard," my reply is that I don't work physically as hard as others.'

Tony never lost his admiration or affection for his father. He always kept close to hand the book *Glenanaar* by Canon Sheehan, which he had inscribed and given to his father as a last Christmas present. Family and employees alike would lose count of the number of times he quoted his father's sayings, such as 'The strongest steel comes from the hottest fire' and, as Michael O'Leary would recall in Tony's eulogy, 'It is better to wear away than rust away.'

The sense of a life cut short by a lifetime of hard, physical work was something that never left Tony Ryan. Perhaps it was no coincidence that he would later tell *Poetry Ireland* that his favourite poem, 'An Spailpín Fánach' ('The itinerant labourer'), was one that he had learnt in school, and it must have burnt deep in 1955. 'For ever more I will not go to Cashel | Selling or bartering my health, | At the hiring-fair, sitting by the wall, | Or a lounger at the side of the street . . .'

Martin's death marked a coming of age for Tony Ryan. Now Shannon offered him the opportunity to honour his father's memory by making something of his life.

Chapter 2

SALARYMAN

For a young man to have employment in 1950s Ireland was an achievement in itself, but to have a position in Shannon Airport was more than just a job: it felt like a gateway to the world.

Living in the Ireland of Tony Ryan's childhood, although not particularly unhappy for him personally, had been a bleak experience for most people. By the time Tony started work, in 1955, unemployment, emigration and the cost of living were all out of control. Some forty thousand people were leaving the country each year. The 1955 census showed the population of the Republic at its lowest level ever. It was a crisis of confidence as much as of economic management. Three different Governments had been elected between 1948 and 1954, each one seemingly worse than the last. Ireland seemed locked in a deadly tailspin.

Yet, in a stroke of good timing, Tony started his working life at the exact moment that Ireland was turning a corner. That same year Seán Lemass of Fianna Fáil gave his famous '100,000 jobs' speech. It marked the beginning of a new approach to economic thinking, developed in consultation with progressive public servants of the era, including Todd Andrews and T. K. Whitaker, that would see the country launched on a path to modernisation.

For many, Shannon Airport already seemed like an outlier for this new approach. Global, innovative and identifiably contemporary, it offered a glimpse of what Ireland might become.

The west coast had been a central feature of transatlantic air travel since the first flight across the Atlantic in 1919. Ireland provided the most obvious stop-off for planes from North America. In 1937 the Government, in a move that was ahead of its time, started work on a new airport at Rineanna in Co. Clare. By the end of the Second World War the new facility—now called Shannon Airport—had four concrete runways, including one of 10,000 feet that could easily deal with the biggest and most powerful aircraft of the day.

On 24 October 1945 the first scheduled commercial flight, an American Overseas Airlines DC-4, flew in from the United States. Soon afterwards all the major American carriers began using the airport. Overnight, Shannon became the most important stop-off on the transatlantic route.

Two years later Shannon's appeal was increased through another innovative move by the state: the introduction of the first customs-free area. This development not only provided international passengers with duty-free goods but also enticed businesses to move to Shannon on the promise of paying no import or export taxes. It was the beginning of a brave new entrepreneurial world that would see Ireland emerge over the decades as a truly global centre of aviation expertise. (For example, Ireland today is a global centre for aircraft leasing, with assets worth more than €80 billion under management, accounting for half the world's fleet of leased aircraft.)

Tony Ryan's arrival at Shannon in the mid-1950s was timed to perfection. Ten years later and the airport would already have begun its steady decline, as newer, longer-range aircraft lessened the need for a Shannon stop-off. But in the fifties Tony seemed to be riding the crest of the future. His birth in Limerick Junction had put him on the 'main line' of national life. Now the airport saw him even better placed. Ireland may have been struggling as a poor outpost on the edge of western Europe; but in Shannon they were at the centre of the transatlantic world.

Tony's starting salary as an Aer Lingus 'counter-jumper'—so named because they lugged baggage up and over the check-in desks—was the reasonable sum of £4 8s 9d, although by the time he had paid for digs in Limerick, bus fares and contributions to help out his mother, there was not much left at the end of a week.

Tony began work on the same day as Christy Ryan (no relation), who quickly became his closest friend and later was godfather to his son Declan. Years afterwards, Tony and Christy together would found Ryanair. Back in the day, they were inseparable, particularly before Tony's marriage in 1958.

Mick O'Carroll, who began work at Shannon the following year, recalls that Tony eventually got himself a Vespa scooter, which he would use to get to the airport, with Christy on the back, riding pillion. 'Tony was one of the few people to have a scooter,' O'Carroll remembers, 'while the rest of us were stuck getting the bus down.'

Life for a young traffic assistant (the women were called 'ground hostesses') in Shannon was a mixture of excitement and the humdrum. Work was based on a four-shift cycle that ran twenty-four hours a day. On any given day Tony might find himself working on the check-in or cargo desk, on the Ship's Papers desk, making sure the paperwork for all aircraft was in order, or in the office on the phones. But the most hectic times always came when big American or British transatlantic carriers touched down.

'Part of our job was to meet every aircraft as it arrived,' recalled one traffic assistant, Frankie Walsh, quoted by Valerie Sweeney in *Shannon Airport*. 'We had to be on the ramp, in all weathers, ten minutes before the estimated time of the aircraft. We stood there in the rain, hail and snow.' When a plane taxied to a halt, steps would be pushed into place. Then the traffic assistants would board the plane, check the paperwork and ensure that there were no diseases or animals on board. The captain would have to sign to say that the plane had been sprayed before the doors had been opened. 'While the passengers still remained on board, the traffic assistant had to disembark,' Frankie recalls, 'go into the main building to deliver the clearance forms, one copy to the health department, one to immigration, one to customs. Only when these procedures were completed to everyone's satisfaction could a ground hostess mount the steps and make an announcement to the passengers that they could disembark the flight.'

Staff members would often find themselves dealing with unhappy passengers traipsing in the rain to a bus or across the open air ramp into the terminal building. 'We tried to provide people with umbrellas,' says Frankie, 'but we lost so many of them when they were whipped out of people's hands by the wind we had to abandon the idea.'

Once the passengers were safely in the terminal, an assistant's job was still only half done. Ship's Papers and manifests had to be prepared for every transit destination. Load sheets and health certificates had to be issued. Only then could an aircraft be cleared for departure.

Transatlantic flights arrived in Shannon either at night or else early in the morning. At such times it was 'all go' for the traffic assistants. Daytime shifts were more relaxed. 'All the effort went into avoiding being spotted doing nothing,' O'Carroll recalled with a smile. There was always more talking to be done about the hurling than about aircraft.

That didn't change much when Tony got a promotion to shift supervisor in 1958. Christy was on his shift, as was a young student, Bronwyn Conroy, the niece of Shannon's lead engineer and later a well-known beauty consultant in Dublin. Conroy recalls that working for Tony was 'really good fun', because 'he was always in good humour and could be extremely funny.' He even allowed her to improve the beauty routines for the ground hostesses. 'When I arrived, all the Shannon girls did was curl their eyelashes and wear Sari Peach lipstick by Gala,' she says. 'By the time I left, nine months later, they all had proper beauty routines!' If a plane landed ahead of schedule Bronwyn even persuaded Tony that the women couldn't possibly go out to meet passengers without having done their faces properly, so it would be all male assistants who were sent onto the tarmac to meet the aircraft instead.

Tony's promotion to shift supervisor ahead of Christy, who had started on the same day, suggests that the management at Shannon recognised his potential above that of his contemporaries. Clearly he had an easy charm and a practical way about him. Conroy recalls that in her nine months at Shannon, at which point Aer

Lingus began its own transatlantic flights for the first time, she was run off her feet. But Tony was known for getting everything done with great good humour, and consequently 'he was liked by everyone'.

Developing a strong team ethic was something that would be important to him throughout his business career, although achieving that through good humour was not. Tony never lost his ability to charm, but those working for him much later on were more likely to be on the receiving end of the 'hairdryer' treatment than of a softly-softly approach.

That new abrasiveness was something that on occasion could surprise or even upset those who had once worked with him at Aer Lingus, when he had been known as a nice guy. Seán Braiden and his wife, Olive, for example, had worked with Tony in those early days. Tony stayed regularly in their apartment on trips to London in the 1960s. When Seán was seconded to Tony's company Guinness Peat Aviation in the 1970s, Olive was dismayed by phone calls to the house at three or four in the morning and by getting 'barked at' by Tony demanding to know where her husband was. 'I was always very fond of Tony,' she recalls, 'but he was a total dictator and difficult to work with. When it came to business, he did what he needed to do.'

That had not been Tony's way at Shannon. Indeed, having shown some management potential, everything suggested that he was on course to be a good company man working in the semi-state sector before retiring with a carriage clock and a generous final salary pension. He had not yet acquired the edge that would see him succeed in business. Neither did he strike anyone at Shannon as being a budding entrepreneur. 'Tony was just an ordinary colleague in those days,' O'Carroll says. 'No-one suspected he had this entrepreneurial spirit, and anyone who says they did notice is lying!'

That ordinariness would be the unspectacular story of the first twenty years of Tony's working life as he moved steadily up the company ladder at Aer Lingus. In 1959, a year after marrying Mairéad, he was transferred to London for a four-year stint, during which he was stationed briefly in the West End ticket office at Bond Street and then at Heathrow Airport. The couple had digs in Maida Vale, where their first son, Cathal Martin Ryan, was born. Not being so dependent on the schedule of transatlantic flights in London, Tony could enjoy a more normal home life with his young family, although, like most fathers at the time, he didn't do much in the way of changing nappies. Britain in the late 1950s had 'never had it so good'. That brought with it some nice perks for the Ryans: Tony purchased his first used car, and the family got a black-and-white television.

Although Tony enjoyed the hubbub of working at Heathrow, Mairéad badly missed Ireland. It was for this reason that when the opportunity came in 1963 to move to the recently opened Cork Airport, Tony jumped at it, knowing how happy it would make his wife. The three years that followed would be among the happiest of their married life. Mairéad was thrilled to be home. A brother for Cathal—Declan Francis Ryan—was born in their first year back. Mairéad's father and Tony began work on the beautiful new house on the hill, with its lovely aspect overlooking the River Lee, just twenty minutes from the airport.

Aer Lingus was heavily invested in making Cork Airport a success, so recruitment for the new venture had been highly competitive. Tony was appointed as a duty manager, although the job, which included shunting luggage from the check-in desk out to the waiting plane, often in the rain, was less white-collar than it sounded.

Colleagues again remember him as a good-humoured and practical supervisor. He was also a good motivator. Mairead Mason, who later undertook PR for Tony in GPA, recalled an eminent surgeon telling her about working for Aer Lingus as a student. The doctor told her that Tony

> was behind the desk, and I was out sweeping the floor. He must have seen an elderly woman struggling with her bags, because he came over and said to me, 'Do you think that lady needs help?' so I went over to help her. He had wanted to teach me the

> lesson, you see, that if someone was struggling, I should go and help. He could have done it himself, but he understood that a young fella will never learn that way. I never forgot that.

In the mid-1960s it would have been easy to see why Tony might have stayed in Cork Airport all his life. Mairéad and the family were happily settled in their lovely new house. His widowed mother, a Corkwoman herself, was nearby. He was popular in work. Ireland, in the midst of the Lemass-Whitaker revolution, seemed on the way up—no longer a place to leave but now somewhere to stay.

But while his fires of entrepreneurial ambition were yet to be ignited, Tony was restless for advancement within Aer Lingus. In 1966 he was offered the chance to go to O'Hare Airport in Chicago as deputy station manager. Chicago was an important part of Aer Lingus's transatlantic operation, and the promotion was a step up in all kinds of ways. But Mairéad, so happy in Cork, was unsure. It was such a long way away. Post was slow. Transatlantic phone calls cost a fortune. The move would be a real upheaval for the family.

Kell Ryan, Tony's younger brother, remembers that the family agonised about the choice for ages.

> I was in his house in Cork the day he had to make the call to say whether he was going to accept the job or not. I'll never forget that, because he had to make the decision whether he was going to uproot from Cork to America. He said he could become station manager of Cork eventually; it was a nice job and he had just built the house with his father-in-law. I guess if he'd decided he was going to stay in Ireland that would have been it.

While every personal factor in 1966 told Tony to stay, ambition instructed him to make the move—just as it had done when his father had moved the family from Limerick Junction to Thurles two decades earlier. Kell reflected:

> Funny, isn't it? Yes or no; the road divides, and what do you do? If it had gone the other way, he probably never would have

left Ireland—would have got manager at Cork Airport and probably stayed there.

Tony departed alone for Chicago, bringing the family out a few months later. He did his best to ease the transition for them, renting a pleasant bungalow in Arlington Heights, about twenty-five miles north-west of downtown Chicago. More rural then than now, the town was only fourteen miles or so from the airport and had a very strong Catholic population. There were also echoes of Limerick Junction to be found, not least in the famous Arlington Park racecourse and the Southwest Chief railway line that ran through the town, taking passengers from Chicago to Los Angeles.

Now aged thirty and occupying a responsible position in Aer Lingus, Tony brought a new seriousness and maturity to his job in O'Hare Airport. 'He worked so hard,' Declan recalls, 'that we didn't see him a huge amount. That's primarily how I remember him in my early years, as incredibly hard-working.'

The transatlantic flight to Shannon left late at night, so most days Tony would not be home until midnight or later. At weekends or on holidays Cathal and Declan might be taken into the airport as a treat with their father. Both were put on their best behaviour. 'It was a respect thing,' says Declan. 'You knew you could have a good time, but you also knew you weren't to mess at the airport.' With Aer Lingus, Tony told his boys, 'you're representing Ireland.'

Working for the airline kept Tony in close contact with Ireland, but living in Chicago gave him an introduction to a different way of life. He became more worldly, observing, although from a safe distance, the race riots and anti-war demonstrations that put Chicago at the top of the global news agenda. More personally, he was changed by the culture and ethos of American life.

Tony quickly came to admire the American ethic of hard work and customer service, and he soon concluded that he needed to change his own laid-back approach. For the first time in his career Tony began to worry less about being good humoured and well liked, and more about setting demanding standards. That didn't always make him popular. Years afterwards he told Marian Finucane of RTE that from this time onwards he began to feel like an 'interloper' at Aer Lingus. Hard work for management seemed more frowned upon than encouraged.

He was unafraid to give his own airport staff a kick up the backside when he felt they needed it. On taking his annual leave he horrified senior clerical staff by appointing an engineer as his stand-in. 'That rocked a few boats,' remembered Derek O'Brien, an Aer Lingus colleague. When staff members complained Tony told them, 'I don't care he's an engineer: he's the best man for the job. Full stop.' It was a story that soon did the rounds throughout the company.

It was also in Chicago that Tony began to emerge as the more familiar hard-bargaining character he would later become. Pat Deasy, his station manager at O'Hare, saw that close up. He may even have been the first to be outfoxed by Tony in a negotiation. When Deasy moved house Tony agreed to buy his previous one. They met at the attorney's office to sign all the paperwork amid handshakes and much backslapping. Only as they were leaving did Deasy realise that he had no cheque from Tony. He mentioned it and was stunned by the response. 'Pat, you know my salary! Where the feck do you think I would get that sort of money? You'll get paid, all right, but you'll have to wait for it.'

'Pat did wait for it, and he got paid,' recalled David Kennedy, later chief executive of Aer Lingus, 'but it was quite some time afterwards.'

The job Tony did in Chicago got him noticed back in Dublin as a hard-working, capable and imaginative manager. In 1968 he was rewarded with a transfer to JFK Airport in New York as station manager, with the task of organising the airline's move to a new terminal. That complex logistical exercise would demand not just long hours but also an ability to think on his feet as, inevitably (like Heathrow Terminal 5 in 2008), things went wrong. 'He'd shown a maverick approach in Chicago,' recalls O'Brien, who became Tony's duty manager in JFK. 'He brought that same sense of not fitting between the tram tracks to New York.'

Tony's role in the terminal relocation introduced him to more new business approaches. He became an important and increasingly influential member of the airport operation committee—demonstrating once again the reputation Ireland has acquired in all kinds of international arenas for competence and diplomacy. He forged close links with his counterpart in Lufthansa, and together they became highly effective advocates of airline rights. Many of these issues would continue as later preoccupations, not least in Tony's attempts to break the monopolies that surrounded fuelling, ground-transportation companies and union labour.

Tony also got a reputation for running rings around officialdom in the airport. This was particularly the case when it came to employing casual workers. Tony used Irish nationals whenever he could, and those from Tipperary most of all. That brought him into conflict with the airport authorities, less for the Tipperary favouritism than for the failure to employ enough American citizens. After several formal warnings he was hauled in front of a disciplinary board, which expressed its displeasure at his hiring record. Tony's reaction was as simple as it was devious. Sure, he said, we don't employ enough American citizens, and that is to be regretted. But we're no different from any other airline. If you go over to the Air France desk the prerequisite for getting a job is that you can speak French. With Lufthansa it's German, and Iberia Spanish. 'So,' Tony told the board, 'if you want to work for Aer Lingus, which is an Irish airline, you have to be able to speak Irish, our national language.' He won the argument, although maybe he was lucky the board didn't immediately test the Aer Lingus staff on their Gaeilge—'and himself,' adds Tony's brother Kell. It was a lesson in how to stay a hair's breadth on the right side of the regulatory authorities.

Tony also had other battles to fight closer to home. His most startling confrontations were with the airline pilots. In the public mind of the 1960s, glamour and prestige still surrounded these sultans of the skies, with their gold-braided lapels, Ray-Ban sunglasses and exotic duty-free cigarettes. By now Tony loathed them as a group, despite once having wanted to join their ranks. 'The pilots used to drive him nuts,' Declan says, remembering his father's rages about them at home.

Seán Braiden agrees. 'There was a culture that the pilots were the be all and end all of flying,' he says. 'Tony never believed in that. He never gave them any space when it came to operational decisions and would be tough. He had his own ideas about how things should be done.'

Above all, that meant getting planes out on time. When Tony felt that pilots were getting in the way of that, and not being team players, he didn't hesitate to tell them in the strongest possible terms.

Eventually the wrangles between Tony and the pilots coming in and out of JFK Airport became so intense that Arthur Walls, general manager of Aer Lingus, flew to New York to see what was going on. What he discovered, Derek O'Brien remembered, was 'a station manager who was very, very effective.' It was an important moment for Tony, because it put him on the general manager's radar as a rising star in the company.

New York taught Tony that he needed to be tough to do his job properly. It also taught him how to enforce his will through a loyal praetorian guard. Christy Ryan, who had worked alongside Tony from day 1 in Aer Lingus, now joined him at JFK as deputy station manager. Tony knew he could trust Christy 100 per cent. Not only had they long been friends and workmates, but Christy had already shown his personal loyalty. Years earlier he had for several months swapped his Heathrow job for the Cork one when a member of Tony's family needed a series of operations in London. It was indicative of the kind of loyalty that Tony could inspire in those close to him.

In New York, Christy became Tony's trusted eyes and ears with the staff, always keeping him up to speed on problems and gossip. Moreover, Christy's taciturn manner helped reinforce the atmosphere of efficiency and serious work to be done that Tony sought to cultivate. It was all a million miles away from the days back in Shannon, when 'all the effort went into avoiding being spotted doing nothing.'

Tony's position as station manager brought with it advantages as well as new challenges for his family. The Ryans had moved to Long Island, living first in Deer Park, Suffolk County, then moving to Garden City, Nassau County, which had been founded by a wealthy Irishman, Alexander Turney Stewart, in the middle of the nineteenth century. 'Garden City especially was a fantastic place to grow up as a kid,' remembers Declan, who recalls wonderful sports facilities and good schools. The family lived in a safe, prosperous area in a comfortable house, with the middle-class 'mod cons' of a colour television and a new car.

Not that Tony had much time to enjoy the pleasures of suburban Long Island. 'You'd see the other dads, doing normal jobs, coming home at five o'clock,' Declan remembers, 'while Tony was doing twelve-hour days, getting home late after the last two flights to Ireland went out around eight o'clock each night.' That left Mairéad with most of the responsibility in bringing up the two boys, who became three in 1971 when another son, Shane, was born.

Aside from taking the boys to the occasional baseball game at Shea Stadium, Tony's principal role in the house was to enforce discipline and to back up Mairéad. He was never afraid to give the boys a good clip round the ear, and the worst crime of all in the household was to cheek their mother. 'Tony became very affectionate in later years,' Declan says, 'but in the early days he was a very stern man.'

Shane, as the youngest, and Declan to an extent, were able to sidestep that sterner side, but Cathal often found himself in the line of fire. Later on, Tony came to adore his eldest son's wit and devil-may-care attitude to life. 'He was the Jack Nicholson of our family,' Declan says laconically. In the 1970s, however, Tony was concerned that Cathal was not showing enough seriousness towards life.

And there was also something deeper. By the time Shane was born the Ryans had been away from Ireland for five years. Tony missed it himself, but more significantly he had the unwelcome realisation that his children were growing up not to be Irish at all. They had American, not Irish, accents; followed NFL and baseball, not GAA; and knew more American than Irish history. Moreover, whatever image they had of Ireland, it was not of Tipperary and the Great Southern Railway but of the bombing and destruction that were beginning to fill the American news broadcasts.

This recognition provoked a strong reaction in Tony: in 1971 he decided to repatriate Cathal to Ireland. There his eldest son would attend one of the country's most prestigious private schools, the Jesuit-run Clongowes Wood, which was famous for its intellectual rigour and its sporting prowess on the rugby field.

This was a big move for the family in all kinds of ways. By sending Cathal, and subsequently the two other boys, to Clongowes, Tony was making a statement about his commitment to the culture of his birth, which was fundamentally different from the Irish-American one. 'He wanted to get the Irishness back into us,' Declan explains. Tony also put on display his own ambition and his unflinching willingness to take hard, even harsh, decisions. The choice of Clongowes itself put aside sentiment, as Glenstal Abbey in Co. Limerick, or Rockwell College in Co. Tipperary, might have been more obvious choices. What united all these options was that they were expensive, involving considerable sacrifice for the Ryans on Tony's public-sector salary.

Cathal's being sent to school in Ireland was a wrenching experience for the whole family, not least for the boy himself. 'Tony would lean over him and say, "Don't cry in front of your mother",' Declan remembers, 'and he understood it, that you don't upset your mom.'

In many ways the move was as difficult for Declan as it was for Cathal. Suddenly he lost his elder brother, who had played the role of hero and principal playmate. Now there was only a baby in the house. 'It seemed gas the first time Cathal went, and I was delighted to see the back of him,' Declan recalls, 'and then I missed him like hell and got upset at Christmas when he was going back and forth.'

That was an emotion shared by Mairéad, who from this time

onwards found that her own homesickness became close to unbearable. Five years earlier she had reluctantly agreed to leave Cork, where she had been so happy, to make the move to the United States. Her experience had been far from the American dream. Tony's long hours kept him away from the house for most of the day, leaving her without much support to pull together the threads of family life. 'I would say eighty to ninety per cent of the parenting was with my mom,' Declan recalls. '"Sympathy" would not be a word that you would use to describe Tony in those years. Mom fulfilled that role in our family.'

Mairéad did a fine job raising the boys, but by 1971 the strain on her was acute. She had gone to Dublin for the birth of Shane, but no sooner had they returned to New York than the baby contracted meningitis. Shane was rushed into intensive care to save his life, and the family had to endure the gut-wrenching experience of seeing him given the last rites. That ordeal forged a special bond with Shane for Tony, who never forgot that his youngest son was lucky to be alive.

There was more drama that Christmas when Cathal returned to Long Island for the school holiday. In many ways this was an extremely happy time for the family, not least because everyone at home in New York found it hilarious how Cathal had 'gone posh' after a few months at Clongowes, saying please and thank you all the time and eating everything off his plate. 'Tony was roaring laughing at that,' Declan recalls.

The good humour only lasted until the end of the holidays. Cathal's return to school was, if anything, even harder on everyone than when he had left the previous September. Whatever instructions Tony might have given to the boys about not crying in front of their mother, it must have been apparent to him by this stage just how unhappy everyone had become. It can hardly have come as any surprise when, in 1972, Mairéad told him she wanted to go home to Ireland.

In so many ways Mairéad was pushing at an open door. Tony missed Ireland himself, especially the hurling and his beloved

Tipperary. Any excitement about life in America had long worn off. In an odd way, Tony didn't even live in the United States: his real life was the no-man's-land of the JFK international terminal. But he did worry about the effect of living in America on his children. Cathal had already been sent home for an Irish education. The same would soon happen to Declan, who was even more American than his older brother, having spent a larger proportion of his life there. That would leave Shane on his own, growing up as an all-American boy. In the early 1970s this meant the context of what one historian calls 'the decade of nightmares' and the sense that drugs and crime were out of control in nearby New York City. Childhood innocence seemed under threat even in the suburbs of Garden City. 'Long Island was a great place to live,' Declan remembers, 'but you don't want to go through your teens there. You grow up too quick.'

On almost every level Tony knew by 1972 that the time had come to go home. It was the right thing to do for his family. Everyone missed Ireland. He could even take pride in having done a good job at JFK as station manager, having overseen the move to the new terminal and managed the greater demands put on the staff by the new Aer Lingus Boeing 747 'Jumbo' jets. All in all, Tony had run a tight operation that was valued by the management back in Dublin.

Yet whatever success Tony might have had as station manager in JFK, the culture of the airline was unfavourable. 'It was not something you did in Aer Lingus,' explains duty manager Derek O'Brien. 'If you went abroad they did not easily or readily let you back home.'

As station manager at the heart of the airline's transatlantic operations, Tony already had the most glamorous and interesting overseas posting. Heathrow would have made a good transfer, but Mairéad had not been much happier in London than in the United States. In the end, says O'Brien, Tony had no choice other than 'to go back to Dublin in a cap-in-hand way' to ask for a transfer into head office.

It was a low moment when Tony made the move back to Ireland, unsure of what awaited him at the Aer Lingus headquarters in Dublin Airport. 'He didn't particularly want to go,' O'Brien recalls, but family needs had taken precedence over professional advancement.

In many ways it was an everyday story. Tony Ryan was a company worker who had climbed up the corporate ladder in a purposeful but unspectacular way to a comfortable middle-management position. Now, for personal reasons beyond his control, he had been forced to slip out of the groove of what was expected of him by his employer. As a result, his career had stalled.

As the plane touched down in Shannon Airport in 1972, bringing the Ryans home to Ireland, Tony could reflect that perhaps the most dynamic period of his life was over. Now in his mid-thirties and apparently going nowhere in Aer Lingus, he had not much to look forward to other than the bland existence of a white-collared administrator in the service of the national airline. The abyss of pen-pushing anonymity opened up in front of his eyes.

Chapter 3

A NEW LEASE ON LIFE

So far, so ordinary: that had been the life of Tony Ryan up to the point when he flew home to Ireland with his family in 1972. Soon things would change, but for that to happen Tony needed one huge of slice of luck. And, as so often in life, that luck came as a result of someone else's misfortune, as fate rattled over the points.

When Tony had gone to the Aer Lingus management 'cap in hand' to ask for a move back to Ireland he had not been given much in the way of encouragement. In the end, however, he got his transfer home because Aer Lingus needed to fill a position quickly, and appointing Tony seemed like the easiest solution.

The airline was putting more resources into its leasing operation. Seán Daly, who had been in the sales department, was put in charge. 'He was a very good personality,' recalls a fellow-employee, Seán Braiden, 'a very striking guy', with exactly the kind of charisma and expertise needed for what would be a difficult sales job on a global scale. But sadly for Daly, shortly before taking the post he was involved in a serious car accident. That put him out of action for a year. Looking for a replacement in a hurry, the general manager, Arthur Walls, who liked what Tony had done in JFK, gave him the job. 'So the way Tony got into leasing was interesting,' says Braiden, 'because he got in by default, really.'

What the 'striking' figure of Daly would have made of the opportunity that now came Tony's way is anyone's guess; but it is no exaggeration to say that Daly's bad luck placed Tony in the right place at the right time in a way that would see him transform his own life and the airline industry.

—

By the early 1970s the global airline industry was in one of its periodic bouts of depression. 'The airline industry tends to have cycles of euphoria brought about by rising markets and rising profits,' explained Aer Lingus's chief executive, Michael Dargan, 'followed by acute melancholia when the pendulum swings the other way.'

By 1972 there was not much doubt about the direction in which that pendulum was moving. On 21 February 1970 a Swissair Convair 990 four-engine jet had exploded five minutes after take-off from Geneva Airport for a scheduled flight to Tel-Aviv, killing all forty-seven on board. That same day an Austrian Airlines jet had narrowly avoided a similar fate, managing to return to Frankfurt Airport after being rocked by an explosion. These two events marked the beginning of a new era of attacks on aircraft, and anti-Israeli terrorist organisations carried out a campaign of such attacks throughout the 1970s. The fear of being blown out of the sky had a disastrous effect on passenger numbers, as well as dramatically increasing security and insurance costs for airlines. The result was a sharp loss of income, accompanied by drastic overcapacity. When the Oil Crisis of 1973 saw fuel prices jump to astronomical levels the airline industry was plunged into 'melancholia'.

Amid the general crisis, Aer Lingus had managed to double down on its own misfortune through a combination of bad luck and bad judgement. For an industry battling against the threat of terrorism, images of the 'Troubles' in the North—where by 1972 the death toll averaged more than one person every day—had, among other considerations, wrecked the tourist industry in Ireland. As if the subsequent loss of passenger numbers for Aer Lingus wasn't bad enough, the chaos of the Irish economy, with inflation spiralling out of control, left its own disastrous mark on a company that made most of its money abroad. In the financial year 1971/2 Aer Lingus and its non-scheduled air-transport arm, Aerlínte Éireann, had incurred a net loss of £2.39 million—the first loss in more than a decade.

Aer Lingus had also been the author of its own misfortune. The decision to buy two Jumbo Jets from Boeing may have looked like good business in January 1967, when the order was placed. But by the time Aer Lingus took delivery of the aircraft, in 1971, it looked like hubris. The 'bubble' of transatlantic air traffic had well and truly popped. Carriers around the world had mothballed their Boeing 747 aircraft. But mothballing wasn't a luxury that Aer Lingus could afford. The company needed to get its Jumbos leased—and to do it fast. Seán Braiden recalls that

> the mission Tony had was to get rid of the 747s—get them out and leased. But he was in territory that he had never been in before. Tony had never been involved in leasing, and I can't imagine why there would be any reason he would have any knowledge or experience of it, because his area of operations had been the airport and what was going on there.

Fortunately the company had already had some success in the area. Historically, Aer Lingus had always suffered an imbalance between its winter and summer operations. This was an industry-wide problem that was more acute for Aer Lingus than most airlines, because it relied so heavily on tourist traffic. Scheduling most of the annual aircraft maintenance for the winter months alleviated some of the problem, but it still left a surplus of aircraft standing around doing nothing for half the year. In the mid-1960s Aer Lingus addressed the problem by leasing out aircraft on long-term contracts in the winter months to carriers in the United States and the Middle East.

The experience had not always been a straightforward or comfortable one. The international nature of the game, involving contracts and property that fell outside the jurisdiction of Irish courts, would often lead to hair-raising and expensive attempts by Aer Lingus to get what it was owed, or indeed owned.

Earlier attempts to lease the brand-new 747s had produced mixed results. After the order for the two Jumbos was placed with Boeing in 1967, Aer Lingus had successfully identified an airline, the low-cost carrier Trans Caribbean Airways, that had peak traffic in the Irish winter months. Trans Caribbean operated between New York, Newark and Washington, DC, and the Virgin Islands, Haïti and the Netherlands Antilles. Tourist traffic on these routes from the north-eastern United States to the sunnier climate of the Caribbean was potentially high, but Trans Caribbean had been unable to exploit this because its fleet consisted of only nine jets. Leasing a Jumbo from Aer Lingus suited everyone. A long-term contract was agreed that would see Aer Lingus provide the aircraft to Trans Caribbean for the high season in the West Indies and bring it back to Ireland for the busy summer on the transatlantic route. Advance payments were to be made at specified intervals. The contract was signed and the arrangement ready to kick in once the 747 came into service in 1971.

However, before the first payment was even made, O. Roy Chalk, the flamboyant owner of Trans Caribbean, sold the company to American Airlines in January 1970 for about $18 million in stock. 'We immediately got worried when we got wind of American's lack of enthusiasm for the contract,' recalls Neil Gleeson, who had helped negotiate the leasing deal. American Airlines had a very large fleet of its own and hardly needed an Aer Lingus 747 to add to the overcapacity it already had. 'As it happened, Trans Caribbean had just missed the advance payment as provided under the contract, which meant they were in default,' Gleeson remembers. 'Our New York lawyers advised that, in view of the default, we were entitled to terminate the contract and sue for our loss.'

It was a high-risk strategy for an Irish airline to take on a giant of the aviation world on home territory, in the United States. But it was a risk that paid off, with Aer Lingus getting a settlement. 'We then had a substantial amount of money', says Gleeson, 'and an aircraft available to lease out again for the winter.'

The experience with Trans Caribbean meant that Aer Lingus by 1972 had developed a certain level of in-house expertise on the legal, financial and operating complexities of leasing out aircraft. What was needed in the context of a depressed global industry was for someone to get out and sell the lease in the new, tougher environment. Hence the appointment in the first instance of Seán Daly, a salesperson. Following Daly's accident, Aer Lingus had turned to Tony because he was available, had a good understanding of routes and carriers, had followed the Trans Caribbean hearings at close quarters in New York, and had brought with him the unconventional turn of mind that his bosses had noticed in JFK.

For the next few months, with his family happily settled back in Ireland, Tony began flying around the world touting for business and trying to get a taker for the Jumbos sitting idly on the ramp back at Dublin Airport. It was a hard and dispiriting job. There was no global shortage of 747s. Dozens upon dozens of planes belonging to airlines from around the world had already been mothballed in the area around Tucson, Arizona, where the dry, smog-free climate helped minimise corrosion. In Seattle, the home of Boeing, a long line of new 747s gathered dust awaiting new owners. It was hardly any surprise when Tony met with rejection after rejection. No-one wanted a spare Irish 747.

That seemed to be the story when Tony started looking for business in Thailand. The country had two commercial airlines. The first was the national carrier, Thai International, which had close ties with the Scandinavian airline SAS and was generally thought to be under the control of the Thai military. That was a non-starter for Tony, but the second designated airline, a much smaller operation called Air Siam, offered a glimmer of potential. It had been inaugurated in 1969 as the brainchild of the entrepreneurial Prince 'Nicky' Varananda Dhavaj, a former wartime RAF pilot and a nephew of the Thai king. His vision was to establish an airline flying across the Pacific, from Bangkok to Los Angeles via Hong Kong, Tokyo and Honolulu. The airline was a minnow in comparison with Thai International, but it had a knack for publicity—even getting one of its planes into the opening credits of the hit television series 'Hawaii Five-O'. Its major competitive advantage was the exclusive right to fly to the United States, including the lucrative LA route. A year after it began flying the route, in 1971, Air Siam sought to expand its capacity and began looking around to lease another Boeing 707.

When Tony arrived in Bangkok he found himself in the frustrating position of negotiating with a company that wanted to lease an aircraft but not the larger Boeing 747s that Aer Lingus had to offer. Tony held several meetings with the chief executive, Virachai Vannukul, trying to tempt, cajole and flatter him into making the 'jump into the big time' with the 747. The two men got along well, but in the end the meetings went nowhere. The risk for Air Siam was simply too great.

Tony left disconsolate at the fact that yet another meeting had failed. Gathering his things together, he headed out to the airport, only to discover that his flight had been delayed. He was left to mooch around, have a snooze, read a book and look over his papers—all the familiar attempts to thwart the boredom and frustration of long delays in the departures lounge of an international airport.

At some point during the wait a light-bulb came on inside Tony's head. Why not give it one last go with Virachai? He found a pay phone and some change, and put the call in. It was the moment that changed everything for Tony Ryan. Virachai, impressed by his tenacity, said, 'Okay, come back and talk to me.' Tony did exactly that and leased him the Boeing 747. 'From that moment onwards', says Fergus Armstrong, a legal adviser to Aer Lingus and later Tony's confidant, 'a perception arose that Tony was a miracle-worker and a man who could do the deal.' Overnight, Tony had become the man who wouldn't take no for an answer.

Dublin might have been delighted at Tony getting one of the Jumbos leased, but the agreement in principle with Air Siam didn't come without its headaches. Reportedly nicknamed 'Air Heroin' within the industry, Air Siam looked like a risky custodian for something as precious as a 747 jet. It appeared to have no cash reserves—any money it had seemed to come from whatever was earned on flights. Air Siam, said the magazine *Asian Finance*, was the 'black sheep' of the region's airlines and not a good credit risk.

That poor reputation caused understandable nervousness back in Dublin. 'It was clearly a high-risk venture involving a company of dubious credit rating,' notes David Kennedy, then assistant chief executive (operations), 'and it entailed sending our most valuable asset—indeed one of Ireland's most valuable assets—to the far end of the world. However, the alternative was to have the aircraft sitting idle on the ground in Dublin, which was not a very attractive proposition.'

Kennedy sent the financial adviser Laurence Crowley to Thailand to put together a deal that would be absolutely watertight. Crowley explains that

> everything had to be watched very carefully. Just like a ship, if you run up debts across the world, you can get writs nailed to your mast and you won't be able to take the ship home until you pay each one of these off on the way back. We didn't want that to happen, and therefore things had to be very tightly organised in terms of guarantees. They were the most difficult things to get, and I worked with Tony to get those guarantees in the end.

A contract was finally signed in the summer of 1973 for the Boeing 747 to operate on the Bangkok–Hong Kong–Tokyo–Honolulu route three times a week. In the first year Aer Lingus would make an operating profit of $3 million from the deal.

Contractual undertakings were backed up by a detailed action plan put together by Kennedy with Tony to make sure that matters never got near a foreign court. For a start, Aer Lingus had insisted on a 'wet' lease (with aircraft, complete crew, maintenance and insurance), which meant that Tony and the 747 flew down to Bangkok with fifteen pilots, twelve engineers and three support staff. Thai cabin crew and co-pilots would be trained by Aer Lingus. Having so many Irish staff members on the ground and in the air made it easier to facilitate repatriation of the plane if the worst came to the worst.

Even these arrangements caused a certain alarm in Dublin. During the Dáil debate on the Air Navigation and Transport Bill in November 1973, Ray Burke of Fianna Fáil demanded that the Minister for Transport and Power, Peter Barry, 'explain the situation in regard to Irish crews flying Irish planes which are on lease to foreign countries.'

Those concerns were shared by Aer Lingus itself. Beyond the arrangement for the wet lease, there was also a confidential plan involving a 'snatch squad' for the 747 and its staff. In the event that Air Siam ran into any kind of trouble, the fear in Dublin was that somebody would slap a lien on the aircraft and hold it on the ground in some place such as Hong Kong or Tokyo. Aer Lingus would have to argue about ownership in the courts of a foreign jurisdiction. 'So we actually had a group of pilots in Dublin', Kennedy recalls, 'ready to fly out to Honolulu, if necessary, to take the aircraft, fly it back to Dublin and then argue about it in an Irish court. That's how concerned we were about the security of the asset.' Indeed when Air Siam ran into financial trouble a few years later, Kennedy did actually 'pull the aircraft back home', and he thought Aer Lingus lucky to have got out with a shortfall of only $1 million in payments from Air Siam.

However risky it might have been, pulling off the deal to get rid of an Aer Lingus Jumbo brought Tony great kudos in Dublin. Colleagues remember that his 'wizardry' on the Air Siam contract excited 'genuine astonishment' in Aer Lingus. The arrangement might have made his reputation, but it also came at a personal price. 'The measures to protect the asset', says Neil Gleeson, 'were where Tony Ryan came in. We put arrangements in place with Tony to ensure he could recover the aircraft at very short notice.' There was, the management at Aer Lingus concluded, 'nobody better to handle that situation than Tony Ryan.' So it turned out that the key to the relationship with Air Siam was that Tony would be sent down to Bangkok to run the operation on a day-to-day basis.

That was not a decision well received at home. Only the previous year Mairéad, homesick and tired of life in the United States, had convinced Tony to return to Ireland. By now she was happily settled in Co. Dublin, with Declan and Shane at home and Cathal close by at Clongowes Wood. It might not have been

Co. Tipperary, but after Long Island it was good enough. Tony may have been spending a great deal of time abroad, but the Ryans as a family were at home once again. So it can hardly have surprised Tony that when he came back to announce that everyone was moving to Thailand it was devastating news for Mairéad. In the end, Tony managed to convince her by saying that it would be for only 'a couple of years'. After that, he promised, he would have made his mark in Aer Lingus to such an extent that he would be able to demand a senior management position in Dublin.

Not the least of Mairéad's concerns was the safety and happiness of her boys in Thailand. That summer had seen revolution overthrow the military dictatorship, and the political situation remained fragile and dangerous. There was a feeling that anything could happen while they were there.

Yet, for all the sense of political chaos, what struck the Ryans when they arrived in Thailand for the first time was its spectacular beauty. At weekends the family would travel to the island of Ko Samet. The beaches and the warmth of the sea were like nothing the boys had ever experienced before. 'Thailand in the 1970s was just incredible,' Declan recalls, 'very unspoilt.'

Bangkok they found a relatively safe and friendly city. While the three-year-old Shane remained at home with his mother, Declan was sent to the English school in Bangkok, where, to his father's evident pride, he continued to assert his Catholicism by getting suspended for refusing to sing the Anglican hymn 'All Things Bright and Beautiful'.

Putting down these kinds of cultural markers was a strong feature of life in the international community. Much of the Ryans' social life centred on the swimming-pool of the British Club in central Bangkok, where the boys got into fierce competition with the Brits, Aussies and Kiwis. In the first year Cathal, who swam for Clongowes, combined with two other Irish boys, the McManus brothers, to win the Gold Ribbon 4 × 100 m relay race at the annual swimming gala. 'Tony loved that,' Declan says. 'He went all around Bangkok boasting that the Irish had won it with three men instead of four, and he was sending letters home saying the only time the Paddys could win is when we're one man down.'

These were enjoyable times for the family; but, just as in the United States, life in Thailand was also taxing for Mairéad and the family. Being on different continents had been tough enough in the more familiar environment of New York. But in Bangkok it involved more sacrifices for everyone, not least the children. Cathal continued to make the long trip back to Clongowes at the beginning of each school term. After Declan turned twelve he joined his brother on the arduous journey. There were no direct flights, so the two brothers had to make their way to Karachi in Pakistan to catch a plane to London. Given that their father was in the airline business, they might have expected him to do a better job at making their arrangements. 'I remember us getting offloaded at Karachi', Declan recalls, 'and ringing Tony in the airport at four in the morning, saying, "Would you ever just buy us a ticket some time?" I only had two quid in my pocket. Luckily, British Airways took care of us.'

For Tony himself, life in Bangkok was all about work. 'He was in charge of everything,' David Kennedy says, 'including responsibility for collecting the rental money on the lease.' To keep the whole operation together involved both dedication and not a little tact. To begin with, there were relations with Air Siam to consider. Tony effectually became no. 2 in the airline, working closely with Virachai Vannukul to make the Boeing 747 route as profitable as possible. But it was also his job to watch Air Siam for any sign of irregularity or financial distress—so he was both friend and informer.

Then there were the Aer Lingus workers to consider. Bangkok was a city with many pleasures on offer. He would tell the staff: enjoy the benefits, but remember that you are here not just as employees of the company but also as representatives of Ireland.

There were also the cultural differences to navigate between the Irish and Thai staff members. This latter aspect did cause some tensions within the Irish group, especially when it came to allowing Thai trainees into the cockpit. At a 'clear the air' meeting on the subject, one staff member asked whether it was really a good idea 'to put these guys in the left-hand seat when they're just down from the trees, for God's sake.' Tony's response was quiet but brutal: 'Okay, I will agree with that,' he said, 'if anyone here can tell me the difference between "down from the trees" and "up from the bogs".'

Smoothing over cultural misunderstandings and sensitivities was also an important part of Tony's job when dealing with the many VIPs touring Asia in the 1970s. One of the trickiest involved Jack Lynch, leader of Fianna Fáil, who visited in 1974. Even before Lynch arrived there had been panic in Bangkok when his plane went missing, leaving Tony on the ground wondering how he would explain to Dublin that he had lost a former Taoiseach. In fact Lynch's plane, flying out from Saigon, had made an unexpected stop in Cambodia, which was in the middle of a bloody civil war. The Vietnamese ambassador to Cambodia was also on board and needed to be dropped off. Flying into Phnom Penh Airport, which was constantly under mortar attack by the Khmer Rouge, was a risky business. Lynch's flight got in all right, but then he had to remain on the plane with no air conditioning or toilets for more than six hours. No wonder that by the time the flight arrived in Bangkok, Lynch was extremely ill.

Tony was waiting with a limousine for Lynch and the former Minister for Justice, Des O'Malley. The journey into Bangkok, on crowded, damaged roads in the monsoon season, was almost as stressful as the plane journey. Lynch, sweating profusely, slept in the back while Tony and O'Malley began chatting. The two would later become close, with O'Malley even acting as solicitor for Tony when he bought Kilboy House in Co. Tipperary a few years afterwards. Perhaps those friendly relations were rooted in the tricky exchanges that took place between them in Bangkok.

Tony asked where the two politicians were staying. When O'Malley told him, Tony turned white. 'You can't say there,' he said.

'It has been booked for us,' O'Malley retorted, 'so it must be all right.'

Tony stood firm. 'I'm taking you to the Siam Intercontinental.'

When they arrived at the new hotel, O'Malley demanded an explanation, but Tony refused. Only much later did he get the story out of Tony that the other hotel had been involved in a sex scandal just a few weeks earlier.

'That's fine,' O'Malley said, 'but why couldn't you just tell me?'

Tony was horrified. 'You couldn't be telling a thing like that to the former Taoiseach,' he explained, 'and sure he might be Taoiseach again!' Tony's mother, like Lynch from Cork, would have been proud.

Tony's working life in Bangkok in many ways must have seemed a souped-up version of his time as station manager in JFK. He may not have been dealing with the day-to-day operational details of flights, but he was still working long hours, coping with staff problems, operating within a foreign jurisdiction, smoothing the way for visiting dignitaries and taking orders from head office in Dublin. To all intents and purposes he continued to look like a solid company man.

Those who visited Tony in Bangkok during this period, however, noticed a dramatic change in his character. When Laurence Crowley went out to Thailand he was astonished by the transformation.

On one occasion the two men took a taxi, with Crowley picking up the tab. 'How much did he charge you?' Tony enquired. When Crowley told him, Tony was outraged that his colleague had been so egregiously overcharged. Tony ran in front of the car and, to Crowley's horror, lay down in front of it until the driver repaid the difference in the fare.

Others too observed a man more entrepreneurial and self-consciously aggressive. One colleague from Aer Lingus was amused to find Tony reading *Winning through Intimidation*, the *New York Times* best-seller by Robert J. Ringer that taught how 'the game of business is played in a vicious jungle.'

Tony was also aware of the change. Later he would tell the story of becoming fixated by a street food vendor he saw on his way to work each day:

> He was a banana-chip maker. His business was to slice, cook and sell banana chips to passers-by. He was extraordinarily skilful, not only in slicing hundreds of bananas into thousands of perfect pieces but also at selling his product. He impressed me and made me think. I felt it a pity that such marketing, technical talent and energy were devoted to a process which sold for a mere penny. There and then I determined that . . . I would apply my energies to developing and marketing a big-ticket product which could sell for vastly more.

Perhaps the most telling witness to the impact on Tony during his time in Bangkok was Mick O'Carroll. The two men had worked together when they started out at Shannon in the 1950s, and they had remained friends ever since. When O'Carroll stayed with the Ryans in Bangkok he was astonished by what he found. The craic between mates was as good as ever, but there was a new element that O'Carroll had never seen in Tony before. 'He was no longer the laid-back, devil-may-care guy', O'Carroll says, 'but a driven businessman getting up at crazy times in the morning, up until all hours and talking about visions of leasing.'

At a relatively late age, heading towards his fortieth birthday, the entrepreneurial heart had finally and, to those who knew him longest, unexpectedly started beating in the breast of Tony Ryan.

Tony's first idea was to launch a business that specialised in aircraft leasing in the Third World through commodity swaps instead of money. 'There are places where they have, let's say, an over-supply of coconuts but they've got no money,' he explained to Derek O'Brien, who was working with him running the Air Siam lease, 'and there are other places where they've no coconuts but they have money, so why can't we lease the planes as a commodity swap?'

When he tested the ground with potential customers, Tony soon found that they baulked at the idea of commodity-swapping their

Jumbos, for example, for bicycles, and the concept was dropped. It was an illustration of how Tony was by now prepared to think outside conventional wisdom to get a business off the ground, even if, laughs Mick O'Carroll, 'it was a daft idea.'

Tony's next idea was more straightforward. He had already successfully leased out planes for Aer Lingus. Now he planned to establish a new company that would act as a broker for airlines around the world that needed to offload surplus aircraft.

On 1 May 1975 Tony became chief executive of a new aircraft-leasing company, Guinness Peat Aviation. He took a 10 per cent holding for a £5,000 investment—a large sum for an Aer Lingus manager, which he raised by remortgaging his house. He also negotiated a performance-based, profit-sharing agreement. The other shareholders, taking 45 per cent each, were Aer Lingus and Guinness Peat, a London investment firm in which the airline was a minority shareholder.

The circumstances of how GPA came into being were complicated. Tony would later claim that he thought up the concept for a leasing company on his own in Bangkok, where 'the original idea was fermenting away'. However, when he returned to Dublin to pitch the idea to Aer Lingus the new chief executive, David Kennedy, poured cold water on it. But when he got a second meeting with Kennedy, Tony turned up with his lawyer—a trick taken straight out of *Winning through Intimidation*—and informed the company that he was resigning in order to set up his own leasing company in conjunction with an Asian airline and an American bank. Recognising that Aer Lingus was about to lose an opportunity, Kennedy caved in and offered Tony the chance to go into business with Aer Lingus. From that position of strength Tony was able to negotiate the ball-breaking contract that gave him profit-sharing and a 10 per cent shareholding that could not be diluted in the event of other investors coming on board. This deal would see his initial £5,000 investment transformed into multi-millions.

The internal company history that GPA later commissioned told a rather more benign story. This version has Tony returning to Dublin in order to resign and launch his own start-up in Asia. When he informed Kennedy, the latter replied, 'Why don't you do it in Ireland?'

That ties in with Seán Braiden's recollection. Aer Lingus had bought a minority shareholding in the Guinness Peat Group, with the idea of having a foothold in the City of London, making financing easier for any new business. But, according to Braiden,

> nothing much happened until Tony came along with the idea of a leasing company. So the view inside Aer Lingus was this was an entrepreneurial endeavour on our behalf which wasn't going to cost an awful lot. If it blossomed, all the better; but if it didn't, then the least it would do would be to solve Aer Lingus's own leasing problems.

So Tony got the go-ahead, Braiden concludes, because he was 'convincing' and 'put a very good story across'.

Kennedy remembers events differently. 'The initial thrust for the establishment of GPA came from Aer Lingus,' he says. The idea was part of an overall policy that Aer Lingus developed during a sharp downturn for the global airline industry to generate profits from activities that were ancillary to the company's main business. That change of direction was approved by the Minister for Transport and Power, Brian Lenihan, Snr, and then confirmed by the new minister, Peter Barry, when the Government changed in 1973.

Aer Lingus wanted to use its own in-house skill base to convert cost centres in the airline into profit centres. Gerry Dempsey, the Aer Lingus representative on the Guinness Peat Group board, presented a list of eight areas of possible collaboration between the airline and the investment firm, including a travel agency, freight forwarding and foreign exchange. Of all the ideas, aircraft leasing stood out as the 'number one' most viable project.

'So we decided,' Kennedy says, 'in collaboration with Guinness Peat, that we would set up an aircraft-leasing company bringing together the financial strength of the bank and the aviation expertise and credibility of Aer Lingus.' It was only at this stage, he suggests, when the decision to go ahead had been made, that Dempsey 'discussed with Tony the concept of his becoming chief executive of this new company.'

Even today the question of whether Aer Lingus received due recognition for the part it played in setting up GPA continues to rankle with Kennedy.

> Tony said that he would have set up a leasing company himself anyway, and maybe he could have done so. But he would not have had the credibility of a City of London bank and a well-reputed airline behind him. It is a pity that in later years he allowed the myth to spread that Aer Lingus was a reluctant participant in the company. Nothing can be further from the truth.

On one level Tony was always happy to give Aer Lingus due credit. He understood that brokerage was the 'raw edge of the industry' and that it often conjured up images of 'one man working out of a garage . . . striving to clinch the one good deal which might set him up for life.' The involvement of Aer Lingus, a well-respected and Government-owned airline, neutered that problem. In fact, one of the early problems the new company ran into was that potential clients didn't always appreciate that Guinness Peat Aviation was an Aer Lingus spin-off at all. The combination of an Irish address and the Guinness name seemed to speak more of pints of stout than of a serious aircraft-leasing business—and what supplies of peat had to do with things was anyone's guess. No wonder the company quickly resorted to operating under the initials GPA—even though Tony himself always preferred the full title.

Tony never wavered in his stance that the original idea for an aircraft brokerage was his. He always maintained that his early soundings in Aer Lingus about the idea for a new company were peremptorily rejected. Soon he found himself frustrated to be in possession of 'valuable market intelligence about someone who wanted a DC-9 and I could do nothing about it.' That was the moment he put an ultimatum to Aer Lingus: back my idea or lose me.

Perhaps in the end it all came down to personality. David Kennedy in 1975 was already a star of the international aviation industry. Appointed chief executive of Ireland's national airline at the age of just thirty-five, he had made it to the top of a business worth $100 million a year in only twelve years. No wonder that *Time* hailed him as the 'whiz-kid' of the airline corporate world.

But Kennedy, whose cool, considered business personality reflected his past as an Irish chess champion, was the head of a semi-state organisation. He was an innovator in his own way, but he was also a manager operating within an environment that demanded due process and order.

Tony Ryan was by now a different kind of animal. Aer Lingus had helped give birth to an entrepreneur. And, as Tony said of himself in 1975, 'I was never going back to the womb.'

Chapter 4

START-UP

'It was a hectic month with many, many inquiries and leads,' wrote Tony Ryan in his first Guinness Peat Aviation report to the board in July 1975. 'It does bring home forcibly that in this industry one must go down many "blind alleys". I estimate that it may be necessary to follow up 50 leads before pinning down some business.' It was a signal of just how difficult things would be for Tony and his fledgling leasing business.

The following month GPA formally began trading in Shannon Free Zone, the international business park next to Shannon Airport in Co. Clare. There were certain obvious advantages to this decision, not least the highly favourable corporate taxation system that gave the new company tax-free status on its profits. There was also the strategic perk that the location, well over a hundred miles from Dublin, was away from the prying eyes of Aer Lingus senior management. Tony already had Aer Lingus placemen breathing down his neck in the chairman, Dick White, and company secretary, David Fleury. The last thing he needed in addition to this supervision was Aer Lingus senior management regularly dropping in on him unannounced to 'see how things are getting along'. Physical distance from Dublin helped ensure autonomy for both Tony and GPA.

Beyond these obvious business advantages, there were other important personal considerations in this choice of location. By setting up in Shannon, Tony Ryan was returning home. When he first raised the issue of a Shannon licence with Laurence Crowley of Stokes Kennedy Crowley during a long flight back to Ireland from Thailand, Tony explained that his main reason for wanting to go to Shannon was 'because my background is Tipperary'.

That mattered to Tony at a profound level. Over the coming years he would find himself on the road and in the sky travelling about half a million miles per annum. But he remained rooted in Ireland because at the end of every trip he came back to Tipperary and the south. Home for Tony always centred on the lines of the Great Southern Railway. His childhood had been spent in Limerick Junction and Thurles, with regular trips down to Mallow to stay with his mother's family. Now he was returning to Shannon and would soon buy Kilboy House in north Co. Tipperary. These touchstones meant that, however far and often he travelled, Tony remained rooted in the terrain of his youth.

Not that everyone welcomed this attachment to the south of Ireland. Tony insisted that employees of GPA had to live near Shannon rather than commute. Eventually many would buy beautiful houses in idyllic spots such as Killaloe or Castlelough on the shores of Lough Derg, but to begin with they often lived in the bleak environs of Shannon.

The Free Zone itself was a barren, featureless landscape of grey concrete, with barely a tree in sight. In addition to the physical harshness, most GPA staff members felt like they were at the far end of the world, or worse. 'Shannon was like the back of the moon,' recalls one employee.

Another early recruit to the GPA team, Graham Boyd, remembers the shock of adapting to life in 'a real backwater'. His journey to work involved driving from his house in Ennis to Shannon on a single-track bog road. At home in the evenings there was only one television station to watch, which began at 6 p.m. with the Angelus. The communications structure was dire. The Boyds were on the waiting list for a telephone line for well over a year. Even when the phone was put in, the line often didn't work. Ringing Shannon from abroad was even worse. This meant going through the international operator, who often had little or no idea where they were trying to ring. 'Caller, can you spell "Ireland"?' became a familiar refrain. 'In the morning you could be doing a deal in New York', Boyd recalls, 'and that evening involved in a hit-and-run with a cow in the middle of a bog road.'

No-one enjoyed finding humour in their situation more than Tony. For years afterwards he would recount with great gusto the story of trying to set up an alarm call from his home phone ('Silvermines 29') in Co. Tipperary.

With an early start the next morning, he had telephoned the local switchboard. 'Hello, Mrs Hoare. Any chance you can give me an alarm call in the morning?'

'What's that then, Tony?'

'Well, you call to wake me up and then you charge me for it.'

'But I can't do that. I haven't got an alarm clock.'

Two hours later the switchboard operator phoned back.

'Mrs Hoare, it's past midnight. What can I do for you?'

'Tony, it's just if you're getting up early, would you ever give me a call, as I have an early start myself.'

Whatever humour Tony found in the charms of rural life, 'backwater' was never an impression he allowed GPA staff to convey to potential clients. From the start he was obsessed with details of presentation and image in order to convey that GPA was a serious international player. GPA's first brochure was a lavish, full-colour affair featuring photographs of Georgian Dublin and Waterford Crystal rather than the concrete jungle of the Shannon Free Zone.

Staff members were also expected to conform to Tony's ideas about how to dress. One colleague remembers that

> his specific notion was that you wear a suit. You wear a suit to the office. You wear a suit when you're travelling. You wear a suit at all times and you look smart. Hungover or otherwise, in hotels at the back of beyond, sitting on aeroplanes—you had to look sharp.

Telephones were expected to be answered after the first ring, irrespective of whose desk they were on, not least because the chances of a call getting through to Shannon were about one in five; each call missed was potential business times five, and it conveyed incompetence. Employees told anybody who would listen how busy GPA was and how many hundreds of thousands of miles they travelled each year.

Even within the Shannon business park, appearances mattered. At first GPA moved into an annex of Airport House, which was functional but drab. 'Within a wet week of being there', recalls one member of staff, 'Tony was on his way out, and we moved into our second office block, which he immediately tried to get called GPA House. It was an image thing.'

The team that first joined Tony in Shannon was small and mainly comprised those he trusted from his Aer Lingus days. Christy Ryan, who had been with Tony from the start of his working life, now joined him on secondment from Aer Lingus. So too did Seán Braiden, a friend from Tony's time in Heathrow. Billy Yeoman and Mary McCarthy, a typist, were also both Aer Lingus. Peter Swift, an executive from the charter airline Britannia Airways, was former Aer Lingus. Of the initial cohort, only Peter Ledbetter, an accountant and former international tennis player, was not connected with Ireland's national airline. Ledbetter became director of finance. Swift dealt with the technical side of leasing agreements. Braiden, Christy Ryan and Yeoman took responsibility for business in specific geographical areas. Tony's role, said Swift, was 'to negotiate the commercial terms of the deal'. And to get the deal in the first place.

GPA's first years were exciting but challenging. 'We lived hand to mouth, with everything operating on a deal-by-deal basis,' recalls Mick O'Carroll, another friend who soon joined Tony in GPA.

Liam Meade, who arrived in 1977, captured the sense of chaos that often accompanied the process of getting deals. 'It was a case of running around with messages we didn't understand, for planes we couldn't find.'

They travelled everywhere and never took no for an answer. Every lead was followed up. The attrition rate for deals was high. 'Of the six likely projects noted in the last annual report, only one materialised,' Tony observed in the report for 1977/8.

The Aer Lingus connection was vital at the beginning in helping GPA even to get in the door for meetings. 'Really we had to play the

Aer Lingus card,' says Braiden. 'You rang up and made an appointment with an airline CEO for "Seán Braiden, Aer Lingus executive", but when you got in the office you did your best to bring it round to leasing.'

That proposition was always a difficult sell. Leasing was still an emerging business, and to most in the industry there was something second-rate, even seedy, about it. Mainstream airlines felt that leasing was not as solid as buying. They were always suspicious about how much the broker was making from a deal. Manufacturers were equally unenthusiastic, as every plane leased was the lost sale of a new aircraft. Therefore GPA was always working against the grain, trying to drum up business in the face of hostility from established players in the industry. The only way to overcome that suspicion was to keep networking in face-to-face meetings, thereby gradually inserting themselves into the day-to-day life of the industry.

The trick for GPA was always to master information—to know which airlines had planes available, when they were available, how much money the airlines wanted for them, and where there were customers who might need them. Tony and his team pored over the vast amount of data that was available to the public from airlines and manufacturers. They became experts in route networks and the fleets of every airline, including the age of aircraft. Often business could be found in the gap between an airline's current needs and the delivery of a new aircraft. Studying orders placed with manufacturers also provided information on when an airline planned to expand its business. That in turn would suggest broader trends about global travel, highlighting regions where tourism was growing, as had happened in Thailand.

Added to this comprehensive study of the industry were tips and gossip picked up around the world. Even if there was no possibility of a leasing deal, it remained vital to meet chief executives and purchasing and planning managers to get a grasp on future thinking by the airlines.

No inconvenience was too great to endure. Braiden remembers one occasion, in 1976 in Seoul, getting a call from Tony telling him to join him in Los Angeles, as he had a possible lead. Braiden's American visa had just days until it ran out, so he went from Seoul to Tokyo to get a new visa from the US embassy, took a Pan Am flight to Honolulu and then another onwards to LA. When he arrived, after more than twenty-four hours of travelling and hanging around in airports and embassies, he was met by Tony, who told him that the potential deal now required them both to return to Seoul. So back they went across the Pacific. 'It was mad, mad stuff,' Braiden laughs.

The Aer Lingus name was vital in setting up many of these meetings, and the company also helped GPA prepare for them. If Tony needed specialists to back up a plan or provide expertise, Aer Lingus offered it. This might include financial analysis of route costings, marketing support or technical advice about what was needed to support a certain aircraft type. That expertise gave GPA an important competitive advantage. It also gave them a financial one, as to have paid for the kind of knowledge that Aer Lingus had in-house would have been impossible on Tony's shoestring budget.

This information on tap enabled GPA to negotiate contracts of great complexity, making deals where the possibility had not even seemed to exist. An early example was the involved lease that Tony put together in January 1977 between Air Siam, McDonnell Douglas and Korean Air Lines. While Tony was in Bangkok managing the Aer Lingus lease, he had assisted Air Siam in arranging a nineteen-year lease with McDonnell Douglas for a DC-10. The plane was put into operation, with McDonnell Douglas providing aircraft maintenance at their headquarters in LA. Everything worked well until Air Siam went bust in 1976. McDonnell Douglas repossessed the plane in a grab while it was on the ground in the US. Even though they had possession, McDonnell Douglas couldn't get rid of it, because legally Air Siam remained the owners. It was a stalemate: Air Siam owned the lease but didn't have the plane; McDonnell Douglas had the plane but not the lease. Inevitably the issue was heading for the courts.

Tony, always on the lookout for an opportunity, now executed what became a trademark GPA manoeuvre. On his travels in south-east Asia he had picked up information that Korean Air Lines was seeking to expand capacity on the route taking workers to the Gulf states. He approached the airline, saying he could get them a cheap lease for a high-density format DC-10. He then went back to Air Siam, saying, in effect, 'You need money up front; you're not going to get your plane back, but I can get you some alleviation of your debt.' A similar pitch was made to McDonnell Douglas: 'You have a plane you can't sell, you're owed money, and I can get you a new deal with an airline that can pay.'

Neither McDonnell Douglas nor Air Siam was particularly happy about the arrangement, as they would both still lose money. But Tony had correctly calculated that each side would recognise that half a loaf was better than no loaf at all.

'That was typical of Tony,' concludes Braiden, whose round trip from Seoul to LA had paid off. 'He could see three situations and knew how to pick his way through the relationships. It took a lot of insight and putting together. It really was a beautiful deal.'

Tony's ability to pull off such complex arrangements stemmed in part from his willingness to fly thousands of miles to secure a contract. He was also rigorous about keeping everybody in the GPA operation on the same page. One of the methods he established early on to achieve this was the 'Monday morning meeting', which became legendary in Irish and international aviation circles. Like most legends, it contained more than its fair share of myth.

'Every time I read anything about Tony Ryan or GPA,' one early employee recalls, 'you get this story about a guy at the morning meeting on Mondays beating the bejaysus out of everybody, and it was cobblers—absolute cobblers.'

Everyone in the organisation was expected to attend the Monday meeting, even if that meant flying in from half way round the world. In addition, there was a daily meeting of whoever happened to be in Shannon. Each gathering took place at the start of the working day, which in characteristic GPA style was at 8:30 rather than the more conventional 9 a.m. that prevailed in 1970s Ireland. The senior person in the office on any given day would chair the meeting. There was a short agenda that consisted mainly of deals that were being worked on. When Tony was in the office he took the meeting himself. Inevitably that meant a more charged atmosphere in the room. In particular, if something had not been done, or if somebody wasn't pulling their weight, he communicated that fact and wanted to know what was going to be done about it. 'But', says one member of the team, 'he wasn't rude: he was forceful, not insulting, and there wasn't blood coming off the walls or the windows rattling. That didn't happen. In fact, if anything, he was a quiet man.'

That quietness could itself be unnerving. GPA staff members would often find themselves sharing long flights with Tony during which he might not speak a word to them beyond the usual basic courtesies. One employee endured a trip to Sri Lanka in almost total silence. 'I thought that was very strange,' he recalled. 'Later I learnt that sometimes he was away in another world, and while you're there you're not the important thing in his world at that point in time. He was planning where he's going and what he's going to say when he gets there.'

The staff at GPA soon became expert Ryanologists, reading his body language for signs of his mood. 'Even when he was saying nothing', one says, 'you could get a vibe from him. You would know if he was frowning inwardly.'

For most, this detachment could be intimidating. For others, particularly when they started in the job, it was humiliating. Graham Boyd found his early days in GPA extremely difficult. He felt bullied by Tony and hated the frequent refusals to talk to him or even to acknowledge his existence. After six months Boyd told Peter Ledbetter that he couldn't put up with this treatment any longer. Ledbetter took him for a pint at Durty Nelly's pub, a few miles from Shannon, and twisted his arm to stay. 'Good things are going to happen here,' Ledbetter told him, explaining that Boyd had yet to prove himself to the boss.

Soon afterwards Boyd did his first deal. He still received little in the way of praise from Tony, but he felt he was treated with a new respect. Suddenly the morning meetings cheered up. 'If you got a deal you would come home on a real high,' he remembers. 'It was a great buzz.' Once a GPA staff member started bringing in business, then and only then did they have Tony's ear.

Tony's detachment, even coldness, was a characteristic that co-workers in Aer Lingus had noticed when he was station manager in JFK Airport. 'He was a very private guy,' recalls Derek O'Brien, who worked under him in New York. 'You would only see him socially every now and again. You could have a few jars with him, but that would be it. He really kept a barrier between himself and people who worked for him.'

Although at GPA Tony could be very considerate about making sure that people had time to spend with their family when they were back from travelling, that sense of distance remained between him as the boss and those who worked for him. On one level that manifested itself as dissatisfaction with their work. While he would sing the praises of his 'talented staff' to the GPA board, that judgement would rarely be heard in Shannon.

'I say this to his credit,' Laurence Crowley judges, 'but he was never content with the status quo. He always thought, This can be better, I can improve this thing, change the model and make it better.'

Boyd agrees. 'If anyone got a deal,' he recalls, 'the response was always why hadn't they got a better one.'

Sometimes that was inspirational; at other times it could be deflating. Only Christy Ryan, who had been with Tony from the beginning, was perceived to be close to him. Other workers found the chain-smoking Christy 'cold', like Tony, and utterly loyal to him. Staff members would be more likely to seek out Peter Ledbetter, as Graham Boyd did, or Peter Swift, as sympathetic voices to intercede on their behalf with Tony.

GPA's major shareholders also found Tony difficult. On the one hand there was admiration for his dedication and willingness to go to the ends of the earth for a deal. A story did the rounds in Dublin

Airport early on about the former Aer Lingus chief executive Michael Dargan taking a holiday in Nepal, only to find the GPA man sitting on his suitcase in the foothills of the Himalayas. 'Why are you here, Tony?' he asked. 'Because I heard they're buying 737s and we might get a lease out of them,' came the inevitable reply.

Dargan's successors, however, found Tony trickier to cope with. While the GPA boss was happy to take advantage of the technical expertise on offer at Aer Lingus—not to mention the savings on cheap flights, hotels and car rental—he was less inclined to take direction from their management. David Kennedy recalls that Aer Lingus nominees on the GPA board were constantly 'annoyed' because 'Tony treated [them] in an off-hand manner.'

They would have been even more annoyed if Tony's comments at the morning meetings had been reported back. 'Will the board come along on that?' Mick O'Carroll recalls Peter Ledbetter asking on one occasion. 'Feck the board!' Tony replied. That was more than just bravado in front of the troops: it spoke of a genuine contempt for his old bosses. 'He had them running around in circles,' O'Carroll says approvingly.

Tony's most difficult task was getting both Aer Lingus and the Guinness Peat Group to take him and GPA seriously. In October 1975 the company achieved its first success when it leased a Boeing 737 to Egyptair on a four-month contract. The following month they began work on a bigger deal with the Japanese trading company Nissho Iwai, which had interests in All Nippon Airways. Four years later Nissho Iwai would become engulfed in a scandal involving illegal kickbacks to Japanese politicians when selling military aircraft on behalf of McDonnell Douglas, Boeing and Grumman. Following the suicide of one of the company's executives and four arrests, the company withdrew from the aircraft-marketing business altogether. However, in 1975 they had 737s to sell. The deal GPA attempted to put together, which was far from straightforward, reveals how everyone in this nascent leasing business was operating less on a wing and more on a prayer.

On one level, everything looked simple enough. Nissho Iwai had their 737 to sell. Aer Lingus wanted to buy another 737, but not until March 1977. GPA lined up an airline, Air Zaïre, to lease the plane in the intervening year, before the Irish carrier needed it. Everyone was happy: GPA would buy the plane, lease it to the Zaïrean airline and then sell it to Aer Lingus. The problem for GPA was that neither Aer Lingus nor Guinness Mahon, which was financing the deal, was prepared to let GPA take the capital exposure of almost a quarter of a million dollars that it needed to buy its first aircraft.

Tony was furious, not least because GPA was set to make that amount in profit from the deal. In the end only a 'gentlemen's agreement' of the kind that still existed in the City of London in the 1970s kept the deal alive. Aer Lingus, as a state-owned company, could not guarantee the $3 million from Guinness Mahon, a private bank, that would finance the deal. The bank, however, took the fact that Aer Lingus would be buying the aircraft as a guarantee in all but name. 'Our only risk', says Ledbetter, 'was Air Zaïre not paying the rent, and we got a four-month deposit from them. So we operated very conservatively.'

Even with the bank and Aer Lingus on board, the final moments of the deal were nervy. Everyone met in London in March 1976 to sign the contract. With the Japanese becoming visibly angry, GPA had to stall until the phone call came through to say that Air Zaïre had made the first payment. Eventually confirmation arrived and, about five o'clock in the morning, the contract was signed.

After eight months in business Tony was able to report that GPA had broken even substantially ahead of its forecast, in fact making a 'small profit'. He had the basis of an 'aggressive team' with 'enthusiasm and ability', ready to take the company to the next level.

Yet the experience with the Air Zaïre lease, he informed the board, had been a bitter one. 'The last-minute rearrangement and distortion of the original concept' was bound to have 'some negative repercussions' for GPA. The 'loss of control' of the Air Zaïre lease was 'unfortunate', because he had wanted this to be 'a showpiece' for the company.

Now he gave his board both a prediction and a warning. 'It is now very obvious', he told them, 'that Guinness Peat Aviation can make substantial profits if supported.' That endeavour required a brave approach. 'Our future is suspect', he cautioned, 'if we cannot put aircraft brokerage on a different level to the traditional broker. We must develop new concepts and ideas.' If GPA failed to seize the moment, there were others ready and able to do so. Continental Airlines had recently concluded an agreement with Citibank to offer a similar service. 'We now have a potentially serious rival,' Tony predicted.

After less than a year in business Tony had already begun to identify a broader strategy for GPA, 'moving', says Laurence Crowley, 'from being a broker to a leaser, which was a big step forward.' Tony now began a relentless campaign to persuade his two major shareholders to allow him to acquire aircraft without having them pre-let. The move from broker to leaser meant upping the risk factor. The current arrangement of acquiring a lease and then finding a plane meant very little exposure unless the lessee went bankrupt. Moving to a new strategy was more risky, but, Tony promised, it would eventually allow GPA to sweep up most of the aircraft of the world—and all the profits that went with them.

'We are inundated with requests for B737 leases for [next] year,' he wrote in frustration to the board at the end of 1976, 'but at this time cannot satisfy a single airline.' The recent upswing in the fortunes of the aviation business meant that it was harder to source efficient jet aircraft. 'GPA must be prepared to accept some element of protected risk in either leasing or acquiring aircraft,' he pleaded. 'Having even one aircraft would allow us some control.'

A few months later Tony returned to the same theme, but this time he was hardly able to contain his anger. Profits were up, to half a million pounds. New staff members were being taken on. But there was frustration within the company about the fact that potential was going unexploited. In particular, everyone was 'concerned at the bank's lack of involvement in our development to date.' Then Tony let rip, writing angrily:

> I accept that frustration is an element in our work but cannot condone long-term continuation of this middleman 'Mickey Mouse' involvement in leases. Frankly our staff are too talented for this grovelling work. Furthermore, by taking a risk we can utilise our expertise and make more money for GPA.

Projects to date had all been short term. The need to acquire aircraft was vital in maintaining cash flow. That would require a credit line of at least $500 million through the Guinness Peat Group to obtain even a reasonable share of the financing market. He told his major shareholders:

> GPA progress to date must be described as interesting and exciting ... I believe we have scratched the surface of an industry that offers fantastic returns if properly structured and supported. Limited risk is necessary if we are to tap this profit potential.

Eventually Tony's badgering paid off: in December 1977 GPA began the process of acquiring aircraft when it signed a contract for a Boeing 747-100, to be delivered in 1981. The following year GPA established a subsidiary, Air Tara, to register aircraft in Ireland. In the meantime Tony consciously began implementing a strategy that moved the company from brokerage to being a wet-leasing operator with access to its own equipment and staff. The financial return was about four times higher. GPA would maintain tighter control over negotiations, leading to longer-term contracts and a build-up of residual value services.

The move into wet leasing was a step change for GPA, but it didn't come without its own frustrations—and even real dangers. A month after the deal with Nissho Iwai, GPA won a deal with National Airways Corporation of New Zealand to lease out a Boeing 737-200. Tony had expressed his habitual irritation that GPA itself could not buy the lease, which was being offered at well under market value, because he knew 'we could make a substantial amount of money by taking a position on the lease.' But he had exclusive rights in marketing the aircraft, which GPA succeeded in wet leasing to Nigeria Airways.

For the nine-month period of the lease, GPA was projected to make $200,000 profit, with more to come if the arrangement was extended. Even after the first two months, the projected profit went up, as the aircraft was flying many more hours than the minimum agreed in the lease. Tony reported:

> It was obvious that if we want great profits we must get into wet leasing [where] the return as compared to leasing the hull only is quite staggering. On the Nigeria lease, GPA will achieve more revenue and profit than the aircraft owners.

For the next few years Nigeria would become the cash cow of his business.

Wet leases also came with their own set of problems. In the case of Nigeria Airways, even getting the aircraft to Lagos was problematic. The man given that task was Seán Braiden, GPA's vice-president for south-east Asia. ('We all got great titles!' he remembers.) He was in Bangkok when Tony ordered him down to Christchurch to collect the aircraft and deliver it to Nigeria Airways. 'It was a B737,' Braiden continues, 'so I could only do two-hour hops right across the world. It took us three days, going something like Christchurch, Brisbane, Darwin, Kuala Lumpur, Bombay, Khartoum, Cameroon and Lagos, where the Nigerians signed for the plane that night.' For Braiden it was then a return trip that went 'Lagos, Rome, London, Dublin, Shannon, back to Dublin, Amsterdam and onwards to Bangkok.' Such was the life of GPA executive, he reflects, although 'Tony was doing that all the time.'

Getting the plane to Lagos was only half the story for Tony and GPA. There were difficulties and delays about changing the aircraft registration from New Zealand to Ireland. That meant paperwork irregularities when the 737 arrived in Nigeria. Accompanying Braiden to Lagos as part of the wet-lease operation were three crew members from New Zealand, who had their passports promptly confiscated by the immigration authorities on arrival. Those crew members then refused to take orders from Nigeria Airways officials, leaving the plane sitting on the ground for three days.

Eventually Tony sent Peter Swift to Lagos to sort everything out. A sum of $12,000 was paid to Nigeria Airways as 'no fault' compensation for the plane not flying. It was money well spent as far as GPA was concerned. Swift recalls that the cheque 'built up good faith with Nigeria and was a sign of our willingness to step up to our responsibilities.'

The relationship turned out to be highly profitable, but it shows how the company had to operate outside the comfort zone of Western airlines to make money. 'It was huge revenue for GPA,' Braiden recalls, 'but it was not an easy area to operate in.' As Tony warned the board, 'conditions are, and will be, extremely difficult.'

The difficulties and dangers involved in international leasing were even more starkly apparent in Iran. In the summer of 1976 Tony arranged the wet lease of two Air Jamaica 727s to Iranair. At the outset there were the usual cultural problems involving staff from two different continents, not least that the Iranians at first refused to work with the black Air Jamaica crew for 'security reasons'. But these problems were ironed out quickly enough, and the leases continued working well until 1978, when they were overtaken by political events in Iran.

By the autumn of that year the events were well under way that would lead to the overthrow of the Shah and his replacement by the religious leader Ayatollah Khomeini in the Iranian Revolution. Almost half the Iranian population was urban, and most of those were poor. As the gap between them and the wealthy elite grew, with an increasingly impoverished middle class, so people began to take to the streets in mass demonstrations.

Observing with concern from Shannon, Tony sent Christy Ryan out to assess the situation. The message that came back from Tehran was unambiguous: 'Abort!' The Royal Garden Hotel, where the GPA team of twelve pilots, eight engineers, one office manager and fifty-eight flight attendants were staying, had already been attacked by rioters. None of the seventy-nine staff members was hurt, but it had been a lucky escape. On 7 November the mostly Irish team flew out of Tehran using one of the GPA 707s.

In Dublin the story was headline news. 'Mercy flight brings Irish girls out of riot-torn Iran', ran the uncharacteristically flushed headline of the *Irish Times*. 'On arrival in London', the paper went on, 'one girl said: "We were virtual prisoners on the 11th floor of the hotel . . . The rioters just went completely berserk, smashing everything they could lay their hands on . . . We just ran for our lives.' No wonder that Christy Ryan was quoted by the *Irish Times* as saying that GPA would not be sending their aircraft or staff back until they were assured it was safe. 'Things were not too good,' he noted with characteristic understatement.

GPA's 'mercy mission' for the Irish 'girls' was just the beginning of the company's troubles in Iran. On 2 January 1979, as the revolution gathered pace, Tony cancelled the Iranair contract and pulled the remaining aircraft out of Tehran. Once the plane was in the air it came under fire from the Iranian air force and was made to land at Tabriz. The Iranians believed that the Shah may have been attempting to flee the country on the GPA plane. It was only when Brendan Swan of GPA assured them that the plane was Irish that 'tensions were somewhat eased'.

This factor was a competitive advantage for GPA that had become a potential lifesaver. 'A country so small as Ireland', Tony said, 'has none of the suspicion that may attach to the big powers, and there is no taint of colonialism. It makes things that bit easier.' Certainly that was the case in Iran, from where the Boeing 707 was eventually allowed to continue onwards to London and then Shannon.

Within two days GPA had signed a new sublease for the aircraft with Air Algérie. 'The luck of the Irish had nothing to do with this,' judged the *Irish Independent*, 'but rather all that flying and an astute awareness of the opportunities there to be seized.'

That sense of GPA as a rising player was confirmed six months later at a press conference in Shannon when Tony announced major leasing and sales agreements on seven aircraft with a total hull value of \$37 million. The deals involved trading with nine international airlines in agreements that were spread over the Far East, the Middle East, West Africa, North America, the Caribbean and Europe. It was the largest aircraft deal that GPA had yet undertaken. Moreover, Tony told journalists, GPA was in the final stages of other negotiations with several major world airlines for aircraft placement and technical and management consultancy, and it already had its own Jumbo Jet on the way.

Clearly GPA was at a tipping-point. From a work-force of eight in 1975, the company would expand to a hundred employees by 1980. As one of Ireland's major foreign-currency earners it was already making a sizeable contribution to the national economy—and the national airline. While Aer Lingus lost £2.9 million on its passenger and cargo services that year, GPA made £1.5 million in profit, contributing £0.7 million to the beleaguered Irish carrier.

'Aer Lingus and the Guinness Peat Group must be extremely happy with the way things are going,' noted Desmond Rushe in the *Irish Independent*. 'So must Tony Ryan, the pioneering brain behind it all. He holds the remaining 10 per cent share and if anyone merited astonishing success, it is he.' Tony was so delighted that he sent the journalist two free tickets to Lagos as a thank you.

Chapter 5

GOING IT ALONE

Kilboy House, Dolla, Co. Tipperary

It might have been only a fifty-minute drive by car, but this rambling, 350-acre Georgian estate was a world away from the railway hubbub of Tony Ryan's birthplace in Limerick Junction. 'There is a sense of gentle seclusion,' he later said, 'a place of utter peace and tranquillity.' The glory of the estate was not so much the house, which was twentieth-century pastiche after the original was burnt out in the Anglo-Irish War, but the glorious parkland that surrounded it. Filled with ancient oaks and chestnuts, with horses and Blonde d'Aquitaine cattle grazing, the property nestled in pastoral tranquillity beneath the Silvermine Mountains. Within a life travelling hundreds of thousands of miles every year, Kilboy became the still point in Tony's ever-turning world.

By the end of the 1970s Tony had come a long way, and not just from Limerick Junction. At the beginning of the decade he had been the Aer Lingus station manager in JFK Airport. Few then would have predicted the kind of success that followed at GPA. He was on the way to creating a $4 billion business that would transform global aviation and see him join the ranks of Ireland's super-rich. Yet it had come at a cost. The building of the company, Tony later reflected, 'required the virtual sacrifice of my private life.'

Tony had bought Kilboy House in April 1976. The Fianna Fáil TD Des O'Malley acted as his solicitor in the sale, bidding on the estate at auction while Tony hovered near the doorway. Eventually Tony got Kilboy for just over £100,000. Afterwards, with O'Malley crowing that the legislation he had passed as Minister for Justice had saved Tony 5 per cent in fees, they went out to Kilboy to look the property over. O'Malley recalls that the house was 'a bit of a wreck'. Everything seemed very neglected and required vast redevelopment. Tony needed to start work on the renovation as soon as possible, he said, because he wanted to create a family home for Mairéad and the boys.

In fact, by the time the house was fit for occupation Mairéad, after a short time in Tipperary, returned to Dublin in order to be closer to the two older boys at Clongowes Wood. This was the beginning of a painful period for the Ryans. 'It was an area of his life that Tony was very sensitive about and felt regret about,' his son Declan remembers. 'There was regret about the marriage, that it broke down, and, like any relationship, there was a lot of sadness associated with that for all of us.'

Tony always accepted that he had asked too much of his wife. She had travelled with him from station to station—London, Chicago, New York and Bangkok—and in all those places she felt desperately homesick for Ireland. When eventually the family moved back home, Tony then began the relentless travelling with GPA that would see him on the road more often than he was at home. Success in business had come because he was such a driven individual. Work consumed him and in the process left very little room for family obligations. 'I travelled ceaselessly, averaging more than half a million miles by air per year,' he said. 'I installed an office in my home . . . staying in touch with the business twenty-four hours a day and planning strategy in weekend sessions with my senior managers.'

On occasion it was hard enough for Mairéad to speak to her husband even on the telephone, let alone see him. In the end the strain simply became too much. They agreed that she could not be expected to live in Kilboy House on her own with Shane when Tony himself was there so infrequently. 'He took the view', Declan concludes, 'that his family life would have to suffer in order for him to achieve success—and it did. Thank God he lived until the age of seventy-two and we all had a great catch-up period later.'

The turmoil in Tony's private life had been caused in no small part by his obsessive commitment to work. The collapse of his marriage if anything only intensified that commitment. He could hardly have put in longer hours than he was already working, but a restlessness now began to take hold of him. It would become the dominant characteristic of the second half of his life. The old happy-go-lucky Tony who had married his childhood sweetheart and been Mr Popular down in Shannon was gone. In his place stood a tenacious, ambitious businessman and entrepreneur consumed by a determination to make it big. That in turn demanded more ambition of GPA. And it meant looking beyond it.

By the end of the 1970s Tony believed that GPA had maximised its efforts as a start-up. The wet-leasing side of the business run by the GPA subsidiary Air Tara was generating decent profits. But Tony wanted more for the company, so from 1978 he began agitating for greater commitment from GPA's major shareholders, Aer Lingus and the Guinness Peat Group. To get their attention he began an aggressive campaign in his monthly reports and at board meetings to highlight what he perceived as their lack of attention and investment. He focused his ire particularly on the Guinness Peat Group. When the bank's placeman on the board tartly reminded him that GPA's business was 'primarily that of an airline leasing company rather than a financing institution', Tony's reaction was immediate and harsh. GPA, he acidly noted, 'would have benefited by even one project being supported by our banking associates, Guinness Mahon.' Their 'degree of participation', he claimed, didn't even come close to matching the brilliant success of 'GPA's track record'.

Frustrated by concerns within Aer Lingus and the Guinness Peat Group about their financial exposure, Tony began looking around for other ways to get more investment into the company. One way to achieve this was through collaboration with another airline. Tony had already had some dealings with Air Canada through leasing negotiations with Air Jamaica, which was part-owned by the Canadian airline. Air Canada's president, Claude Taylor, had praised the professionalism and dedication of the Irish company during those negotiations. When Tony suggested that there might be an opportunity to join forces, Taylor sent a vice-president to the west coast of Ireland to discuss the matter over lunch and a round of golf. This began a long period of complicated negotiations over several years. There were no lengths that Tony would not go to in order to achieve a deal, including, Graham Boyd recalls, leg-wrestling on the floor of a Montréal restaurant with the wife of an Air Canada VP.

Tony's initial plan was to establish a separate relationship with Air Canada, although it soon became apparent that a joint venture with a non-Canadian company would cause 'political embarrassment' in Montréal for the state carrier. Not wanting to lose the deal, Tony went to the GPA board to argue that Air Canada should be allowed to buy into the company. It was an easy suggestion for Tony to make, as his own 10 per cent share would remain undiluted in the process.

Having previously been infuriated by the timidity of the GPA board, Tony now turned those same concerns back on them. Why not spread the risk, he argued, by bringing in greater investment? GPA was now exposed to the tune of $2 million. That figure 'would be eliminated by Air Canada taking a significant stake in the company.' Moreover, the sixty aircraft the Canadians were planning to lease through GPA promised profits 'of at least $20 million'.

When Tony presented his plan to the board, the Aer Lingus representatives were incensed. To some extent their reaction stemmed from a wariness about sharing an Aer Lingus spin-off with another airline. But the real anger came because they felt that Tony had acted outside his authority. The non-executive director, Maurice Foley, expressed fury that Tony had presented the board with a 'fait accompli'. What followed, noted the chairman of the board, Geoffrey Knight, was 'very abrasive'.

Over the course of several meetings Tony persistently clashed with Foley about the project. He demanded that the board recognise what a deal with Air Canada might mean for the future of GPA. 'The fact that one of the world's leading airlines is willing to consider such an offer shows remarkable faith in the business and management of GPA and is our most exciting development to date,' he told them. GPA could only win from such a 'liaison with one of the world's major scheduled airlines.' There was now 'the very real possibility of Air Canada going it alone' if it was pushed out of the GPA deal. Instead of a new investor, GPA would end up with a new and powerful competitor.

In the end, Aer Lingus backed down, recognising that GPA had to get capital from somewhere. 'GPA had grown successfully and needed more equity capital,' the airline's chief executive, David Kennedy, recalls. 'Aer Lingus was reluctant to invest more equity but wished to continue its support.' Although the Aer Lingus board members continued to express severe reservations, summed up by Foley as 'the worry of GPA becoming dominated by Air Canada', they grudgingly nodded through a recommendation to invite the North American airline to join GPA.

To seal the deal, Kennedy held personal talks with his Air Canada opposite number at an International Air Transport Association conference in Manila. Kennedy says he was

> very friendly with Claude Taylor, and he and I got together at the airline meeting. I told him that Aer Lingus was very supportive; we believed the company was well run and that it was likely to continue to grow successfully. Air Canada then came in as equal partners.

In May 1980 Air Canada took a 29.3 per cent share in GPA for an investment of $7.3 million.

Whatever Kennedy told Taylor, the process of bringing Air Canada into GPA had revealed the extent of distrust towards Tony that existed on the GPA board and within Aer Lingus. There was a feeling that he had got too big for his boots, was too sharp and had too little respect for the Aer Lingus tradition. Kennedy suggests that there was

> a very strong sense of loyalty throughout the company. The concept of public service was actually very strong and meant something to us. Tony Ryan's was a different approach—a different business culture. And it would have made some people uncomfortable, to say the least.

This clash of cultures came spectacularly to the fore immediately after the partnership with Air Canada had been forged. In the summer of 1980 Tony stunned Aer Lingus with plans for his own airline to compete on routes with the national carrier. It was the beginning of the road that would eventually lead to Ryanair.

—

Competition had become the name of the airline game by 1980, with the United States taking the lead. In 1976 Senator Edward Kennedy had begun congressional hearings on the government's regulation of the airlines, primarily trying to flush out why prices were so high. The following year a new president, Jimmy Carter, made deregulation a central plank of his administration. To lead the Civil Aeronautics Board he appointed Alfred Kahn, an Ivy League professor who had made his reputation with a pioneering study, *The Economics of Regulation.* 'Wherever competition seems feasible', Kahn declared, 'my disposition is to put trust in it much the same way as I do in democracy—as a manifestly inefficient system that is better than any of the alternatives.'

Kahn quickly began to dismantle fare and route controls, working to 'remove the meddling, protective and obstructionist hand of government, and to restore this industry, insofar as the law permits, to the rule of the market.' Indeed, where the law did not permit, he changed it. In 1978 the US Congress passed the Airline Deregulation Act, which liberalised the airline market by allowing for new carriers and cheaper fares. As if to lead by example, Kahn also made his own federal agency redundant, declaring that CAB would close for business on 1 January 1985.

One of the most prominent new entrants into the market was Freddie Laker's Skytrain, which from 1977 offered a low-price, no-frills transatlantic service. Pan Am, the American market leader on the route, made its contempt clear, with one executive noting that everyone would now 'have the pleasure of losing money together'. To see off the Laker challenge, Pan Am and other leading International Air Transport Association airlines soon launched a price war with Skytrain that would put Laker out of business by 1982. It was an early indication that, in a deregulated market, plucky newcomers would have to fight hard not to be eviscerated by the big beasts of the industry.

Deregulation in Ireland would have to wait until 1984, when a parliamentary revolt over an 'anti-competitive' Air Transport Bill led to an upheaval in the Irish airline industry. Sean Barrett notes in *Deregulation and the Airline Business in Europe* that in the last year of regulation the protected Aer Lingus had 2.2 million passengers; by 2008/9 four Irish airlines in the deregulated market carried 72 million passengers, of which Ryanair had some 68 million. However, at the beginning of the decade, according to Barrett, himself a key figure in the process of deregulation, 'Ireland was an unlikely source of contestability in European aviation.' Despite high fares, there was huge public affection for the national airline, with many seeing it as the projection abroad of Irish nationhood and *céad míle fáilte*. That sense of it as a national ambassador had been illustrated in September 1979, when an Aer Lingus Boeing 747 jet, *St Patrick*, brought Pope John Paul II to Ireland. It was the first time a pope had flown any airliner other than Alitalia (offering in its own way a pontifical boost for airline deregulation).

Politically, too, Aer Lingus remained tightly bound to the instruments of the state. Crucially, the airline kept an unyielding grip on the regulatory functions of the Department of Transport, which meant that any attempts to bring down prices were ruthlessly crushed.

Yet if ever a country was in need of airline deregulation it was Ireland. At that time, remembers GPA's Graham Boyd,

> Ireland and Portugal were about the only countries in Europe that had only a single, state-run airline. Aer Lingus and TAP Portugal were two of the most inefficient airlines in the world, with the worst passenger miles per employee. Monopoly state airlines were the worst. The passenger statistics on the London–Dublin route had not changed in twenty years because most people couldn't afford to fly.

Tony Ryan saw an opportunity to shake up the market in this context of international deregulation and contrasting Irish stagnation. In the summer of 1980 he called Boyd over to Kilboy to discuss putting a proposal to the Government for a new licence on the Shannon–JFK transatlantic route. Joining them was the marketing and PR consultant Jim King. He would quickly become one of Tony's most trusted lieutenants, known in GPA circles as 'His Master's Voice' for his total loyalty and discretion. King's initial doubts on his arrival from Dublin that weekend in June were not about the airline plan: he was horrified at how Tony was renovating Kilboy in a fashion more akin to a Californian ranch than to an estate of Georgian origins. King laughs that when they first met Tony was

> visually ignorant, had no appreciation of painting, sculpture or anything like that. He had affection for craftsmanship, things like stone walls, but it's an example of how he pursued what interested him.

Once King had put his aesthetic concerns to one side, he quickly recognised the radical nature of Tony's idea.

> He had already seen something in the leasing world and exploited it. Now it was the airline. He sensed there was change coming. He had no confidence that Aer Lingus would lead that change and knew he would be in conflict with them if he did it. But he simply went ahead anyway. He was a greedy man in the best sense: if this change was going to happen, he wanted to be in there with as large a position as he could get.

Tony's initial proposal was a radical pitch to private investors and the Government for a new airline, Irelandia, to transform 'the least-developed aviation nation in Europe'. Ireland needed another airline, Tony argued, not just to increase the efficiency of Aer Lingus but also to prevent foreign airlines filling an obvious gap in the market. The first phase of the operation would see Irelandia running flights out of Shannon to New York, Boston and London. Over time it would become a hub for flights to European, American and worldwide destinations. Fares on the initial transatlantic routes would start at the bargain price of £160 return.

By August, Tony had refined his pitch in a new draft.

> The keystone of Irelandia's operations will be low overheads, efficient operations and forceful marketing . . . Irelandia will respond to the deregulation philosophy currently implicit in American aviation policy and now gaining ground in Europe. Deregulation is a word that appears offensive to most national airlines; nevertheless, in the long term deregulation combined with competition is the only method by which the travelling public will enjoy low fares.

Tony kept working on his proposal for Irelandia throughout 1980, bolstering the conceptual language of the paper with hard data on potential directors, shareholdings, capital structure, plans and forecasts. Peter Ledbetter quietly met executives from the Shannon Free Airport Development Company, who told him they would 'support the project in principle' and advised on who might be sympathetic in the newly established Department of Industry, Commerce and Tourism, as well as in Bord Fáilte. 'The way to succeed', Ledbetter reported back, 'was to have a strong local champion supporting the application and [they] mentioned the Minister for Industry and Commerce, or alternatively to have such a strong case that internal pressure within the civil service pushed the scheme to a valid conclusion.'

Fortuitously for Tony, the minister in question was Des O'Malley, to whom he gave regular briefings on Irelandia and the possibilities for deregulation. Less fortuitously for those plans, Fianna Fáil lost office in June 1981. It was reported by the news magazine *Magill* that O'Malley had been poised with 'a proposal to "Lakerise" the North Atlantic operation . . . [and] that Tony Ryan of Guinness Peat should be allowed to run a service to New York from Shannon.'

Support from O'Malley would have helped Tony jump the difficult first hurdle for Irelandia: the opposition of Aer Lingus. Nevertheless, Ireland's national carrier continued to be its own worst advocate during this time of international revival in the airline industry. In 1981 the company would lose £15 million on the North Atlantic route. 'Aer Lingus has a total staff of 6,800, of whom 1,500 work on the North Atlantic operation alone,' noted *Magill*. 'They employ more people than they fly passengers per day.' No wonder there were calls, fiercely resisted by Aer Lingus, for 'Lakerisation'.

Deregulation may have been a dirty word in Aer Lingus, but when, in early 1981, executives at the company finally got wind of the full extent of Tony's plans for Irelandia, the name Ryan became an even dirtier one.

'It came to our attention in Aer Lingus that Tony was trying to set up another airline, Irelandia,' David Kennedy recalls, 'and at that time he was actually precluded contractually from starting an airline.' Trust was even further eroded when Tony requested permission to buy an equity stake in the freight airline Aer Turas. Board members were instructed to administer a dressing down. Dick White, who had been the founding chairman of GPA, protested to Tony about 'philosophical differences in the conduct of business'. Maurice O'Kelly of Guinness Mahon was even more forthright. 'Tony, this is outrageous,' he thundered. 'You cannot, you should not be doing this, trying to set up an airline in competition to the airline that set *you* up. This is the wrong way of going about things.'

Tensions now quickly increased. When details of Tony's plans leaked he threatened to issue the GPA board with an injunction. 'Frankly, I was very concerned at the possible irreparable damage that such loose talk could cause,' he submitted.

Fearing an unpleasant legal battle, Geoffrey Knight, chairman of GPA, telephoned O'Kelly in an attempt to mediate. Instead he only fanned the flames. The call, 'the purpose of which', said O'Kelly, 'was to send to me a mild rebuke from Tony for discussing this matter, and my views thereon,' became the final straw for him.

O'Kelly resigned from the board on 13 May 1981, offering as a departing gift a scything blow against Tony and his style of management. 'My reason for resigning', he wrote formally to Knight, 'is that I no longer have the necessary degree of confidence in the judgement, ability, intelligence and integrity of the Chief Executive.' A year earlier, when expressing doubts about the Air Canada investment, O'Kelly had warned that GPA, 'despite its fantastic profit record', was becoming dangerously 'dependent on one or two people for its ongoing success'. Now he believed that the man who more than any other *was* GPA had run out of control.

'Maurice O'Kelly was incensed', says Kennedy, 'and regarded it as unethical for Tony to compete with one of his major shareholders and the company which had initially set him up in business.' Kennedy himself was more sanguine. 'Personally I didn't particularly like what was happening, but I recognised that these things happened in business.'

Relations between Tony and Aer Lingus remained tense throughout 1981. Kennedy remembers that 'we had some conversations in Aer Lingus' about replacing him, although these were always 'fairly inconclusive'. Those plans only firmed up when Tony overplayed his hand.

The rumpus over Irelandia fed a growing and undisguised contempt within Tony's circle for the GPA board and the public-sector mentality within Aer Lingus. In contrast, they considered themselves a breed apart. They were pioneers operating without constraint at the frontier of international aviation. There were no subsidised lunches and gold-plated pensions for them. They had different rules. GPA and Irelandia were ventures for the brave. 'Tony certainly didn't behave like the gentlemen of the board,' Jim

King says. 'David Kennedy never would have behaved liked that. But then David Kennedy never would have set up an airline.'

That sense of invincibility mixed with frustration led Tony towards a risky strategy. On 13 November 1981 he wrote to Geoffrey Knight saying he wished to resign as chief executive. He cited the 'considerable strain' of his role and the 'almost constant travelling'. He followed up with a more formal letter on 7 December making the same point. No doubt Tony expected Knight to throw his hands up in horror. Instead the chairman calmly put the matter to members of the board, who, he informed Tony on 28 January 1982, approved the idea.

A tense game of cat and mouse followed in the next months. Knight was a phlegmatic character; based in London, he had an inevitable detachment from the politics of the Irish aviation world. Above all he was a practical man, who now took Tony at his word and began searching for a new chief executive. He suggested that Tony might like to 'continue your association with the company' in a non-executive role, perhaps as deputy chairman. Tony replied nonchalantly that the position 'would be of considerable interest'. In reality he never believed he would be leaving his executive post.

Everyone at GPA, including Tony himself, thought he was irreplaceable. 'It was theatre for the Aer Lingus board,' King recalls, 'because what would they do without Tony Ryan?'

Knight believed he knew the answer to that question. He had his eye on just the man to replace Tony and now set out to headhunt him. On 19 April he wrote confidentially to Kennedy that the 'ideal candidate for this position would be Maurice Foley, having in mind the changing needs of the company in its next stage of development.' Foley had been a fierce critic of what he saw as Tony's casual approach to the board. He was widely admired, not least by Tony himself, for his fine strategic and analytical frame of mind. Knight conceded that

> you would find it very difficult indeed, if not impossible, to release Maurice for this appointment. However, I think that you

> will agree with me that it is critically important that we ensure the continued success of this remarkable company which, up until now, has owed so much to the personal drive and initiative of Tony Ryan. It could, in my view, very well start to lose a good deal of its impetus when Tony is not available if we are obliged to settle for a new Chief Executive of mediocre calibre.

Eventually, after much persuasion, Kennedy concurred. Foley was approached and he expressed interest. The process of succession had begun.

Tony initially expressed enthusiasm about bringing Foley aboard, thinking neither that Kennedy would release him from Aer Lingus nor that the candidate himself would be interested in the position. As the transition process began to move forward, however, the reality of losing executive control of GPA began to hit him.

Tony showed his full range of emotions at a hastily arranged meeting with Knight in London on 1 June 1982. He expressed resentment at being kept out of the loop. 'It seems incongruous', he protested, 'that as a significant shareholder and Chief Executive, the conditions and terms for the new Chief Executive are taking place deliberately without any reference to me.' There was also anger at being pushed aside, as 'I do feel my current role is being usurped.' And for the first time in the process, Tony revealed a touch of vulnerability. 'I genuinely am worried,' he finally admitted to Knight.

His concerns were well founded. On 7 June, Knight wrote to Tony in a tone that was so off-hand that the chairman could hardly have made it clearer that the Ryan era at GPA was nearing its end. Obviously he hoped Tony would stay in touch with GPA, but 'any future role for you in the company must be very dependent indeed on agreement and understanding between you and your successor.' Maurice Foley had already been offered the chief executive post, Knight casually reported, so perhaps Tony could 'talk to Maurice'. Knight hoped to get everything tied up by July 'so that we can make public our intentions before too many rumours start to emerge.'

Tony was horrified. Overconfidence had resulted in the imminent loss of control of the company he had founded in 1975. The previous financial year he had made almost £10 million in profits for GPA, five times more than projected profits for the company. He knew he had 'an intuitive feel for aviation' and a leadership style that got results. Now the company was saying, 'Thanks for that,' and moving on without him. With projected profits of £32 million for the period 1981–5, that would be leaving someone else to cash in on his hard work—literally, in fact, as he had already told Knight he would be selling his 10 per cent interest in the company.

Back in Kilboy, alone, it all seemed like madness. A small part of Tony had meant the resignation offer. He was forty-five years old, working a punishing schedule, travelling hundreds of thousands of miles a year. No-one could maintain that lifestyle. Friends had heard him talk more about his father, who had died young after a lifetime of punishing physical work. Inevitably there were thoughts about packing it all in and enjoying the money he had made. Then there had been a contradictory impulse. Tony remained a man of ambition. He had ideas and strategies for changing aviation. Yet in GPA he was still thwarted by Aer Lingus. In the light of the Irelandia experience, he had thought, Why not just say, 'Feck 'em'? and then do precisely that as their competition.

Confronted now with the reality of losing everything he had built up, Tony understood that he had made a terrible misjudgement. Instead of cursing himself, he addressed the problem head-on with an act that was as shameless as it was brazen: he simply withdrew his resignation.

On 16 June 1982 Tony wrote to Knight and the GPA board not in apology but in confrontation. 'Your letter of 7th June has not alleviated my worries about the position which has now developed within the Company,' he announced. 'The matters to which my resignation gave rise have not been resolved, and more seriously, a general situation has developed which is extremely threatening to the Company's welfare.' Moreover, 'as a shareholder', he was 'very concerned by your statement you are very far down the line in your discussion with [Maurice Foley].' Therefore he had only one course of action. 'The situation leaves me with no alternative but to now withdraw my resignation as chief executive.' In an aside for Knight, he added, 'Geoffrey, we genuinely have a difference of opinion. Indeed I am disappointed that you cannot accept the priorities as I see them.'

It was a defiant performance and one that might just as well have come from *Winning through Intimidation,* the book Tony had enjoyed so much in Bangkok. In the end his chutzpah meant he kept his job, although as a compromise he had to accept Foley joining GPA in the new position of president—in effect as no. 2.

Decisive action had saved the day, but Tony had learnt an important lesson: to prosper he needed to operate from now on with more sophistication and subtlety. Never again could he allow an establishment man like Knight to put him in check.

Chapter 6

A PINT, A PAPER AND AN ELECTRIC SHOCK

The seven months between Tony's resignation and his subsequent withdrawal of that resignation had been a bruising time, but the effect on his team at GPA was just as profound. The 'masters of the aviation universe' atmosphere in the Shannon Free Zone had been replaced with something altogether more circumspect. Uncertainty stalked the corridors of GPA. The staff gossiped about whether Tony was in or whether he was out, who might be replacing him, and what impact it would have on their own prospects. There was something deeper at work as well. Suddenly GPA executives began to see themselves as others saw them—and it prompted a fleeting crisis of confidence.

In the end, Liam Meade, who had joined GPA in 1977 as director of operations, put this concern directly to Tony. In the summer of 1982 he wrote telling him frankly that 'a reappraisal of the *kind* of company we are, and more importantly the kind of company *we need to be* in the future is essential to the continued well-being of GPA.' They had generated a strong business from 'six pulsating years of globe-trotting and driving'. Much of that business had come their way 'because of the particular aura developed around the new Shannon company with a highly motivated chief executive supported by a hard-working team.'

But, Meade continued, 'I submit that in 1982 we are perceived slightly differently.' Now the company was seen as 'opportunistic, greedy, slightly parasitic, unyielding'. The market was behaving 'defensively' towards GPA, and the company needed 'to equip itself to overcome this reaction'. That meant a new skill set and image, 'a *different* GPA—one that radiates sophistication; professionalism; stability and maturity and that brings valid products to the market at fair price.' To achieve this 'transformation', Meade concluded, 'will require a commitment to organisation and its development that has been lacking during our initial years.'

Opportunistic, greedy, parasitic, unyielding; lacking in sophistication, professionalism and maturity—it was a harsh judgement on the first six years of the company that Tony had built from nothing. A year earlier, while Tony was busily planning for Irelandia, it would have been impossible to imagine a member of his staff having the audacity to write such a note. Now the strain of the previous months was visible, not least in the chief executive himself.

Tony seemed uncharacteristically vulnerable and fragile. Even such loyalists as Jim King, who formally joined GPA in July 1982 as executive vice-president, noticed that Tony had begun to retreat into himself. 'He was cheesed off with the trouble from Aer Lingus,' King recalls. 'He drank quite heavily and was incredibly restless—very, very restless.' It was a characteristic that King would come to regard as 'maybe depression, because his moods would swing quite a lot.'

Other staff members at GPA also noticed that Tony had become increasingly withdrawn. He appeared less frequently in Shannon, often working from the 'bat cave' office that had been put into the basement at Kilboy. He less and less often took the infamous Monday morning meetings. Inside the GPA offices Maurice Foley, installed as Tony's no. 2, became the more visible face of day-to-day leadership. 'Maurice was extremely efficient, hard-working and all those things,' one executive recalls, but many suspected that the Aer Lingus man was there to keep 'an eye on all that was going on'. Foley was respected for his organisational capacity, but the staff were unsettled. 'Different animal, different culture,' one executive says. 'From that moment onwards Tony was not as in your face. You would never see him rambling around the corridors. He would always be in his office—in fact he moved into a new office—so he wasn't accessible.'

The restlessness that Jim King had noticed was about more than disillusionment with Aer Lingus. Tony had made a success of GPA, making a personal fortune in the process, yet he seemed to be searching for new challenges and opportunities. Irelandia was still rattling around inside his head, but the political and business circumstances were not yet ripe for such a move in Ireland. 'I think he was frustrated,' says the architect John Meagher, who had met Tony in 1980 and would become a close friend. 'He was going into board meetings, going into his office and meetings with banks and aircraft manufacturers. He adored the whole business of aircraft, but he was just bored with pushing paper and money around the table. It's almost as if he felt nothing real was happening.'

Tony's initial impulse to satisfy this desire for a wider role was to look for a public outlet to match his growing interest in the arts. GPA had already emerged as a prominent and imaginative sponsor of the arts in Ireland. In 1980 it had sponsored the influential international art exhibition Rosc in Dublin (a sponsorship that was withdrawn three years later, after 'the snub', Tony fumed, of 'the selection panel [that] did not regard the work of a single Irish artist as being good enough to include in the exhibition').

In 1980 Tony had told the board of his strong belief that GPA should 'find methods of making an appropriate contribution in other ways to the enrichment of the country, including its cultural and artistic development.' Over the decade this would develop into high-profile sponsorship that included the prestigious GPA Book Award, the GPA International Piano Competition, the GPA Emerging Artists Awards, GPA Music in Great Irish Houses and the *Irish Arts Review*, as well as many other national and local projects. Tony always insisted that 'big names' be attached to these projects, which, for example, saw the likes of Graham Greene and John Updike come to Ireland to adjudicate on the literary prize. These names brought with them 'high visual identity with strong media coverage' for GPA.

However sophisticated GPA's arts sponsorship became, in many ways Tony had fallen into it more by way of social bravado than of any grandiose strategy for the company's role within the artistic world. That same year he had found himself at a dinner hosted by the modernist architect Michael Scott. With eleven people present, thirty-three bottles of wine were drunk. 'Tony was having a ball of a time,' remembers John Meagher.

> Michael Scott said to him, 'Listen, Tony, we're in serious trouble about Rosc. We need somebody to finance it.'
>
> So Tony said, 'How much is it?'
>
> '£55,000.'
>
> 'No problem, I'll do it.'
>
> So Tony woke up on Sunday realising what he had committed to and had to call his board at 8 a.m. Monday announcing he was spending all this money. There was uproar!

For the board it was just one more example of Tony 'going rogue' and a precursor to the rows that would soon follow about his plans for the new Irelandia airline.

As it turned out, Rosc was not the only time that Michael Scott would land Tony in hot water. In 1985 Scott sold a death mask of James Joyce to GPA for £16,500. Scott was to have presented the mask at auction, but the private sale to Tony beforehand was hailed as 'saving' the fragile plaster cast for Ireland. Stephen Joyce, the author's controversial grandson, thought otherwise. He protested loudly that such a 'private and sacred' artefact should never be sold. Moreover, he suggested, the mask was not even Scott's to sell. He conceded that Tony had acted honourably in buying the mask. Nevertheless, Joyce wrote to him in the strongest terms urging the return of the mask to the Joyce Museum in Sandycove, Co. Dublin, where it had resided (next-door to Scott's house) for the previous two decades. If matters were not satisfactorily resolved Joyce would change his own will to exclude all Irish institutions from bequests of the James Joyce items in his possession or over which he had control.

In the end, Scott backed down, offering to repay Tony and return the mask to Sandycove. 'What a relief!' exclaimed the eminent painter Louis le Brocquy. 'The following day we met Tony Ryan in Kildare Street and he was quite willing to go along with this.' In fact, the mask remained in Tony's possession until at least 1991. He didn't like to be threatened by anyone, least of all a man like Stephen Joyce, whom he despised.

By the time of the death-mask affair, Tony was already established as an influential cultural figure. He may have started out as an accidental patron of the arts, but by 1982, in despair from his battles with the GPA board, he had sought to develop a role for himself in the artistic life of the country.

That summer he wrote to the Taoiseach, Charles Haughey, who was also closely associated with Rosc, to propose a new Forum for Business and the Arts. 'The essential task of the Forum', he wrote, 'would be to promote an alliance between business and the arts at the highest level.' His ambitious programme endeavoured to 'promote understanding of the role of the arts in our society', including their 'commercial value', to assist companies and institutions 'in formulating sponsorship policies', to 'stimulate the purchase of art objects for corporate collections' and to encourage the 'sponsorship of openings and other events'. All this was to take place within a new tax framework that would encourage businesses to support the arts. To start discussion, Tony offered to host a seminar for senior figures in business, politics and the arts.

'All in all, I think your idea of a seminar is a good one,' Haughey replied. 'GPA by its enlightened sponsorship of the arts can certainly claim the right to take the initiative in organising it.'

This first foray by Tony into the politics of the arts marked the beginning of a civic engagement that would last for much of the rest of his life. Although he understood that, for many in the arts world, it was his cash rather than his taste that interested them, the very relationship between money and culture was a topic about which he now began to think deeply.

'Art is not seen as a necessity by the mass of people or their politicians,' he told a seminar on arts funding in 1984. 'It is regarded as a luxury—or at best an indulgence.' While those who loved the arts knew that this was not the case, 'our persistent mistake is to presume that others always agree.' The role of business, he continued, was to fill the gap that had been left after the 'age of religious and aristocratic patronage'. That meant making judgements about quality and popularity. The competition for sponsorship was 'fierce'. Choices had to be made and 'uncomfortable issues' faced. 'In the province of the arts, no more than in any other field of Irish life,' Tony observed, giving expression to a broader philosophy, 'the loud and persistent call is for yet more grants, more subsidies, more neutering security. We are in danger of becoming a politically bought, hand-out society with a growing disapproval of the spirit of self-sufficiency, because it exposes our timidity and laziness.'

Tony was keen to secure more money for the arts; but art itself was 'a product that has a value and price'. Therefore artists should 'aspire for commercial success, not shrink from the judgement of the marketplace.' They should welcome the 'excitement and satisfaction' of an environment for artists in which 'the public would have an informed appreciation' of their work and be 'eager to pay for it'. Business could support the arts on that basis. 'The arts deserve more help from business,' Tony concluded, but 'investment in the arts should be in respect of achievement and contribution—not a handout.'

Over the coming decades Tony would frequently despair at the unwillingness of the artistic community to engage with him in any way other than by putting their collective hand into his wallet. On one notorious occasion in 1994 he invited a select gathering of artists to Kilboy for a symposium with the Minister for Arts, Culture and the Gaeltacht (and later President of Ireland), Michael D. Higgins, to 'advise/influence him on the direction of government policy'.

The event was meant to be a think-in; in the end it became a drink-in. Over the course of the weekend the assembled arts figures laid waste to Tony's wine cellar, including more than two hundred bottles of his best claret. 'It is unfortunate that the final session was influenced by the dinner the night before,' Tony lamented afterwards. 'I had some points to raise.'

It was a refrain that Tony would repeat time and again when dealing with the arts world. He believed he had a serious contribution to make through funding and in applying the lessons of business 'to make radical changes by restructuring the management of the arts in Ireland.' More often than not this led to exasperation rather than fulfilment, never more so than as a Government appointee on the board of the National Gallery of Ireland.

In many ways Tony was temperamentally unsuited to sitting as an ordinary board member. The quiet meeting rooms of Merrion Square were unaccustomed to the kind of frank speaking found on a Monday morning in Shannon. What perplexed Tony most was the triviality of what was discussed. 'I have found the meetings and attitudes most wasteful,' he complained in 1987 to another board member, Bryan Alton, well known as Éamon de Valera's doctor. 'Frankly my most exciting meeting was the last one, when I had the opportunity of smoking a cigar!'

Tony's response to this situation was an action plan to put the National Gallery on stronger financial footing. It was a radical proposal that included 'privatising a small percentage of the gallery' and 'selling off art that the director and the board would regard as not being of significant importance.' The result would be that the gallery would 'benefit from refurbishment and improved facilities and in addition would gain from having new surroundings and paintings on display in terms of attracting more visitors and promoting art to a wider audience.'

The idea went nowhere, with the chairman, Bill Finlay, refusing even to put it on the agenda for a board meeting. GPA's Seán Donlon, who, as a former secretary-general of the Department of Foreign Affairs, understood politics in the public sector better than most, told Tony sadly afterwards, 'You have obviously invested a good deal of time in fulfilling the obligations imposed on you by your appointment to the board, but it is becoming very clear that the prospects of your being able to achieve what is needed through continuing your active membership are, at best, remote.'

Tony concurred and wrote to the Taoiseach in 1988 to resign. 'The Gallery now is leaderless', he explained, and 'in a rather sorry structural state'. Meetings were spent on 'total triviality'. There was no point in staying. The two men met the following week, and Haughey, despite Tony having been appointed by Garret FitzGerald, persuaded him not to resign by promising that Pádraig Ó hUiginn, secretary-general of the Department of the Taoiseach, would 'monitor the situation' and ensure 'visible action' at the gallery.

In reality Tony would have preferred an opportunity to become chairman of the board, but a businessman in charge would have been a step too far for the gallery. Tony remained on the board for eight years. His disillusionment became even stronger when he came to believe that the gallery wanted him to fund their new Millennium Wing.

He declined the opportunity and instead directed his efforts towards a new museum in Limerick to house the fine collection of John and Gertrude Hunt. That project, too, would come at a moment of major upheaval in Tony's life, and, just as in 1982, art would offer an immediate release from the dramas of GPA.

One unexpected side-effect of Tony's emergence as a cultural figure in the early 1980s was a dramatic change of image. It might have been a rebranding; perhaps it was a mid-life crisis. Either way, it seemed like a visible sign of renewed confidence and individuality after the setbacks over Irelandia and the resignation fiasco, as well as a demonstration of a new artistic sensibility. Out went the dark, pinstripe three-piece suits he had worn around the world; in came a succession of expensive cream linen suits. Black lace-ups were succeeded by natty Gucci loafers. Plain white shirts were replaced with striped pastels, with fashionable contrasting white colours.

The change caused sartorial panic in certain quarters at GPA, as staff members, wanting to ape the boss, felt the need to experiment with their own dress. There were a few unsuccessful attempts to mimic Tony's new flamboyant image; most settled for wearing a billowing silk handkerchief in their top pocket, as Tony himself now did.

The effect of Tony's new image was striking, and it made an immediate impact on those encountering him for the first time. The lawyer Robert Greenspon, who was recruited to GPA from the United States in 1984, remembers the day he met Tony.

> Maurice Foley had put on a lunch at his house on the shores of Lough Derg. We all went out to meet a boat coming up the Shannon, and there on the bow was this figure in a white suit, with a flower in his lapel and wearing a bright-red tie. It reminded me of [the writer] Tom Wolfe and had the same kind of impact. This was definitely someone out of the ordinary. You don't meet many people like that in the business world. So I knew I was going to like Tony Ryan straight away, even if I also sensed that he was going to make life interesting, to say the least.

Tony's change of direction in 1982 was about more than a new set of clothes: it was a shift in how he saw himself. He had made the transition from Aer Lingus employee to successful CEO, but in doing so he had acquired an entrepreneurial frame of mind. That was not something that could be contained within the confines of GPA and its relationship with Aer Lingus. His first attempt to break out—Irelandia—had failed, or was at least dormant. A venture into cultural politics with the Forum for Business and the Arts was an interesting diversion but not one to exploit his entrepreneurial drive. What Tony desperately wanted by 1982 was a serious business opportunity. Instead what he settled on was ownership of the *Sunday Tribune.*

The '*Trib*' had gone into liquidation that October after a disastrous attempt to launch a sister paper, the *Daily News.* A month later Tony bankrolled the purchase of the Sunday title for the sum of £5,000. To his colleagues it seemed an odd decision even at the time. 'He told me what he was contemplating and asked what did I think,' Jim King recalls. 'I used McConnells [advertising agency] to give us an objective report. Their view was that it had limited prospects and that the competition for advertising revenue was so severe that the big established names like Independent Newspapers would almost certainly squeeze it out.'

In fact, Independent Newspapers was one of the reasons that Tony went ahead. Among his greatest skills when looking around for ideas was an ability to see what worked elsewhere and then give it his own unique twist. This had been the way he had transformed a salaried job leasing a couple of Aer Lingus Jumbos into a multi-million dollar business. Later it would be how he would use the low-cost, no-frills model from the United States to create an airline that eventually became Europe's biggest carrier.

In 1982 everything was more personal. The *Sunday Tribune*, suggests Michael O'Leary, later CEO of Ryanair, 'was all about trying to do down Tony O'Reilly and have political clout. He had to buy a newspaper because O'Reilly had a newspaper.'

The two Tonys, both born in 1936, would endure a fractious and competitive relationship over the coming decades. Yet if imitation is the sincerest form of flattery there can be little doubt that Tony Ryan admired the way in which O'Reilly had established himself as the most well-known businessman in Ireland. In part that high public profile was due to O'Reilly's international rugby career, which gave him an identity outside business. He had made his money by rising through the ranks to become chief executive (and later chairman) of the American food giant Heinz. In the early 1970s O'Reilly bought all the voting shares in Independent Newspapers, giving him a further public profile as the proprietor of the mass-circulation *Irish Independent* and *Sunday Independent*.

Later, after being awarded several honorary doctorates, the GPA founder would style himself 'Dr Tony Ryan' in imitation of Dr Tony O'Reilly, who held a PhD in agricultural marketing. Now he imitated him with the purchase of a national newspaper. Tony's misfortune was to choose to do so with the brilliant but combustible Vincent Browne.

'We didn't get on in business, because we are too alike,' Browne wrote with typical candour after Tony's death. 'Not that I had any of his entrepreneurial genius or his energy, but we were similar temperamentally: stubborn (just a tad on my part), short-tempered (just a tinge on my part), sometimes irrational (very occasionally on my part).'

Browne had approached Tony in the autumn of 1982 about the possibility of buying into the *Tribune*, with Browne himself as editor. The initial outlay for the title may have been just £5,000, but the estimated cost to relaunch the paper was closer to ten times that amount. The first edition was due to come out on 17 April 1983.

From the outset Tony's relationship with Browne was fraught. To some extent this was Tony's own fault. He had no experience in running a newspaper and never really understood the culture. A receptionist at the *Tribune* recalls Tony's absolute bafflement on turning up early one morning at the newspaper's office only to find the place entirely deserted other than herself. Browne played on this inexperience and for the next year drove Tony to exasperation.

It was inexperience that led Tony to make the beginner's error of not putting his own person in charge as managing director. In part this can be explained by the quality and reputation of the man Browne recruited for the job. John Kelleher was the highly respected controller of programmes at RTE1 television. To poach him from the state broadcaster was a coup for the newspaper, giving it immediate gravitas. But Kelleher was not Tony's appointment, which immediately left the new proprietor on the back foot.

From day 1 there were problems at the *Tribune*. Browne was an outstanding journalist, but his editorial and management style has often been thought haphazard. 'The *Sunday Tribune* is like "Dallas",' noted one reporter, referring to the popular 1980s television programme, 'except that Browne's editorial style is like JR, and his business acumen is closer to that of Cliff Barnes.' Tony didn't like either, and soon the proprietor and his editor were engaged in a series of rows that became legendary in media circles and beyond.

The *Tribune* in its earlier incarnation had been a sober affair, run by Conor Brady, who went on to edit the *Irish Times*. Browne brought a different approach. As the editor of *Magill* he had built a reputation for finding scoops, delivering outspoken and often outrageous editorials, and generally making a nuisance of himself with the political and financial establishment. The relaunched *Tribune* gave him the opportunity to play a similar game on a bigger stage. It quickly became a campaigning newspaper, week after week running stories such as 'Free Nicky Kelly' (a member of the Irish Republican Socialist Party convicted of the Sallins train robbery in Co. Kildare and who was subsequently given a presidential pardon). Many of the *Tribune* stories centred on the Provisional IRA, which had developed a relationship of trust in Browne. After several weeks of these stories, Tony began to worry that somehow he had got himself caught up with the IRA and that his newspaper was turning into the republican organisation's newspaper of choice.

What tipped Tony over the edge, however, was an interview with the chief of staff of the INLA—a splinter group of the Official IRA ('the Stickies'). Dominic 'Mad Dog' McGlinchey was by this stage the 'most wanted man in Ireland', and the following year he became the first republican extradited by the Irish state to the North. In November 1983, without consulting Tony, Browne interviewed McGlinchey at a safe house believed to be in Cork, where McGlinchey openly admitted to Browne that 'we were involved mainly in the killing of UDR [Ulster Defence Regiment] men and policemen, and we did a fair few bombings of police barracks and towns. I don't think a town wasn't blown up. They all got a touch—Killalea, Bellaghy, Portglenone, Magherafelt, Maghera, Castledawson, Ballymena and lots of others.'

A friend recalls that when the interview was published Tony 'went mad, because he mistakenly thought Vincent had republican sympathies.' Tony's son Declan believes that his father's reaction might have been different if the strongly worded editorial that appeared inside the paper had been on the front page—'although they probably would still have fallen out about it,' he concludes.

Tony summoned Browne and Kelleher to his house in Wellington Road in Dublin for what turned out to be a spectacular confrontation. Present at that meeting was the young man Tony had just taken on as his first personal assistant, Denis O'Brien. A long-term acquaintance, Greg Jones, had written to Tony in January to recommend a friend's son from Trinity Bank in Dublin who 'seems to have the energy and personal attributes which you in the past looked for.' Tony met him and was sufficiently impressed to give him a job. O'Brien would go on to become one of Ireland's most significant entrepreneurs, building up a multi-billion telecoms business.

When Browne and Kelleher arrived for the meeting, O'Brien showed them into the living room, where they found Tony in a state of blind rage. O'Brien recalls that,

> as they walked in, Tony said to Vincent, 'You're a fucking INLA cunt,' and the next thing Tony swung at him. So Vincent then whacked him one, and they started to brawl. Johnny Kelleher was speechless, because he thought he was going to be CEO of a newspaper, instead of this kind of drama.

Browne records a slightly different series of events, admitting that the two men 'squared up' before being 'dragged apart' just as 'a blow was about to be struck'. Either way, Tony's relationship with Browne never recovered.

Kelleher soon left the newspaper. That departure left Browne as editor, managing director and financial controller. The results were not happy ones for Tony. There would often be phone calls to Kilboy on Friday evenings saying the paper couldn't come out unless money for the printer was immediately made available. Ulster Bank would phone to say that the accounts didn't balance for the week, with cheques going out for double the sums that were coming in.

Tony came to believe that there was some manipulation of the cash flow to engender a sense of crisis and get more money out of him. 'Eventually', O'Brien recalls, 'Tony said to me, "Find somebody to go in and run that newspaper for me".' The man

O'Brien suggested was his brother-in-law, the accountant Eugene O'Neill. After just a few weeks O'Neill reported back that he felt he could get no co-operation from Browne or the *Tribune* staff. 'There was a mutiny against him,' says O'Brien.

The showdown came at a meeting of the board in Kildare Street in June 1984, less than three months after the *Sunday Tribune* had relaunched. Most of those present were Tony's appointees, including Peter Ledbetter and Arthur Walls (a future chairman of Ryanair) from GPA, Donal Flynn (Tony's personal accountant), Denis O'Brien and Eugene O'Neill. Also present was the former Minister for External Affairs and chief of staff of the IRA, Seán MacBride, who was Browne's mischievous appointment on the board. Tony had the numbers to do whatever he liked; the question was whether he had the will to keep going with the paper.

After initial business was out of the way O'Neill proposed that Browne be sacked, but he did it so nervously and timidly that it failed to register. 'He so mistimed his intervention that nobody paid any attention,' Browne says.

The next attempt, according to Browne, was better co-ordinated. O'Neill announced that the company was insolvent. Tony then said he would not invest any more money. Finally, Flynn announced that he was resigning as a director.

What followed was bedlam. MacBride theatrically pointed at Flynn and spat out the name 'Schuschnigg'. That historical reference to the Austrian chancellor who had caved in to Hitler left most people nonplussed, but Flynn seemed to understand only too well. He rose from his chair to storm out, only to get stuck trying to squeeze past Arthur Walls. 'Some of us—including Tony—were in fits of helpless laughter at the chaos of it all,' says Browne. Amid the hubbub, Browne announced that he would buy the paper. Tony wearily concurred, having finally decided that the game wasn't worth the candle.

As he left the meeting, however, all Tony's anger and frustration at Browne suddenly spilled over. 'Tony went mad,' O'Brien recalls. He rushed at Browne, fists flying, but in the process gave a glancing blow to MacBride. In a performance worthy of his mother, the legendary Maud Gonne, MacBride went down like a pro, screaming in his famous lisping French accent, 'He has hit me! He has hit me!' Browne expressed 'outrage' and was 'encouraged by a wink from Seán to join in the drama.' Eventually Tony left the building, furious but glad to be rid of the entire commitment.

'About a week later', says O'Brien, 'Vincent came down and we did a deal with him. That was that, and Vincent was off.' Tony was glad to see the back of him and the paper, but his losses had been astronomical. Press reports suggested that Tony had lost about £600,000. 'It was much more than that,' O'Brien says. 'He lost well over a million, if not more.' Vincent Browne, O'Brien concludes, 'was the only guy that out-negotiated Tony that I ever saw.'

The *Tribune* had been a disaster for Tony, yet despite the rage he demonstrated in his personal confrontations with Browne, he quickly moved on. 'He had got into a furious temper about it,' John Meagher says, 'but then he just said, "That was a mistake," and got rid of it in his head.'

Tony's ability to draw a line under misadventures was the counterpoint to the periods of 'black dog' depression he often suffered during periods of stasis. Meagher got to see both sides. At times, Tony could be morose, even silent, for days on end. On one occasion, when they were in Mexico for three weeks, Tony said almost nothing for ten days while he brooded on some unrelated problem. Meagher kept gabbling away at breakfast, lunch and dinner while Tony stared gloomily at the table. 'He did suffer from some kind of depression,' Meagher reflects. 'Sometimes people who are very creative and live that kind of life—it sometimes comes with the territory.'

Meagher also saw the volcanic temper that lay beneath an essentially still façade. 'I saw Tony in fights,' he says, 'not just one punch, lots of punches, big bust-ups. If somebody had annoyed or upset him he would just lose his rag totally and blow up and let them have it.'

Tony's anger over the *Tribune* and his propensity to turn in on himself might have produced a retreat to Kilboy to lick his wounds. But instead he simply pressed delete and moved on. It was a characteristic that was perhaps among the most important features of his emotional armoury. Tony was never afraid of failure. His tempers and slides into depression often coincided with periods of frustration when projects weren't going according to plan. Once they failed, however, the worrying stopped and he started thinking about other initiatives, which brought a corresponding lifting of his spirits.

That resilience proved to be a particularly useful attribute in the 1980s as Tony lurched from one apparently quixotic venture to another. One such project was the purchase of the Old Schoolhouse in Dunquin, on the Dingle Peninsula. In fact, the 'old' house was no such thing. Built of concrete and faced with stone for an authentic look, it had been part of the film set for *Ryan's Daughter*. 'Tony was down there on a beautiful, clear sunny day,' Denis O'Brien remembers, 'and he had a couple of jars, saw it and said, "Now wouldn't it be great to buy that." He never used it afterwards—never went near the place—but he just liked it!' Declan Ryan recalls that the auctioneer had told his father that it was the most westerly property in Europe, 'so he used to console himself with that for having wasted his money on it.' Years later Tony would consider establishing a writers colony to 'initiate a bard culture', but the plans fell through for lack of interest.

Another project was an attempt to apply to build a high-powered European satellite in conjunction with the state-run RTE and Telecom Éireann. The Government, afraid that the investment was too risky, ended up blocking the move. In fact the company that eventually won the licence, Astra, would lead the way in the communications revolution that followed, not least as the main provider for Sky Broadcasting.

Closer to home was the purchase of his own pub, The Pike Inn at Birdhill, Co. Tipperary. On one level the initiative could hardly have been more personal. 'The GPA crowd would drink in Durty Nelly's [in Bunratty] after work,' recalls Gerry Power, who started in the company in 1985, 'but then from Nelly's to home was too long a drive, whereas from Birdhill it was, like, fifteen minutes. So Tony wanted to have a pub closer to home.'

The Pike Inn was in a terrible state, so John Meagher was asked to restore it. Denis O'Brien, who managed the project, estimates that about £750,000 was put into the renovation of what was renamed Matt the Thresher. 'I couldn't believe that,' O'Brien laughs. 'I just thought, Holy feck—that much into a pub!' But he later came to see that Tony's gastropub concept was ahead of its time. Gerry Power agrees. 'His idea was to establish Matt the Thresher and then recreate the formula around the world. Nowadays there isn't a capital city anywhere without an Irish pub, but he was at the forefront of branding that idea.'

Tony would eventually sell the pub in 1987. He had told Meagher when they looked at the original Pike Inn that he wanted to buy the place because 'one of my ambitions in life is to get a free pint and a free newspaper.' The *Sunday Tribune* and Matt the Thresher had provided him with scoops of different kinds, but neither had turned out even to be cheap, let alone free.

Friends were amazed at how sanguine Tony was about the disappointments he had endured away from aviation. Owning the *Sunday Tribune* had brought Tony the kind of press that was hellish to endure for such a private man. His consolation was that elsewhere, in the business press, he was beginning to receive the kind of international attention that profiled his achievements in aircraft leasing rather than dust-ups with Vincent Browne. The former subject may have garnered less gossip in the Horseshoe Bar at the Shelbourne Hotel, but in the wider scheme of things it mattered more.

That was certainly the case with a profile that appeared in December 1983 in the prestigious financial magazine *Fortune*. In many ways the tone of the feature, both admiring and perplexed, was typical of the international reaction to this entrepreneurial success story from Ireland. 'GPA has come from nowhere in 1975 to earn $8.7 million on assets of $100 million in [this] fiscal year,' it reported. 'Those returns—world class by the standards of the highly-leveraged leasing industry—flow into GPA's improbably provincial home base at Shannon Airport in the west of Ireland.' The implication was clear enough: How had Tony Ryan built a multi-million-dollar business, making himself a reported personal fortune of more than $7 million, from a place that was 'remote and not particularly well connected to the world by airlines or even telephones'?

Tony himself provided readers with the answer.

> I don't want to sound arrogant, but we've learned the market very well. We've never been wrong in valuing an aircraft. As I have a large equity in the company, it concentrates the mind that you have to get it right. An error could be a very painful experience.

No wonder, then, concluded *Fortune*, that 'in the increasingly free market for air travel, many airlines are likely to specialise in marketing what they know best—schedules and service—and leave their hardware problems to specialists like GPA.' And to Tony Ryan, the man they christened 'the airlines' golden middleman'.

Profiles in magazines such as *Fortune* helped facilitate Tony's vision of expanding GPA's international reach. His objective was to grow profits by 35 per cent a year for the next five years. To meet that target required a major push into the American market. The United States was home to almost half the world's airlines. If Tony could make serious inroads into that market, he knew he would achieve his goal not only of making GPA the biggest leasing company in the world but also of transforming how the airline industry conducted its business. 'Forty years ago', he mused, 'it was incongruous for a shopkeeper not to own his own shop. Nowadays, retailing and real estate are thought of as separate businesses.' His aim was to make the same true for airlines in their relationship to jet planes.

Civil aviation was going through a period of radical change by the mid-1980s. Deregulation in the United States had increased the demand for aircraft, and new 'anti-noise' legislation was making older planes obsolete. With many airlines reluctant to commit money to buying aircraft, the level of leasing shot up even among prestige carriers. By the end of the decade, for example, British Airways would be leasing a third of its planes. These figures implied rich pickings for companies like GPA, which suddenly found their services greatly in demand. Indeed, the problem increasingly became not demand but supply, and the capital to finance it.

By the time of the *Fortune* profile there had already been one false but not unhelpful dawn for GPA in breaking into the important American market. When the airline Braniff had entered bankruptcy proceedings in 1982, the company's secured creditors enlisted GPA to carry out a technical evaluation on the entire fleet. It was a plum role, not least because an appointment in such a high-profile case attracted publicity for GPA and reinforced its reputation as a trusted judge of value in the market. 'We interviewed a number of people,' remarked one of Braniff's lenders, 'but GPA brought the broadest experience to the problem we had to solve.'

Tantalisingly, there was also the prospect of further advantage: if Braniff was unable to reorganise to the satisfaction of the courts and the creditors, GPA would be asked to dispose of the entire Braniff fleet, bringing in a potentially huge commission on more than sixty aircraft. In the end, Braniff managed to offload a third of its fleet to another airline, which was enough to finance a restructuring. GPA missed out on the ultimate prize, but it did get a hefty fee, along with a raised profile and reputation in that all-important American market.

It was no coincidence that GPA's first major American deal followed shortly afterwards. In 1983, taking advantage of airline deregulation, America West Airlines raised $19 million in a public offering to finance a 'no frills' service operating out of Phoenix,

Arizona. The time-scale for America West was incredibly tight, with a planned launch within months. The message to GPA was simple: get us seven 737-200 aircraft by the launch date and you've got yourself a relationship. There followed a period of frenetic negotiating and scrambling around to acquire an additional four aircraft to supplement the three that GPA already had to hand.

On 1 August 1983 America West made its first flight into Phoenix, where hundreds of local residents were waiting under a giant banner proclaiming *Welcome to the Valley!* GPA had delivered for the airline. 'They're very creative people,' judged an approving America West investor. In return it was clear to Tony that America West was GPA's 'most significant new customer'. In the coming financial year alone the airline would contribute 9 per cent of GPA's annual profits, with further expansion to come. What was particularly gratifying was that a successful entry into the American market had been based on good judgement more than luck.

After airline deregulation, Tony had taken the decision in 1982 to set up an American subsidiary. This made GPA geographically better placed to capture new business with the low-cost American airlines that were expected to proliferate within the new deregulated market. Graham Boyd was sent to New York to set up an office, before an eventual move in 1983 to Stamford, Connecticut, the upmarket home of many *Fortune* 500 companies. In effect the role of the company, named GPA Corporation, was to hustle for business and facilitate deals in the United States. Contracts were always signed in tax-free Shannon, meaning that GPA Corp. got taxed only on its finder's fee. Such was the success of GPA Corp. that it would soon be going head-to-head in the United States with Steve Udvar-Házy and International Lease Finance Corporation, the California aircraft-leasing company that was GPA's only major rival.

The deals with America West, and those over Braniff, raised GPA's visibility in the United States, which in turn helped the company attract American investors. GPA was by now a dynamic force in the industry, but in many ways it remained a 'boutique' operation. Tony wanted GPA to take advantage of the deregulation dogfight by upping its 3 per cent of global aircraft inventory to 5 per cent. To achieve this, GPA would need to find a bolder strategy, matched by an equity base of about $200 million. 'GPA is good at "putting out fires"', judged Juan O'Callahan of TAI, the company's research arm, but it risked 'losing out' in times that were 'interesting (perhaps dangerous)'. The strategy was perilous but offered the potential for vast reward: a stake in a global market projected at an annual $13 billion for as far as anyone could see.

To expand and meet Tony's objective to make GPA the biggest leasing company in the world required considerable capital and investment. The breakthrough came when Tony gained an introduction to the influential Australian investment banker James Wolfensohn. Although Wolfensohn was temperamentally a different kind of character from Tony, the two men had a similarity in age and background, as well as a cultural affinity based on the historical ties between their two countries. Wolfensohn, however—whatever his outsider origins as an Australian—was the ultimate insider in New York financial circles. He had recently been a candidate for president of the World Bank and would later assume that role in 1995. In the early 1980s his investment firm, James D. Wolfensohn Inc., was among the most prestigious in the world. When he took a look at GPA he liked its potential and agreed to present the company to American Express and General Electric Capital Corporation for potential investment.

Tony was exultant, particularly at the prospect of going into business with GECC, the investment arm of one of America's most famous businesses. As Maurice Foley noted, 'if you look for a US financial institution that's interested in aviation and that's not a bank you come very rapidly to GECC.' Indeed GECC was one of the biggest players in the aviation industry, with its CF6 family of engines in the 1980s powering wide-body aircraft that included the Boeing 747 and 767, the Airbus A300, A310 and A330, and the McDonnell Douglas MD-11. Investment by General Electric in GPA would represent a massive breakthrough for the Irish company in terms of prestige, access to capital and the continuing expansion of its North American base. In addition it would bring Tony into contact with Jack Welch, General Electric's already legendary CEO. The two men, a year apart in age, would get along well in person, although eventually the relationship would end in tears and public humiliation for Tony.

Negotiations with GE proceeded throughout early 1983, with Wolfensohn brokering the deal. The objective was to facilitate GPA's expansion into the American market, 'where airline deregulation has greatly increased opportunities'. In April, GECC agreed in principle to buy an equity interest of just over 22 per cent in GPA for a total consideration of $18 million. Tony's personal 10 per cent holding in GPA remained undiluted. 'The agreement to come on board reached by GECC this week,' Tony enthused to Wolfensohn, 'represents one of the most significant milestones in GPA's history.' As he wrote in his next annual report, the investment not only 'significantly enhanced the strength of the balance sheet' but also ensured that GPA could 'take advantage of trading opportunities without the need to have bank financing in place in advance.' In other words, Tony could let his GPA dogs off the leash.

'Without any question,' Tony wrote afterwards to Welch, 'the single most significant development for GPA since its formation in 1975 was the investment made by GECC in 1983. While the GECC shareholding equalled that of the other corporate shareholders, the size and financial muscle of GECC clearly [surpasses] their combined total strength.' GPA, Tony believed, had 'at last obtained a near-perfect shareholder mix in terms of motivation, interest, financial capacity and nationality.'

Alas for Tony, that turned out not to be the case. The relationship with GECC quickly soured. In part this was a clash of cultures—not national but of size. GECC was a big corporation within a giant one. It had little history of owning minority stakes in other companies: GE as a group rarely bothered with businesses it didn't control. In fact it made no secret of the fact that the initial investment in GPA was just the beginning of its commitment, which most analysts presumed would lead to a friendly takeover.

A significant aspect of the GECC deal was that an initial public offering (IPO) was expected for shares in GPA either in London or in New York. With a new investor of the quality of GE on board, and with GPA providing (to quote *Fortune*) 'world class' returns, the timing could hardly have seemed more propitious. 'We all believe a successful flotation to be in the best interests of the company and the shareholders, including GECC,' Tony told Wolfensohn. The information memorandum that was prepared for the GECC deal stated explicitly that 'the company and certain or all of its shareholders intend to make an initial public offering of the shares of the company as soon as possible after the current offering.'

The GECC deal was approved by the GPA board on 23 May. A date in a month's time was set for the IPO, and a prospectus was prepared. Then it was delayed until September. The GECC deal still went ahead on 19 August 1983. Shortly afterwards the IPO was postponed indefinitely.

It is hard to know exactly what game Tony was playing. Having been so gung-ho about the IPO when he had GECC on the hook, his rapid about-turn once he had reeled them in is difficult to explain. Initially Tony had given the GECC executive vice-president, Gary Wendt, the impression that they were in it together, as Jim King recalls.

> I'll always remember the day that the GECC involvement was agreed, with Tony and Gary down on their knees, with their backsides up in the air, drawing up structures and all the rest of it on the floor in Kilboy . . . When we were finished we walked down to the pub in the village and had a few pints. That was how the agreement took place.

However, Tony now fell back on the excuse he often used when backtracking on a given issue: operational difficulties. Simply put, he told Wendt, an IPO would get in the way of everyday trading. 'Our commercial development has been less than it should have been,' he explained, blaming the complexities of negotiating a private offering to GECC and a potential IPO at the same time. That inevitably had 'serious implications for the normal operations of the company' and was something that GPA must consider 'in reviewing future plans for a public issue'.

There was no question that the previous few months had been technically difficult, but more important to Tony and GPA was the sudden unpleasant realisation that GECC was picking up the company on the cheap. The $18 million that GECC had paid for its 22.7 per cent stake in GPA implied a valuation for the company of about $80 million, or nine times its previous year's earning. Tony and his senior executives believed that the company was worth considerably more. 'GECC got a private placement discount,' Maurice Foley noted. 'For now we'll invest our new equity and turn this company into an even stronger vehicle.'

That approach might have worked for Tony, but it was never a situation that was going to suit GECC for long. 'The General Electric System relies on intense management involvement', wrote Wendt, 'and finds itself frustrated when its expectations are not met or its influence unimportant.' Exactly a year after GECC bought a stake in the company, Wendt told Tony of his 'desire that GECC have as great an involvement with GPA as possible.' Seven months later he announced that GECC was pulling out of the company.

The blow, when it came, was unexpected. At a GPA board meeting in London on 29 March 1985, Wendt casually announced, under 'any other business', that GECC would be selling its stake in GPA. It was the kind of ruthlessness that would later see Wendt engulfed by a notoriety that went well beyond the business pages of the national media. The announcement was 'shattering' for Tony. His first reaction was one of fury at the manner of the announcement. 'I should have been told privately in advance of GECC's position on such a vital subject,' he wrote angrily to Wendt afterwards. 'I can envisage nothing more likely to erode the confidence or progress of a company than such a precipitous action by a major shareholder.'

Along with his official letter as CEO, Tony also included a private note scolding Wendt. Only weeks earlier Tony had agreed a new deal to become chairman of GPA (with executive powers), with a further $10 million investment. 'Had the GECC position been advised to me in time, I would not have agreed to enter into the new agreement,' he complained, adding menacingly, 'I believe I have been the subject of misrepresentation.'

That threat was too much for Wendt, who fired back angrily 'to express concern over the tone' of the official letter and the personal note. 'GECC reached its position after careful consideration of the factors surrounding GPA and expressed this position to its fellow shareholders as soon as practicable,' he countered. 'Innuendos that we are acting unethically and in a manner which is detrimental to the other shareholders are uncalled for given the circumstances.'

Undeterred, Tony attempted to go over Wendt's head by appealing directly to Welch. He conceded that there had been 'a learning curve period for both parties' involving 'certain inevitable cultural and style differences'. He reminded him that GECC's $18 million investment was now worth 'in the region of $56 million today'. But most of all he complained about Wendt, presenting him as incompetent, discourteous and duplicitous. His initial announcement, made 'without any notice whatsoever', had come 'as a bombshell'. Wendt had then left him 'under the impression that GECC had reconsidered its position.' Later he 'categorically stated GECC's intention was to sell', only then to do another about-turn by saying that 'further GECC Board review was required'. Inevitably such 'vacillation has been extremely disruptive' and raised 'serious questions' for both companies. Therefore, Tony concluded, 'I would like the opportunity of personally meeting with you at the earliest opportunity.'

The letter was a dud. Within Welch's multi-billion GE conglomerate, GPA was nothing more than loose change. In 1983 it had looked like a tidy way to handle some of the problem accounts within GECC's commercial airline portfolio and a means to develop new business activity in used-aircraft refinancing. Now that the relationship had failed to work as expected, Welch and GE simply bailed out. Welch replied offhandedly by asking Tony to 'contact

Mr Wendt', adding that, 'hopefully, we can resolve this issue to our mutual advantage.'

It took another seven months for GECC to divest itself of a stake in GPA. 'With the transaction closed and the check cleared, please be assured that all hatchets have been buried,' Wendt wrote cheerfully to Tony afterwards. 'In case you're not familiar with that American phrase, it means no ill feelings remain and that best wishes are granted.'

Tony didn't bother to reply. More important was the declaration from Wendt in an earlier letter. 'GECC and GPA', it said, 'should be viewed more as competitors than partners.' This wouldn't be the last time he would cross swords with General Electric. At the time, however, Tony hardly seemed to care. As GECC departed, the American share of GPA's business had jumped from 16 per cent in 1981 to more than 60 per cent in 1985. The company's move into the American market, helped by the GECC capital and prestige, was paying off. GPA Corp. now had a smart new office in Connecticut, opened by the Taoiseach, Garret FitzGerald, as Tony's mother looked on. 'I cannot think of a prouder moment,' Tony said afterwards.

Chapter 7

LONDON (LUTON) CALLING

Waterford Airport, 8 July 1985

It was a low-key place to begin a new era. Despite the famous crystal glass and 'sunny south-east' weather, Waterford was neither an important commercial centre nor a draw for overseas tourists, in the manner of Cork, Kerry and the west. The city was a relative backwater, albeit a charming one. Not many people needed to fly in and out, a fact amply demonstrated by the size of the plane waiting on the stand that day. The white twin-turboprop Embraer EMB 110 Bandeirante had a capacity for only fifteen passengers. Space was so tight that the flight crew had been recruited primarily on the grounds of height: attendants had to be under 5 feet 2 inches even to stand up straight in the aircraft.

In many ways this service was not much more than a quick-fix solution to a minor business problem. Guinness Peat Aviation had recently acquired a job lot of planes: three jets and the Bandeirante. The jet aircraft were straightforward to lease out, but there was little demand for the small twin-turboprop. Rather than the plane being left wasting in Shannon, it had been sent off to Waterford to service a new route to Gatwick Airport. The annual number of passengers was expected to be not much more than five thousand.

When the former Aer Lingus chief pilot, Captain George White, turned over the engine and the twin-turboprop spluttered into life, he could not have known that he was firing up a revolution in European travel. For this was the first flight of Ryanair, the airline that would go on to dominate commercial aviation on the continent and change the way Europeans thought about the very notion of travel.

On a symbolic level the Bandeirante could hardly have been better chosen, the name coming from that of the Portuguese adventurers and treasure-hunters of the sixteenth and seventeenth centuries. In the case of Ryanair, everyone knew the adventurer behind the operation. First there was the name of the airline. Then there was the shamrock on the tail fin of the aircraft, which to anyone looking closely was made up of three Rs. Each represented a Ryan—Cathal, Declan and Shane—and they were the three children of the finance and brains behind Ryanair: the GPA boss, Tony Ryan.

'Mr T. Ryan is not in any way involved with Ryan Air,' Declan Ryan had written to a potential investor only a few months before. That may have been technically true, but everyone, not least Declan himself, understood that Ryanair was Tony's project.

Five years earlier Tony had been frustrated in his plans for Irelandia. The ambitious project would have seen the new airline competing directly with Aer Lingus on the prestigious transatlantic route. That initiative had provoked fury among Aer Lingus executives, especially because many of them considered GPA to be an Aer Lingus company and Tony, by extension, their employee. On that occasion he had been forced to back away from the plan, but he never stopped thinking about a low-cost, no-frills competitor to the national carrier. By 1985 he had improved his tactics. There was no point in taking on Aer Lingus head-to-head. Tony needed to establish the principle of competition without engaging in a direct fight.

Late in 1984 Tony invited his old friend Christy Ryan down to Kilboy. The two men had started out together in Shannon in the 1950s, and Christy had been part of the GPA start-up. More recently he had been general manager of the small airline Aer Arann, running a scheduled service from Shannon to Dublin. He could be a difficult character—'Christy is Christy,' wearily noted one personnel report at GPA—but Tony trusted him. It was a bond that went back to when they were just lads on the back of a motorbike, happy with their jobs as counter-jumpers in Shannon.

Christy had an idea for running an air-taxi service out of Waterford, his home county, but he had been unable to raise the capital. Tony, on the other hand, despite his losses on the *Sunday Tribune*, had millions in tax-free dividends from GPA burning a hole in his pocket. He had already tried without much success to get a hydrofoil ferry service operating across the Irish Sea. Now he wanted to get the airline project back up and running. Christy was no entrepreneur, but he was a trusted friend and a highly accomplished manager. It was no surprise that Tony should want him involved in Irelandia, not least because he was the ideal mentor for the other key figures in the new airline.

Ryanair was not just a business investment for Tony: it was a family one. He saw the project as an ideal way to get his two eldest boys back home to Ireland and, in a trust shared equally with Shane, who was still at school, to start them off in business. Declan was working in the United States for America West. Cathal was flying Boeing 747s as a co-pilot with Air Lanka. The two had acquired the necessary background and experience in aviation. Now they could return to run their own company under the watchful eye of their father and his oldest, most trusted friend. 'It's disgraceful that so many youngsters have to leave the country,' Tony told friends. 'I want my boys to follow me into the aviation business, but there are no jobs. So we'll create our own airline, because Ireland needs it.'

Over a few pints in Tony's local pub in Dolla, he and Christy worked out their plan for the new airline. After the previous tricky experience with the GPA board over Irelandia, Tony wanted plausible deniability over his involvement. It was for this reason that he initially baulked at Christy's idea of trading under the name 'Ryanair', preferring instead 'Trans Tipperary'. But Christy wanted the Ryan name on the plane, so in the end Tony reluctantly agreed. It made little difference in the long run to Christy, who dropped out early in the project and always felt that his name had been written out of the Ryanair story.

On 28 November 1984 the company was formally incorporated as Danren Enterprises, soon changing its name to Ryanair Ltd. The ambition of the original business plan, dated 2 March 1985, was uncharacteristically modest. 'Ryanair's overall strategy for Year One', it stated, 'is based on achieving break-even or better operations with a single Bandeirante competing in two distinct but complementary markets.' This identified, firstly, a night-mail service operated under contract to either An Post or a leading courier company such as UPS and, secondly, cheap passenger charters to special events such as football matches at locations not serviced by scheduled airlines. The immediate objective was to secure 1,339 hours of business in the year from 1 May 1985, when the company would begin trading.

The key to pricing would be 'a degree of flexibility', with an average mark-up on direct costs of 65 per cent, increasing to 100 per cent 'where the market will stand it'. Working on these figures, the business plan confidently predicted: 'Preliminary projections indicate that these (or equivalent) Market and Price Targets will enable the company to achieve approximately break-even results in its first operational year.' The initial equity funding, supplied by Tony, of £250,000 (in addition to £35,000 in start-up costs) would be 'sufficient to keep the Company in credit at all times.'

It was on the basis of this business plan that Ryanair made its formal application on 5 March 1985 to the Department of Communications for a class C operating authorisation to run the Bandeirante. The two shareholders of the company were listed as Cathal Ryan (90 per cent) and Christy Ryan (10 per cent). On the board they were joined by a chairman, Ken Holden, who had acted as a consultant for Tony at GPA, and Declan Ryan, who became company secretary. To cover Tony himself, the application stated in explicit terms that the company 'has no direct or indirect connections with any other company in Ireland or elsewhere.'

The first, difficult months might have given even Tony pause for thought about his involvement in the new enterprise. The Waterford–Gatwick route itself was popular enough with a niche market. Local businesspeople immediately recognised the advantage of an air taxi to London without the bother of the two-hour drive to Dublin or Cork. Moreover, Gatwick was a 'proper' airport, with an excellent rail connection to the heart of the city. The idea of having breakfast at home in Waterford, lunch in London and dinner back home in Waterford had an obvious appeal. Less attractive was the endless circling of Waterford Airport, waiting to land before getting diverted to Dublin. Aircraft could land at Waterford only when the cloud base was above 800 feet (as opposed to 300 feet at the rival Cork Airport), which meant, the *Irish Times* reported, an 'unacceptably high' number of Ryanair diversions to Dublin, 'with consequent damage to customer relations and Ryan's reputation.'

Other problems for the fledgling airline surrounded its management. Part of the original concept behind Ryanair in 1984/5 had been a tie-up with Club Travel, a prominent Irish travel agency for both scheduled and charter flights. They acted as the principal agent for the new airline. In June 1985, a few weeks before the first flight took off, the owner and operator of Club Travel, Liam Lonergan, was appointed managing director of Ryanair. He brought energy and marketing savvy to the airline but had little experience of the aviation industry. That led to a series of spectacular rows with Tony, who quickly lost faith in him. Five months after he was appointed, Lonergan resigned. 'A number of things came to a head in the last ten days or so,' he said, 'and I felt it was not appropriate to continue on as managing director.'

Tony was glad to see him go. Lonergan, through Club Travel, had been an important part of setting up Ryanair, but he had never been Tony's man. To replace him Tony now turned to Eugene O'Neill. The young accountant had not had a particularly auspicious beginning to his career with Tony. He had been chief executive during the unhappy experience of owning the *Sunday Tribune*. Then he had run Tony's investment vehicle, Irelandia (the name was rescued from the original airline idea), where the most notable bit of business had been the disastrous purchase and subsequent sale of a B&I Line hydrofoil. No-one, least of all Tony, doubted O'Neill's ability. He just needed him to be lucky the third time round.

Not that luck was the main currency now at work with Ryanair. From the beginning, Tony had viewed the unsatisfactory Waterford route as the 'sprat to catch the mackerel'. Once it established the principle of competition with Aer Lingus, he could turn to his real target: the Dublin–London route. A new business plan outlined a vastly more challenging project than the initial document of March 1985. Now the scope of Tony's ambition was revealed for the first time: Ryanair's five-year objective was 'to become firmly established as Ireland's second airline.'

Tony was prepared to invest huge sums and take vast early losses to meet that objective. By the end of 1986 Ryanair would have recorded a deficit of £2.2 million.

These were losses that Tony was prepared to bear, because he recognised that the times demanded it. He had wanted to compete with Aer Lingus five years earlier, but he backed away, as the context of the day had been wrong. By 1985, however, that context had been transformed beyond recognition. There could hardly have been a more propitious time for bringing the fight to a complacent national carrier. In the space of a year Ireland had metamorphosed from one of the most uncompetitive airline environments in Europe into one of the most cut-throat. That world was made for Tony Ryan.

The new aviation environment had seemed a long way off in the summer of 1984, when the Fine Gael-Labour Party coalition Government introduced one of the most draconian anti-competitive pieces of legislation in the history of the state. The Air Transport Bill was a direct response to the Government's failed legal attempts to stop Transamerica Airlines and various Irish travel agents selling tickets for Transamerica's charter flight service from the United States to Shannon. The Minister for Communications, Jim Mitchell, had sought an injunction from the High Court to prevent ticket sales on the grounds that it interfered with the Government's right to control air fares. The High Court granted the injunction against Transamerica but ruled that the minister could not control fares set by travel agents. Moreover, when Transamerica appealed to the Supreme Court even this injunction was overturned. The Government prepared to appeal but in the meantime set about changing the law to close the competitive loopholes the court case had revealed.

The penalties the Government sought to introduce were enough to put off any agent selling a cheap airline ticket: a £100,000 fine, two years in prison and the loss of a travel-agency licence. Such was the punishment for 'undermining the system of control' within Irish aviation. 'The minister's powers would be undermined,' the Government argued. 'Discounting and other malpractices could take place on a scale that would undermine approved tariff structures and could have serious implications for airlines generally and for Aer Lingus in particular.'

The introduction of the bill was met with fierce opposition within and outside the Dáil. Leading economists, headed by Sean Barrett, publicly denounced it as being 'to the obvious detriment of the fare-paying public' and 'wholly at variance with public pronouncements on the need to encourage efficiency and lower cost', adding that it 'further lowers public confidence in our legislators'.

In the Dáil, opposition was led by Des O'Malley. As a TD for Limerick East, he had taken a strong interest in GPA. It was through Tony, O'Malley says, that he first became interested in the lack of competition within Irish aviation and the problem of the Aer Lingus monopoly. Over the years, at meetings and dinners, Tony had briefed him on how deregulation was transforming the worldwide aviation industry, particularly in the United States, and he constantly urged him to take on the issue within Ireland. In many ways he was pushing at an open door, as O'Malley's own political thinking was already developing towards the free market. By 1985 he would have established a new political party, the Progressive Democrats, committed to the liberalisation of Irish markets. In the United States and Britain a similar process had put airline deregulation and privatisation at the forefront of the debate. It was no surprise in 1984 that O'Malley, by now an independent TD after losing the Fianna Fáil whip, should have chosen such ground on which to plant his flag.

Tony kept close to O'Malley during the debates, supplying him with information when it was helpful. Not that O'Malley was a stooge of Ryanair: he pursued the issue with tenacity, taking advice from voices outside the industry, most notably Barrett. He also used contacts developed in Europe during his time as Minister for Industry. By the mid-1980s the European Commission was keen to encourage competition in aviation. It supplied O'Malley with key statistics and expert analysis with which to bolster his case.

To this barrage of academic and bureaucratic information O'Malley added his own skill in framing the debate to maximum effect. The Dutch airline KLM, he pointed out, was being paid half a million pounds a year by Aer Lingus *not* to fly to Dublin, thereby allowing the Irish carrier to charge up to £500 for a return fare to Amsterdam. How did they get away with it? he asked. Because the Department of Transport was the 'downtown office of Aer Lingus'. The phrase stuck, because it perfectly conveyed the image of a cosy or even corrupt relationship that put the interests of the airline above those of the Irish people.

When the Air Transport Bill was read for a second time, on 27 June 1984, the Government's complacency was demonstrated by the minister, Jim Mitchell, not even being present for the debate. Instead, the minister of state, Ted Nealon, outlined how the bill would 'close off a loophole . . . in the general national interest.'

'Is it in our national interest,' O'Malley baited Nealon, 'that this should be so, or will we continue to make the mistake of equating Ireland's national interest with the health of Aer Lingus's balance sheet?'

When it came to the vote on whether to take the bill to the next stage, the opposition whip, Bertie Ahern, sensing an opportunity, announced that his party would not be supporting the Government on the Air Transport Bill. That decision was straight politics. The Fianna Fáil leader, Charles Haughey, liked to oppose everything he could that was not his own policy when out of office. (Fianna Fáil, for example, opposed the Anglo-Irish Agreement in this period but later worked it successfully in government.) Now their opposition, along with sufficient discontent from free marketeers on the Government's own benches, was enough to stop the bill in its tracks. Mitchell soon announced that he would be parking the legislation in order to better appraise the issue.

'Air fares bill hits turbulence', reported the *Irish Press*. It was turbulence for some, clear air for others. Tony had been exultant at the failure of the Air Transport Bill. The door of airline deregulation had been held ajar; Tony now went barging through. Within five months Ryanair was incorporated and the principle of deregulation established with the Waterford–Gatwick route.

In April 1985 Ryanair applied for a licence to operate on the Dublin–Luton route. Again it was a clever choice: an unfashionable airport outside London to which Aer Lingus did not fly at that time. It was subtle competition rather than head-to-head conflict with the national carrier. Over the next eight months Tony quietly lobbied Jim Mitchell and the Taoiseach, Garret FitzGerald, who was regularly invited to Kilboy and would eventually join the GPA board as a non-executive director in 1987.

These personal contacts were vital to what happened next. Ireland was still getting the hang of the processes of deregulation. Later, more transparent procedures for putting a service or utility out to tender would be adopted; but in 1985 having a word with the minister seemed to be enough.

It turned out to be a win-win situation. The Government had a problem with hostility from the public and the Dáil, including its own backbenchers, about a deeply unpopular air-fares policy. Now here was Tony Ryan, someone with an international reputation in the aviation business, offering to get them off the hook. Give us the Luton route that Aer Lingus doesn't want, Tony told them, and all your problems are solved.

The political expediency of the decision was reflected in the strange scenes in the Dáil when it was announced on 4 December

1985. The committee stage of the Air Transport Bill had been resumed. The chamber was almost empty following the excitement of a controversial statement on European affairs by the Taoiseach immediately beforehand. Now, during discussion of an opposition amendment to the Air Transport Bill, Mitchell pulled a rabbit from his ministerial hat. 'It is appropriate to announce now', he declared, 'that I have approved in principle a new air service from Dublin to Luton, return, costing £99. I have given Ryanair the go-ahead, and it will be announced by my department later today.'

A moment of stunned silence was interrupted by audible laughter from Des O'Malley's direction. Mitchell ploughed on, passionately declaring himself 'among the most ardent advocates of liberalisation of air transport' and 'all for an open-skies policy throughout the European Community'.

'At last I am beginning to see the fruits of my labours!' O'Malley jeered. He then sought assurances that it was 'a genuine £99 fare and not full of all kinds of restrictions.' When he received them, O'Malley hailed the moment as 'a great step forward in terms of Irish aviation policy' and 'quite an event'. He even congratulated the minister.

Meanwhile, it was left to the Ceann Comhairle to point out from the chair that the minister's unscripted change of policy had broken procedure. 'The minister has announced it, and the deputy has welcomed it,' he complained, 'and neither was in order.' After all, the minister's announcement was a *volte-face* on the bill under discussion, which had been put before the Dáil in his name.

Having the Dublin–Luton licence granted was a triumphant moment for Tony, but it was also one with immediate dangers. As the *Irish Times* pointed out, 'Ryan Air strongly deny that Cathal Ryan is a stalking horse for Tony Ryan. Were this to be the case, it would prove embarrassing for the elder Ryan, who is a partner in Guinness Peat Aviation.' The newspaper continued mischievously: 'The national carrier would not take too kindly to him starting an airline in competition with Aer Lingus.'

Years afterwards the chief executive of Aer Lingus, David Kennedy, would happily admit that the advent of Ryanair was good for the national airline. 'To look out the window at Dublin Airport and see a Ryanair aircraft sitting there was a wake-up call,' he says. At the time, however, there was only anger and bemusement within Aer Lingus. Kennedy didn't even bother seeking assurances from Tony about his role in Ryanair, because everyone accepted that the GPA boss 'was involved, absolutely'.

That involvement itself prompted fury within Aer Lingus, but so too did the way in which Tony had got the licence. 'He found it so easy to get a licence from the Government without any formal tendering process,' Kennedy complains. The Dublin–London route was the 'most profitable part of the Aer Lingus network'. For Tony to get a piece of that action, even though it was to Luton, without a proper bidding process or a requirement to take on other public-service requirements stuck in the craw of everyone at Aer Lingus.

Sometimes that displeasure felt personal. When Derek O'Brien, who was on unpaid leave from Aer Lingus at the time, was tapped up by Tony in January 1986 to join the new airline as commercial director, he found himself hauled into the offices of the national carrier. 'We've heard a rumour that you're thinking of joining Ryanair,' he says he was told. 'If this is so, your unpaid leave is cancelled and we expect you back in the office by Monday. If you don't turn up we will assume you've resigned.' O'Brien didn't need time to think it over. 'It was "Goodbye and get lost" from Aer Lingus,' he says, 'so I just said, "Stuff it," and decided that I would join Ryanair anyway.'

Over the next few months Tony focused on getting the airline ready for its inaugural flight to Luton on 23 May 1986. He had to maintain the illusion of an arm's length relationship, so most of the meetings took place down in Kilboy rather than in Dublin. There was no detail too small for Tony to consider, right down to the quality of the desk in the new booking office that would open in Dublin's south city centre. In many ways that desk, individually designed and constructed, was an early indication of the dichotomy at the heart of early Ryanair: while Tony wanted the airline to be a low-cost carrier, he also wanted it to be elegant and in some ways classy. Cheap and cheerful, he would remind everyone, 'does not have to mean shite.'

Eugene O'Neill was the man tasked with selling the Ryanair image. Among the many old hands that Tony had brought in from Aer Lingus, there was a certain bemusement, even annoyance, that someone with so little understanding of the aviation industry should have been asked to run the new airline. But it was for their experience that those more seasoned figures had been recruited. What Tony wanted from O'Neill was pizzazz—a youthful face that could put Ryanair forward as a contemporary, populist and entrepreneurial alternative to the staid, out-of-touch Aer Lingus.

O'Neill was perfectly suited to the role of master of ceremonies. Flash, even brash, he also had a winning way that combined charm and a knowing look that said, 'Sure it's gas, isn't it!' He would organise publicity stunts for each new Ryanair initiative, involving bagpipers and lots of pretty women. Everything shouted that you could pay more money to fly Aer Lingus if you wanted, but whatever your age or class you would have more fun on Ireland's second airline.

Dressing in natty Armani suits and occupying a vast, expensively designed office in Dawson Street, O'Neill also seemed to represent something else new. He was the next generation of businessman—the heir to Tony's class of 1936, which had done so much to transform the landscape of Irish business. The 'Celtic Tiger' was not yet born, but O'Neill in 1986 was an early prototype for a kind of businessperson that would become familiar in the following decade. He had confidence in himself and also in Ireland as a place where things could happen. In the context of the mid-1980s, with the economy in tatters, that belief offered a much-needed burst of optimism. 'Eugene O'Neill is a young man with big ambitions,' declared the *Irish Times's* 'People' profile. 'Ryanair's 30-year-old managing director plans to make the company one of the most successful in the country.'

Among Ryanair's trickiest first tasks was convincing people to fly to Luton Airport. It had been made famous for all the wrong reasons in the 1970s by a television ad for Campari featuring the actor Lorraine Chase. Chatted up by a 'posh' suitor, her character pointed out in a chirpy Cockney accent that she had wafted not from paradise but from Luton Airport. There was probably no television-owner in England or Ireland (where ITV was readily available) who didn't immediately have Chase's voice come to mind when thinking about that unfortunate airport.

The snob value surrounding Luton Airport might have counted for less than people imagined. Heathrow Airport, after all, was next to Hounslow, a destination visited by few of the millions of travellers who passed through each year. More problematic, however, was the fact that Luton was outside London and had poor transport connections. Yet even this was a mixed blessing. On the one hand it allowed Ryanair to set its own fares, as it was not competing directly with Aer Lingus on one of the London routes regulated through bilateral agreements between Ireland and Britain; on the other hand it put the new airline at a disadvantage with passengers who wanted to fly directly to the capital. Tony's answer was as simple as it was brilliant. 'Just call it London anyway,' he told O'Neill. And so the Dublin to 'London Luton' route was born.

The onward-transport issue was harder to solve. With no underground railway line into the city centre, unlike at Heathrow, passengers were confronted with having to catch a bus, get a shuttle connection to the train station or pay an expensive taxi fare. It would turn out to be the major irritant for passengers in using the service.

Another issue to be neutralised was the fact that the journey with Ryanair took half an hour longer than Aer Lingus's to Heathrow. Ryanair's air operator's certificate was surely the only licence in the world in which the exact type of aircraft had been dictated. 'It was another example of the "downtown office" syndrome,' Declan Ryan suggests. Tony had originally planned to fly ancient Vickers Viscount aircraft on the route, but in the end he paid out £3 million to Dan-Air for two second-hand BAe 748 turboprop aircraft that could accommodate forty-eight passengers. These were still noisier and slower—'marginally slower', Tony corrected—than the jet aircraft that allowed Aer Lingus to give passengers a quicker, smoother journey to London. Eventually Ryanair would force the minister's hand with a typically cheeky ad announcing that they would soon be flying jets, 'subject to government approval'.

Down at Kilboy, Tony was constantly urging the Ryanair team to come up with imaginative solutions to these and other problems. But he also believed that if the price of a ticket was right, the paying public would understand that, like taking a bus instead of a taxi, the cheap fare made up for any minor inconveniences.

That the issue of price was Tony's ace in the hole was confirmed the day before Ryanair's first London flight. With the clock ticking down, the three big airlines operating across the Irish Sea each launched an assault on Tony's newcomer in an obvious attempt to spoil his big day. Ryanair was operating the route to London Luton for £99 return. Now Aer Lingus, British Airways and Dan-Air all announced that they were slashing their round-trip fares to Britain to £95. It was a declaration of intent: you wanted competition, the move said, so here it is.

Ryanair might well have reacted with anger and outrage. Instead they used humour to make a point. 'At last the penny has dropped,' quipped the Ryanair chairman, Arthur Walls, CEO of Clery's department store, before announcing that the airline had dropped its own prices to £94.99. It was a clever one-liner that reinforced Ryanair's image as a cheeky newcomer thumbing its nose at the big operators while helping to bring down prices for the ordinary punter.

What could have been a depressing beginning to the new service was instead launched in party style at Dublin Airport. O'Neill sent the first flight on its way amid the hoopla of pipers and cheerful banter. The inaugural passengers were presented with commemorative glassware. Among the first on board were top brass from Aer Rianta and Bord Fáilte, accompanied by the Aldermen and Burgesses of the City of Dublin. Tony's boys were there to receive congratulations on getting their new venture off the ground. RTE cameras rolled to capture a 'historic' day in Irish travel. In fact, amid the general excitement and jollification, it would have occurred to only the most observant that the one person who was missing was the man paying for everything. Tony Ryan, unwilling to undermine the assertion that Ryanair had nothing to do with him, did not attend the maiden flight from Dublin to London.

At Kilboy the following Saturday, however, Tony's commitment was to a different matter. He grilled O'Neill and his team on the first days of operation, wanting every detail. Then it was on to strategy. Aer Lingus slashing prices had been a warning. Ryanair could expect no favours from the national carrier. The rumour, vehemently denied, was that Aer Lingus had set up a special unit to target its low-cost, no-frills rival, taking aim at both price and reputation. Tony had seen what Aer Lingus could do to newcomers in the market. The previous year it had enveloped and then crushed the small independent airline Avair. The lesson Tony drew from this was that Ryanair had to establish itself quickly as a proper competitor to Aer Lingus. To run Ryanair as a small-scale operation was asking to be overwhelmed by the behemoth that was the national carrier.

Tony now laid out a threefold strategy to bite at the ankles of Aer Lingus. Firstly, Ryanair had to remain competitive on price no matter what Aer Lingus did to undercut it. Secondly, it had to go head-to-head with Aer Lingus in the publicity war that was already under way. When Aer Lingus launched a series of snarky advertisements deriding 'cosmopolitan Luton Airport' and enquiring why anyone would fly there instead of to a real London airport, Ryanair hit back in kind, asking if it was really worth paying an extra £150 'for breakfast'. That approach made an advantage of the 'no frills' aspect of Ryanair and emphasised the importance of price. Similarly, the fiftieth anniversary of Aer Lingus that year was greeted in tongue-in-cheek style by Ryanair with a poster of a giant birthday cake with a huge slice missing. These and other publicity stunts captured the popular and critical imagination. In 1987 Ryanair won the *Sunday Tribune* advertising campaign of the year award for its broadsides against Aer Lingus.

The third element of Tony's three-pronged attack was in many ways the most audacious. If Ryanair wasn't to be seen as a pipsqueak in comparison with Aer Lingus it had to do more than talk big: it had to act like a significant carrier. That meant expanding its fleet, looking beyond the Dublin–Luton route to find niche markets ready for development, and sometimes taking on Aer Lingus on its major routes. This policy would see Ryanair embark on a major dash for growth in the next two years, pulling in obscure routes such as Knock–Luton while simultaneously offering direct competition to Aer Lingus on the strategically critical route to Manchester.

That growth would be an expensive business for Tony, who over the coming years would have to dig deeper and deeper into his pockets to keep Ryanair aloft. Yet he was sustained by the belief that Ryanair had identified a new market that would transform commercial aviation, making it democratic and popular in ways that would have been unthinkable in the days when he started out in Shannon or worked amid the glamour of JFK Airport.

That Tony understood this new market better than anyone else was highlighted by the difference between Ryanair and Aer Lingus on price. While Aer Lingus had attempted to spoil Ryanair's party with a price slash in May 1986, the real contrast between the two companies on fares came in the small print. A Ryanair passenger bought a return ticket at the advertised price. For an Aer Lingus passenger the cheap fare was available only on a super-apex ticket bought a month in advance for a stay that had to include a Saturday night. That arrangement was all very well when planning a family holiday months in advance, but if you lived in London and someone in your family died in Dublin you might end up paying hundreds, if not thousands, of pounds to bring everyone home for a funeral that would take place in days. With Ryanair you just booked the flight at the normal price.

In happier times, Irish people began making more frequent and often spontaneous trips between Dublin and London. British tourists visited Dublin in greater number, making the city a favourite weekend destination. And workers who might otherwise have left Ireland at a time of economic hardship were now able to fly home at the end of every week. Derek O'Brien recalls that

> we had plasterers going to London, commuting for £94.99, which was unheard of before. And what's more important, they were bringing their wage packets back to Ireland. That was thanks to Tony Ryan's vision, no question. My own belief is that in the beginning he saw it as an investment in the country rather just a money-making enterprise.

Two months after the launch of the Ryanair route to Luton the verdict came in from the voice of the Irish establishment. 'Still a few hitches, but Ryanair's price is right,' announced the *Irish Times*, which had sent a reporter to judge the experience. Yes, there were problems with the transport system getting from London out to the airport, but Luton Airport itself had actually turned out to be quite agreeable, with 'an excellent duty-free shop far superior to the boxlike structure provided for the Irish flights from Heathrow.' Businesspeople on the flight 'love the flexibility it gives them without the vast expense of a £200 ticket.' Everything was rooted in the 'big advantage Ryanair has over every other airline', namely the price of tickets and no restrictions. All in all, concluded the newspaper's slightly surprised reporter, 'Ryanair was a pleasant experience.'

Middle-class Dublin exhaled in relief. Permission had been granted to travel Ryanair. The airline would never be posh, but it had become socially acceptable (and would be explained in ironic, slightly apologetic tones at dinner parties in south Co. Dublin). Now the phones never stopped ringing in the Dublin booking offices as passengers fought to get seats. A year after launching the Luton service Ryanair proudly announced that it had flown its 250,000th passenger. Tony had shown that a new airline could begin to compete with Aer Lingus in Ireland. The next question was whether it would make him any money.

Chapter 8

BETTER TO WEAR AWAY THAN RUST AWAY

By 1986, as Tony Ryan turned fifty, he seemed to have the world at his feet. Ryanair had been successfully launched. GPA, despite the difficult private placement after GECC divested its shares, was about to enter a new period of astonishing global ambition and growth. For Tony this expansion would mean growing international prestige and vast dividends paying him multiple millions each year. Instead of wasting that money in areas where he had no expertise, as with the *Sunday Tribune*, he was now investing in an industry in which he had well-honed instincts and expert knowledge.

Ryanair in the beginning would cost him millions more than he lost on the *Tribune*, but Tony always believed that the low-cost, no-frills model would see the airline come right in the end. More to the point, Ryanair, unlike GPA, was a company that Tony could call his own. He was beholden to no-one. There was no majority shareholder to lord it over him or clip his wings. The entire project, despite being seen by many as a plaything, was all of a piece with the way that Tony had come to think of himself.

By the mid-1980s Tony looked the very model of a modern entrepreneur. Friends and colleagues had already noticed the change in his sartorial taste: cream suits, Italian shoes and distinctive pastel-coloured shirts with white collars. But nothing seemed to announce his change in status and attitude more than the arrival in 1985 of a personal driver. In many places in the booming mid-1980s, not least London and New York, a driver was often the first thing anyone with money looked to acquire. But Ireland was not booming, and in a society that often frowned on those who got above themselves—'Who does that fella think he is?'—such a status symbol inevitably sent out a message.

'Tony became more and more removed from the minions of the place,' says one of the earliest GPA recruits. 'You would meet him socially from time to time, but not with the regularity that you had in the early days. You didn't know from then onwards whether he was travelling or in Kilboy or what he was doing.' The hiring of a driver suggested to many, including his colleagues in GPA, the general sense of Tony's withdrawal behind the walls of Kilboy and the forbidding doors of a Mercedes-Benz.

Tony Ryan was no longer one of the boys. He was rich. He was the boss. He was in charge. Ireland's leading universities even gave him a new honour to play with—'Dr Tony Ryan'—which prompted sneers from many. But for the boy from Limerick Junction who had never been to university these awards showed respect ('For robing purposes, my height is 5'9" and cap size 7½,' he advised Trinity College, Dublin, in 1987). University had not been an option for young Tony Ryan. Instead, these famous Irish institutions were now coming to him.

Behind the walls and honours, life for Tony went on, all observed by the man he had employed in the new position of driver. If no man is a hero to his valet, Tony Ryan was the exception to the rule. Certainly that was the case with Derek Doyle, who was taken on as driver and general Man Friday in 1985. 'I saw all sides of him,' Doyle says. 'He was an extremely fair man, although he had a short fuse on the little things. But on the big things very often he was extremely sanguine and just said, "That's life, so".' Doyle worked for Tony for more than twenty years until the latter's death in 2007.

> He would tire you out all right. You could be doing weeks on end of morning, noon and night—starting at 6 a.m. and still out at two the next morning—so it would be tough going. But he would always sense if I was getting frazzled and would come into the kitchen in good humour, saying, 'Derek, it's going to be

quiet tomorrow. Why don't you take it off.' So he would push you to breaking-point, but could be good too.

More than most, Doyle got to see the tastes of the private man away from the spotlight. Whereas formal dinners at Kilboy would be characterised by fine food and expensive wines, Tony's habits at home were much plainer. He still loved his fry every Sunday morning. Dinners at home were of the kind that his mother might have made back at 83 Railway Cottage, and he enjoyed nothing more than his favourite cabbage and bacon. There were concerns about middle-aged spread, with frequent bans on puddings in order to help keep his weight down. That didn't stop Tony appearing regularly in the kitchen when he could smell sausages or bacon under the grill.

In contrast to the man at GPA who let everyone know where they stood, Tony often seems to have tried hard not to trouble or upset his private staff. Each morning, for example, Doyle would include grapes in Tony's bowl of fruit at breakfast. Finally, one day Tony rang down and said, 'Derek, I don't like grapes.' Uncharacteristically it had taken him two years to say so. 'I was one of the few people, actually, that he didn't bollock,' recalls Doyle, who nevertheless witnessed some of the terrible tongue-lashings dished out to others. Over the years, he came to realise that Tony instinctively took to or against people for whatever reason, and that there wasn't much changing his mind. 'You either got on with him or you didn't,' he suggests. 'There was no grey area. If he liked you, then you were fine. If he didn't, then it didn't matter what you did, how good you were—it was curtains.'

Doyle also became an important character in the lives of GPA and Ryanair operatives when it came to gauging the mood of the boss. At GPA House in Shannon people would keep an eye out for the Merc parked outside to know if Tony was around the building. 'If you really wanted to get Tony's ear', says one, 'you checked with Derek, because he knew what was happening, where Tony was going and what time his flight might be.'

Tony was often at his happiest away from Shannon. More and more he seemed to welcome and embrace the rhythms of life in the countryside. Photographs from the mid-eighties show a completely different side of his personality when down at Kilboy: relaxed, informal and visibly happy. In the fields with his cattle, dressed in a shabby sheepskin coat and muck boots, hair awry and stick in hand, he inevitably looks a long way from the image he cultivated in business. But neither does he look like a millionaire playing at 'country squire'. Tony simply looks at one with himself and his surroundings.

Arthur Finan, the farm manager who arrived at Kilboy shortly after Doyle, remembers that Tony liked nothing more than wandering the estate to see what was going on. 'You would have these guys working away on the farm, cutting timber with a chainsaw, their trousers half way round their backsides,' he remembers, 'and Dr Ryan would come up on them and tap them on the shoulder and say, "How's that going?" and chat. He thought the world of them.' He deferred to them when it came to estate matters, even when they came into conflict with other areas of Tony's business dealings.

Finan recalls one day at market in Ennis selling cattle from Kilboy and getting a call from Tony saying he had looked at the figures with his PA and didn't think the selling price was high enough. 'Bring them home,' Tony told him. Finan was rankled by the unprofessionalism and by having his judgement called into question. 'I can't come back,' he explained, 'I'm in the middle of selling your cattle, and I'm about to go into the ring.' Down the line, Finan recalls, he heard the PA launch into an attack, 'which really upset me'.

When Finan got back to Kilboy he went to see Tony with his letter of resignation. 'Arthur, if you leave,' Tony told him, 'then I'm going to sell this farm.' It was an exaggeration, of course, but for the next twenty years Finan heard no more about the farm figures versus proposed figures drawn up by an accountant. 'One animal won't make the same as the next,' Finan explained to Tony. 'They might all be white Charolais cattle, but they don't all make the same money.' Tony accepted that, and the matter was never raised again. The PA, thwarted in his agricultural ambitions, instead ended up maximising Tony's investment in Ryanair. His name was Michael O'Leary.

As well as these simple pleasures of rural life, Tony also developed the more traditional pursuits of the country gentleman. About this time he became friends with Ken Rohan, one of the best-known property developers in the country. The two men began shooting together regularly at the Ballinacor estate, near Rathdrum, after which Tony would stay at Rohan's beautiful Charleville estate, in Enniskerry. 'No more than me, Tony wasn't one of the great shots of Ireland,' Rohan recalls, 'but we enjoyed the thrill of it and the social aspect.' Again it was a side of him that many didn't see. 'Besides being an incredible entrepreneur,' he says, 'Tony loved his fun and had a lovely, mischievous sense of humour. We enjoyed shooting each other's birds instead of our own, which was even more fun.'

It was about this time that Tony began to take his lifelong interest in horses more seriously. He had been drawn to the 'sport of kings' since boyhood, when he would stand on the roof of the family cottage to watch racing at Limerick Junction. In 1986 he had only one mare, Kilboy Concorde, at the farm. When she had a foal Tony had asked Jim Bolger, the famous trainer he knew through Maurice Foley, to take a look. That horse, Father Phil—named after Father Philip Fogarty, the boys' headmaster at Clongowes—won several races before breaking its leg and being put down. Then another colt, Monsignor Phil, started winning races. So as the mare kept producing, buyers started arriving. Tony bought a second mare, Diamond Fields, for £270,000. Her first foal made 375,000 guineas at Newmarket and herself went on to produce a number of winners. 'He was incredibly lucky with horses,' reflects Finan, who often thought that equine success gave Tony more pleasure than any million-dollar business deals.

It was enjoyment that would later see Tony purchase the Castleton horse farm in Lexington, Kentucky, at the centre of the thoroughbred horse world. There he would lavish time and money on breeding stock, with notable successes including Catchascatchcan, whose first foal, the drily named Antonius Pius, fetched €1½ million as the farm's first yearling through the sales ring. 'He made a big impact in the thoroughbred world in a short space of time,' says Julian Dollar, who worked for Tony before moving to the famous Newsells Park Stud. 'He would never have called himself a fantastic horseman, but he was able to make very astute business decisions. He was an amazing character.'

Time in the pasture with the cattle in Kilboy, shooting weekends, the horses and the acquisition of a driver—it would be easy to imagine that Tony was slowing down. He even bought a house in Ibiza, to which he repaired each June for sunshine and relaxation. And while it was easy to point to evidence to the contrary, not least Ryanair, as proof that his restless energy and ambition remained unabated, there was no question that Tony was consciously adjusting the balance of his life.

To some degree this was simply the enjoyment of the considerable fruits of his equally considerable labours. But it also addressed a deeper fear. His own father, Martin, had died at only fifty-four, just a few years older than Tony himself now was. Tony always believed that Martin, worn down by the demands of life on the railways, had essentially worked himself to death. Tony may have had more in the way of creature comforts than Martin, but the millions of miles he had travelled and the constant stress of running businesses in the high-pressured world of international aviation would, he feared, eventually take their toll.

At various times Tony seriously considered complete withdrawal. 'He talked about that a number of times,' recalls David Kennedy. 'He spoke to me about the fact that his father had died quite young. His father had died in his fifties of a heart attack, and Tony was quite conscious of this.'

In the end the acquisition of a driver, together with more time spent at Kilboy, became the concession to age, but Tony's father remained very much on his mind from now on. In 1990, at precisely the same age at which his father had passed away, Tony watched his mother turn the sod for the Martin Ryan Institute at University College, Galway—a tribute from a grateful son. Above the door would be placed the lesson that Martin had taught Tony as a boy and by which he continued to live his life: 'It is better to wear away than rust away.'

At a time when Tony was thinking about his relationship with his father, his own role as a father was giving him particular satisfaction. He had seen less of the boys growing up than he would have wanted. Now Tony felt he was doing something to help and encourage the two older boys, Cathal and Declan, in a way that had not been possible when they were younger. He was pleased to be giving them a platform in the business world through Ryanair. More importantly, he was thrilled to be working alongside them and, best of all, to be spending time together regularly.

Cathal and Declan were very different in personality, but each reflected a side of their father that Tony himself could now relate to. The wilder, more combustible Cathal reminded Tony of his younger self. Declan, more thoughtful and reflective, connected with the man that Tony had become. He was proud of both and now began a new kind of relationship with them as men, not boys, and it was one that would give him pleasure for the rest of his life.

Meanwhile, with Shane, his youngest boy, who was still at school, Tony now had more free time than when the two older sons had been growing up. In particular, father and son developed their relationship around a shared love of racing, which would later see Shane become a successful international horse-breeder at Tony's farm in Kentucky.

Navigating the difficulties of the split between Tony and Mairéad had been difficult for everyone concerned. The two separated but never divorced. Nevertheless, by the mid-1980s Tony had managed to move on in his personal life. In particular he developed an intense relationship with Miranda Guinness, Countess of Iveagh, that lasted close to seven years. It could never have been a low-key affair. Tony was by now one of Ireland's most prominent millionaires. Miranda was among the most prominent society figures in Ireland, and her comings and goings lit up the society pages. *Irish Tatler* even named its society page, 'Miranda's Diary', in her honour. She was married to Benjamin Guinness, third Earl of Iveagh, until their marriage collapsed in 1984 under the pressure of his battle with alcoholism.

'She was the perfect clothes horse,' says Lucinda O'Sullivan in *The Little Black Book*. 'Tall, slim, beautiful with dark auburn hair, twinkling eyes, and a wonderful soft, plummy voice.' Everyone who met Miranda seemed to fall in love with her, and Tony was no exception. 'He was very much in love with her,' says Denis O'Brien, who was Tony's PA in the early 1980s. Even when the relationship eventually floundered, about 1991, the two remained close friends. No-one would ever hear Tony speak a bad word about Miranda. 'The fondness was still there,' says Ken Rohan. 'He didn't move on and forget.'

As well as bringing a new dimension to Tony's emotional life, Miranda was also an important influence on his style and tastes. 'She polished him,' O'Brien says. 'It was like polishing a diamond, because he always had the interest, but she developed his taste.' To some degree this was social. Wealth had brought many things into Tony's life, but Miranda represented the kind of 'old money' that no amount of dividends could bring a working-class lad from Limerick Junction. She smoothed his way in fashionable and artistic society, often saving the day.

Seán Donlon of GPA saw this first hand during the visit of Graham Greene to judge the first GPA Book Award. Greene, frail and ill by this time, found the public outings extremely stressful. 'Miranda really rescued [events] in Dublin when things got rough,' says Donlon. 'Greene couldn't cope with big crowds, so she brought him out of buildings and sat him down and got him a glass of whisky. He didn't particularly click with Tony, but he certainly clicked with Miranda, who really minded him for the few days.'

Tony never learnt to enjoy Miranda's social set, and in photographs, stuffed into 'black tie', he rarely looks happy or

Martin and Lily Ryan: Tony's parents at Keane's Points, Limerick Junction, Co. Tipperary, c. 1935.

Christening day: Martin Ryan with Tony, aged three months, at Keane's Points, 1936.

'Trains were in my blood': Tony, aged around two years, wearing his father's fireman's cap, at Limerick Junction.

The railway children: (*from left to right*), Tony, Kell, Simon, Mary and Rena Ryan, with their parents Lily and Martin, at Bohernamona Road, Thurles, Co. Tipperary, c. 1950.

Tony (*back row, far right*), Simon Ryan and Rena Ryan (*second row, fourth and fifth from right*) at the National School in Monard, Co. Tipperary, c. 1943. Of the twelve children whose feet are visible, seven have no shoes.

Visit to Glenstal Abbey, Co. Limerick, 1948. Tony (*far right*) with Michael Cleary, Tony Wall, Pádraig Garman, Gus Mahoney, Seán Carey, Leo Mc Namara and Declan Mooney. (*Courtesy of John [Seán] Carey*)

'Counter-jumper': Tony in his Aer Lingus uniform at Bohernamona Road, c. 1955.

American Dream: Tony (*far left*) watches Minister for Transport and Power, Brian Lenihan, Snr, open the Aer Lingus-Irish terminal at JFK Airport, New York, 7 May 1971.

The boredom begins to show: Tony (*far right*) visibly outgrowing middle management at Aer Lingus. JFK Airport, c. 1972.

Mr GPA: (*clockwise, left top*) T.A. Ryan, chief executive; Boeing 707 in GPA livery; GPA Boeing 737 on wet lease to Air Lanka, Sri Lanka; GPA Boeing 737, one of two on long-term lease to Aerotour, France.

A new image: Tony in the Library at Kilboy, Dolla, Co. Tipperary, mid-1980s.

Always embracing a bull market: Tony on the farm at Kilboy.

Des O'Malley in 1982, when he was Minister for Trade, Commerce and Tourism. Both in and out of government, O'Malley was a forceful advocate for airline deregulation. (© *Photocall Ireland*)

Editor Vincent Browne in the offices of the *Sunday Tribune*, c. 1983. (© *Photocall Ireland*)

Tony with the Taoiseach and future GPA Board member, Garret FitzGerald. The coalition government led by FitzGerald awarded Ryanair a licence for the Dublin–Luton route in 1985.

Dr Tony Ryan: commencement ceremony at the University of Limerick for the award of an honorary doctorate, 1992.

'There's space for everyone here': As Minister for Tourism and Transport in 1989, Séamus Brennan (pictured with Kerry Airport chairman Bryan Cunningham) promoted the 'two airlines' policy that allowed Ryanair to grow. (*Courtesy of Kerry Airport*)

'Better to wear away than rust away': Lily Ryan breaking ground for the Martin Ryan Institute, University College, Galway, 1990, with Captain Cathal Ryan on the left. When this photo was taken, Tony (*hidden*), 54, was very aware that his father had died at the same age.

Tony in February 1992, shortly before the failure of GPA's share flotation. (© *Getty Images/ David Levenson*)

'To look out the window at Dublin Airport and see a Ryanair aircraft sitting there was a wake-up call.'—David Kennedy, Aer Lingus.

With Bill Clinton, Dublin Castle, 1 December 1995. After the failure of GPA, Tony was already on his way back up with Ryanair.

Protégé: Michael O'Leary at the Ryanair offices in Dublin Airport, 1999.
(© *Photocall Ireland*)

With Richard Branson. 'Dear Richard, The correct spelling is *Bollix*. Warmest regards, Tony.' Takeover talks between Virgin Express and Ryanair collapsed in 1996.

The House that Ryan Built: Lyons Demesne, Co. Kildare.

The front gate at Castleton Lyons in Lexington, Kentucky. (© *Alamy*)

Ryanair chairman David Bonderman at the company's AGM, a year after taking the airline public in 1997. (© *Photocall Ireland*)

Tony with the jockey Kevin Manning and a groom at Leopardstown racecourse. Horses had been a passion since childhood when he could see the Tipperary racecourse from his house in Limerick Junction. (© *Healy Racing*)

Tony with his friend Ed Walsh (*left*), founding president of the University of Limerick, and Dublin City University president, Ferdinand von Prondzynski, at the DCU Ryan Academy, 2005. (© *Irish Times*)

The front gate of Lyons Demesne on 5 October 2007, the day that Tony was buried. (© *Collins Agency*)

Ireland's Aviator. Tony in his Aer Lingus uniform in October 1957 and at the Pima Air and Space Museum, Tucson, Arizona, shortly before his death in 2007. Between these two photographs being taken, Tony Ryan had transformed the global aviation industry.

comfortable. However, what really did give him pleasure was the way Miranda seriously entertained his aspirations as a collector of art and restorer of property. Miranda had already transformed the Guinnesses' sepulchral Farmleigh estate in the Phoenix Park to renewed Georgian splendour. Later, to critical acclaim, she would restore the dilapidated Palladian mansion at Wilbury Park in Wiltshire. Miranda enhanced Tony's understanding of the decorative arts, helping him to think about the lines of a room and judge the weights of silks and fabrics, the scale of furnishings and the quality of paintings that would be hung. Although Tony continued to support contemporary artists, it was from this time onwards that his tastes moved back in time as a serious collector of Stuart and Georgian art.

'Miranda had an incredible sense of aesthetics, as she showed with her own house in England,' Rohan says, 'and Tony was very good at asking for advice.' It was Miranda, says Ann Reihill, publisher of the GPA-sponsored *Irish Arts Review,* who 'taught Tony about the finer points.' Almost as a practice piece, he bought an elegant white stucco Georgian house in Pelham Place in London's fashionable South Kensington, which he and Miranda redesigned together.

Working on Pelham Place with Miranda served as Tony's apprenticeship for his later and most important project: the stunning restoration of Lyons Demesne in Co. Kildare. The pleasure that Tony got from this new departure was great, and, according to his friend Jim King, he threw himself into it. 'Once he opened up to the visual arts he became really very, very knowledgeable. So Miranda had a huge influence on his life and development.'

Not that such a development took place at the expense of Tony's business ambition. It is a common enough trait for entrepreneurs to lose their edge as new-found wealth brings comforts and pleasures to distract from the hardcore business of making money. That was not the case with Tony Ryan. He may have had occasional thoughts of mortality, but for all the pleasures on offer as a modern Medici, collecting *objets d'art* and dispensing patronage, Tony in the mid-

1980s remained as committed as ever to the global expansion of his principal business interest, GPA. For Tony's ambition, far from diminishing, now seemed unbounded.

At an American Chamber of Commerce in Ireland luncheon on 1 May 1985, Tony made it clear just how all-encompassing those aspirations had become. The previous five years, he declared, had been a 'coming of age' for GPA. The company had expanded to a fleet of eighty-seven jet aircraft and 109 employees, and enjoyed a compounded annual growth rate of 35 per cent. Yet, Tony suggested, it was just a beginning. After all, 'although GPA may have the industry's largest pool of operating lease aircraft, we never lose sight of the fact that it is currently less than 1 per cent of the world fleet.'

Now the company needed to be 'suitably ambitious' in order to move to the next stage. He declared:

> I believe we have arrived at a staging-point from which we can grow GPA from a small company into a medium-sized one. My objective for my next appearance here, on 1 May 1990, is to be able to confirm to you that GPA will by then have achieved a billion-dollar asset balance sheet. It is quite within our capability. To attain it we need improve only marginally on our rate of growth until now.

It was a bold claim, not least because it came as a major investor, General Electric Credit Corporation, was pulling out of GPA. In order to fill the gap left behind by GECC, and to match the ambitious plans for future growth, Tony needed capital—and he needed it fast. That money might have come from a public flotation, but there were concerns about whether the markets, potentially spooked by the coming withdrawal of GECC, would fetch up a share price that matched the company's valuation.

There was no question, Morgan Grenfell bank in London advised, that the GECC factor would have 'a significant negative impact'. In a private offering, however, the GECC departure 'could be minimised'. In all likelihood, it concluded, GPA should be able to raise as much privately as it could publicly. That was enough to convince Tony to look for private money. The strategy would be simple, he told his no. 2, Maurice Foley: 'Raise one large chunk of money in the United States and another in Japan.'

Morgan Grenfell, working in conjunction with First Boston Bank in the United States, quickly identified a massive potential investor: the insurance giant Prudential. The withdrawal of GECC, rather than deterring Prudential, actually seemed to encourage it. Provided that another major investor could be found, it was 'looking good for $30–40 million' and was prepared to accept 'a non-voting instrument with a stock purchase conversion option'.

Securing this investment in the United States kept Tony on familiar tracks. The road east, looking for money in Japan, however, was a new departure. In November 1985 Tony led a GPA team to Tokyo to introduce the company to Japanese trading firms and major banks, including some that were already small-scale investors. The culture shock was profound. Whereas the GPA business culture had often taken advantage of a certain Irish informality of style, it was not an approach that worked in the more stratified and formal Japanese business world.

Tony was prepared for this difference, having spent a great deal of time in the Far East, but, even so, the contrast was marked. At every meeting vast numbers of officials turned up (twenty-three at the first session with Mitsubishi), completely swamping the five-man GPA team. Each meeting involved elaborate courtesies of introduction and endless enquiries about the minutiae of hotels, timetables and transport. In addition, the hospitality schedule was brutal even for Tony, who could always hold his own, with its emphasis on after-hours drinking of Scotch.

By the end of five hectic days burning the candle at both ends, Tony was able to report back to the GPA board on a fund of good will established and, more importantly, offers of credit and investment. In particular, leading institutions, including Mitsubishi, Orient Leasing and the Long-Term Credit Bank of Japan, were 'giving serious consideration to an investment'. Indeed it soon became apparent that, far from having to chase Japanese investment, Tony and GPA would be able to choose a partner.

Eventually the choice fell on the Long-Term Credit Bank. The negotiations, complicated by a time difference of nine hours, were convoluted and hair-raising. In March 1986 Tony flew to Tokyo to push the deal through as the clock counted down to the deadline of 31 March. Matters were further complicated when the *Financial Times* picked up the story of a potential new investment. Finally the deal was signed with only two hours remaining to the deadline, with frantic out-of-hours phone calls to AIB Bank to make sure that the money could be moved between accounts in time.

On 3 April, at a press conference in London, Tony made the announcement that GPA's private placement of $100 million of convertible preferred shares, led by the Long-Term Credit Bank and Prudential, had been oversubscribed at $115 million. This represented 'the largest tranche of equity capital ever raised by an Irish company.' The deal, Tony added, had secured GPA's potential for growth over the next five years, during which time the company would 'aim to control 3 per cent of the world's jet aircraft and 20 per cent of the operating lease market.'

It was an astonishing story of success—not least for Tony himself. His own holding in GPA was now valued at $22½ million, in addition to the vast tax-free dividends he earned each year.

There was one other number that caught the eye at the press conference on 3 April. Aer Lingus had made a profit of $14 million in the deal by selling part of its stake in GPA. Tony Ryan, who within weeks, with Ryanair, would start to compete head-to-head with Aer Lingus on the Dublin–London route, had just made the national carrier the equivalent of its entire pre-tax profit for the previous year.

It had been a remarkable turnaround. Almost exactly a year after Gary Wendt's announcement that GECC was pulling out, Tony and GPA emerged stronger and better capitalised, with a new frontier opening up in the Far East. Tony's confidence had been momentarily shaken by the GECC failure. Now he roared back, with self-assurance at full throttle, and prepared to launch an audacious move to consolidate GPA's position by taking over—and taking out—his principal opposition.

International Lease Finance Corporation was founded in California in 1973 by Steve Udvar-Házy, with the father-and-son partnership of Leslie and Louis L. Gonda. Their business focused primarily on North America, while GPA was largely based outside that region. Each had a different style and ethos. ILFC, despite going public in 1983, had maintained the tight family-centred ethos of its origins as a start-up by Hungarian emigrants to the United States. They had a much smaller staff than GPA, outsourcing financial operations and other tasks, and in general were less aggressive in the marketplace.

By the mid-1980s the two companies had become locked in a battle to become the pre-eminent specialist lessor within the aviation industry. On a certain level, travel seemed to be in only one direction. Early in the decade, ILFC's total assets had been three times those of GPA, with bigger pre-tax profits. Now, by 1986, GPA had leapfrogged ILFC in assets and profits. Over the next two years, as GPA's annual profits grew by 49 per cent, ILFC's would actually drop slightly.

Yet despite this apparent position of strength, Tony understood that, in reality, ILFC had by 1986 got the jump on GPA. Two years earlier, armed with additional investment achieved by going public, ILFC had shifted its strategy towards new, rather than used, aircraft. By the end of 1985 half their fleet comprised new aircraft. That year they placed a large order with Boeing for thirty-two new aircraft, extended to fifty-four in 1986. That was the year that GPA got its first new plane.

Over the next few years GPA and ILFC, in order to knock each other out of the game, would compete for orders, culminating in a $3.2 billion order for GPA in 1988, immediately countered by a $5 billion order for ILFC, this amount being trumped eleven months afterwards by GPA announcing a $17 billion deal. The following year, 1990, ILFC cashed in its chips by selling out for $1.3 billion to the insurance giant AIG.

However, in 1986, as Tony announced new capital at his London press conference, GPA and ILFC were themselves engaged in uneasy talks about a possible takeover or a merger. GPA had initiated contact in late 1985 to ask about acquiring an interest in ILFC, which had responded cautiously by advising that any acquisition by GPA would have to be for the whole company, including buying out all shareholders. At a meeting to discuss a possible deal Udvar-Házy told Tony that 'any bid would have to be at a premium or current market value (c. $275 m) to have any chance of success.' Tony countered that he was thinking of a figure closer to $180 million. 'If those are the figures we're looking at,' Udvar-Házy retorted, 'why don't we buy you?'

In April, armed with new finance, GPA came back with a more serious proposal outlining what would be in the deal for both sides. Tony and Udvar-Házy met in London for a 'very constructive conversation'. George Magan, the director at Morgan Grenfell who handled GPA's affairs, wrote to the ILFC founder Leslie Gonda with a proposal to initiate formal negotiations 'under the strictest confidentiality', in the expectation of creating the 'strongest and most effective operator in the industry' and 'significant increased value for the existing shareholders'.

The timing of the move was not coincidental. Certainly Tony wanted to make a play for ILFC in an attempt to neutralise a competitor. However, what concerned him more was the potential threat if ILFC was taken over by a major investor. Indeed his greatest fear was that GECC, having failed in its efforts with GPA, might now turn its attentions to ILFC. 'There is the possibility—and the danger', Juan O'Callahan later wrote to Tony, 'that GE could now acquire ILFC with its fine portfolio, order book and clients . . . GPA must not be dwarfed—in fact, GPA must become significant or dominant.'

The problem for GPA was that ILFC, while happy to flirt, consistently went coy when it came to making any kind of commitment. 'Our position', Leslie Gonda wrote on 5 May 1986, 'is, very simply, that we don't see any advantage or benefit to ILFC by joining with GPA.'

When Tony went back in 1987 the answer was the same. 'ILFC has concluded that the proposed structure by GPA has no merit for ILFC or its stockholders,' Udvar-Házy bluntly informed Tony. The two men had planned to talk in Ireland a few days later. Now Udvar-Házy cancelled the meeting.

In many ways Tony's reply got to the heart of the problem. 'I am disappointed that it was necessary to cancel the meeting last weekend,' he wrote to Udvar-Házy, 'as I believe it would have given us time to tease out some of the issues we discussed and the apparent differences of philosophies between our companies.'

What he might have added was 'and ourselves'. For in many ways the differences between the two men, together with their apparent lack of personal empathy, symbolised and exacerbated the culture clash between GPA and ILFC. Tony and Udvar-Házy, both outsiders in their different ways, had set up their companies through their own entrepreneurial initiative, effectively creating the new industry of airline leasing. Neither was inclined to cede that ground, or their company, to the other. In the end, when the question boiled down to whether GPA would buy ILFC or vice versa, the inevitable answer by 1987 was simply to call the whole thing off.

Chapter 9

CRYING ALL THE WAY TO THE BANK

The late 1980s would be a period of extraordinary success for Tony Ryan and GPA. In 1983 the company had made net profits of $9 million. By 1987 that annual profit had risen to $68 million. The following year, profits were up again, to $101 million. In 1989 the figure would rise to $152 million. By the beginning of the new decade GPA profits would hit $242 million.

All told, it was an unprecedented tale of success for an Irish company, and one that made Tony rich. In 1990 his bonus alone was $86 million. That wealth brought increasing influence and public visibility. Yet any resentment at Tony's great wealth seemed dissipated by his other role as the man behind Ryanair. Here he was cast as the Robin Hood of Irish aviation, robbing rich Aer Lingus to bring low-cost air travel to the lives of thousands of ordinary people who might not otherwise have been able to afford it.

'We were seen as the darlings of aviation in the early days,' the commercial director, Derek O'Brien, remembers. 'People always seemed to be saying to me, "Ryanair? Yes, you're fantastic!" wherever I went.'

Tony may not originally have wanted the airline to bear his name, but now Ryanair was making him a household name—and a popular one at that.

Much of the credit for that popularity was due to the dynamic young team that Tony had put in place to run Ryanair. Cathal and Declan Ryan were both major shareholders. Eugene O'Neill, Tony's former PA, had gone in as chief executive. O'Neill was a brilliant showman, an all-singing, all-dancing representation of what Ryanair was about. Where Aer Lingus seemed staid, comfortable, establishment—the kind of airline chosen by your snooty aunt from Howth—Ryanair was younger, hipper, less class-conscious. O'Neill, dubbed 'Mr Armani', after his designer of choice, was the embodiment of the demographic that Ryanair passengers aspired to be and, indeed, often were. And whether you were a labourer on your way to a building site in Britain or a couple flying out on a mini-break, as you looked around at your fellow-passengers of various classes and ages there was a shared assumption among almost everyone: Ryanair had made life easier and more fun.

That sense of enjoyment was something that O'Neill transferred to the Ryanair offices. Staff members greatly admired him for his style and the good humour he brought with him each day into work. He was a driven individual but one who managed to inspire loyalty and devotion among most who worked alongside him. Ryanair might have started out with just a couple of slow planes, a Government that was ambivalent about whether it wanted the airline even to exist, and a national carrier that was determined to crush it, but it behaved from the outset like a genuine contender.

For all O'Neill's positive energy, in the end it was his business strategy that provided Aer Lingus with the opportunity to strike. To an extent, he was stuck in a dilemma. His plan was to present Ryanair as a genuine alternative to Aer Lingus. That meant talking big and making sure that actions followed words. There was no point running a softly spoken niche airline. The example of Aer Turas, swallowed up a few years earlier by Aer Lingus, showed the defects of such an approach. Ryanair had to pitch itself as a genuine competitor to Aer Lingus—the plucky underdog tweaking the nose of its bigger rival.

But O'Neill chose to fight the wrong battle with Aer Lingus. Instead of following the original Dublin–Luton model (a low-cost, no-frills service to an unfashionable airport) in order to compete *in parallel* with Aer Lingus, he decided to face them head-on. In 1988, emboldened by further EU deregulation, he embarked on an ambitious dash for growth, establishing routes to airports to which Aer Lingus already offered services.

The most audacious of these routes was to Manchester, which Aer Lingus saw as the hub for its European operations. Their response was brutal. Aer Lingus upped the number of its flights, taking advantage of an existing relationship with Aer Rianta in Dublin Airport to schedule earlier departure times than Ryanair. Aer Lingus also launched a price war, undercutting whatever fares Ryanair offered. 'This was insane behaviour,' says Derek O'Brien, 'because Aer Lingus were getting into financial trouble by this stage and was losing money hand over fist.'

It may have been insane, but it worked: within months Ryanair ceased its service to Manchester. Taken together with similar competitive failures on routes to Liverpool and Glasgow, this meant that no sooner had the 'dash for growth' begun than it juddered to an embarrassing, costly stand-still.

O'Neill, chastised and humiliated, now began to carp about the rules of the game. It wasn't fair that Aer Lingus should engage in what he saw as anti-competitive practices. Take them to the EU Competition Authority, he demanded of Tony, and sue for damages.

That request was the moment Tony woke up. Since the foundation of Ryanair in November 1984 he had looked on the airline as a labour of love. It had satisfied his instinct to advance the cause of deregulation in the airline market and had allowed him to take the fight to Aer Lingus in the most direct way possible. It had also provided a neat way to work with his boys in Ireland. Tony had kept a keen eye on the project as it came together and had enjoyed the high-profile successes that Ryanair had scored. But he was less enamoured at getting shafted so comprehensively by Aer Lingus, not least because the failure attached to his own name, with 'Ryanair' emblazoned on every aircraft. Now his chief executive was asking, through the instrument of the national carrier, to sue the Government, upon whose good will the very existence of Ryanair rested. It would be an act of suicide, Tony concluded.

Once Tony began to lose faith in O'Neill he started to take a closer look at what was going on inside Ryanair. To accomplish that task, in May 1988 he sent in his new PA, Michael O'Leary, to interrogate the books.

Tony had first run across O'Leary when the latter was a tax trainee in Stokes Kennedy Crowley (later KPMG). O'Leary had worked under Gerry McEvoy, whose accounts included advising both GPA and Tony personally. 'Michael was very ambitious and probably could have been a partner in KPMG,' says McEvoy of his young apprentice, 'but he was impatient to do his own thing. I imagine that he would probably say he would never have been interested in being a partner—that he had more lofty ambitions!'

It was through McEvoy that O'Leary was introduced to Tony. 'Michael was working on the [Kilboy] farm accounts,' McEvoy recalls, 'and got to know Tony a bit.' O'Leary might have been just one more of the faceless number-crunchers who crossed Tony's path daily, but he had a couple of features that helped him stand out. First, he was educated at Clongowes Wood and had been at the school at the same time as Cathal (two years older) and Declan (two years younger). Although their difference in age meant that the boys had not been friends, that common ground meant that Tony and O'Leary could talk easily about a shared world. Second, O'Leary even then had the kind of chutzpah that Tony admired. 'I called him up one weekend', O'Leary remembers, 'because there was a scheme—not a tax dodge, but a grey area—and I said to him, "Look, I'm not allowed to say this at SKC, but I think I can save you some money"'.

That claim must have struck a chord with Tony, because shortly afterwards he decided to offer O'Leary a job in GPA. The difficulty was that Tony couldn't find him. 'I got a phone call one day, asking where was Michael,' remembers Laurence Crowley, a friend and director in Stokes Kennedy Crowley. When Tony discovered that O'Leary had left to run his own newsagents he was livid. 'Nobody told me!' he thundered. To compound the irritation, no-one even knew where the shop was. 'So Tony apparently travelled around dozens and dozens of newsagents in Dublin looking for Michael until eventually he found him,' Crowley says. Tony then offered O'Leary a job in GPA, but it was turned down. A few months later he came back and tried again. In the end O'Leary said he wanted to come and work as Tony's assistant. They agreed that O'Leary would get paid 5 per cent of any money he made.

By the time O'Leary walked through the door at Ryanair he had already established a rapport with Tony based on straight talking and a forensic analysis of the books. It is striking when talking to anyone who saw the two men in action together, especially in the early days, that they all tell a version of the same story to explain the success they enjoyed. O'Leary, they say, put specifics on Tony's ideas. 'Tony was a visionary,' sums up Crowley. 'Michael was a doer, a deliverer.' That made them a perfect match.

Finding someone to match Tony's imagination and courage had never been an easy task for him. Sometimes that was because those he picked ended up lacking the necessary skills for the job. At other times it was because they didn't have the strength of character required to tell Tony when to back off. And at still other times it was because they lacked faith in Tony's instincts when every rational instinct said, 'Abort.' In part this was often Tony's own fault, as he found it almost impossible not to interfere when others had been tasked with implementing his ideas.

The fact that he could be ferocious in his criticism added a personal dimension to any relationship. In Denis O'Brien, his first PA, Tony had found someone who would stand up to him and whose entrepreneurial spirit matched his own. Now in Michael O'Leary he had discovered someone who would also stand up to him and whose managerial talent far outmatched his own. It was O'Leary who could make Tony's vision fly, and he also possessed the self-confidence to clip Tony's wings when necessary. On occasion that would lead to spectacular rows between the two men, but Tony always understood that talent-spotting the young accountant, as he had done with O'Brien, was among his most important calls. The eventual decision to put O'Leary into Ryanair was described by him as the best deal he ever did.

By 1988 Ryanair was 'a mess of unmerciful proportions', O'Leary recalls.

> They had great PR, but where was all the money? They were producing accounts showing them making money, and yet there was a huge hole, with cash running out the door. They were making assumptions about passenger numbers and fares paid, they didn't seem to know what half the costs were, and there was hardly any accounting system. It was a shambles. So I was sent in to try and find out what the hell was going on.

Three weeks later O'Leary went back to Tony and delivered the news: 'This is a fecking total mess.'

Tony now instructed O'Leary to draw up an action plan of how to put the airline on a more stable footing. When O'Leary presented that report to Tony on 26 August it made for stark reading. The company would need 'a *minimum* funding of IR£3 million to see it through to April/May' the following year. Thereafter, every lever had to be pulled in order for the company to make money. 'THIS COMPANY MUST NOW BE PROFITABLE,' O'Leary wrote. 'It has established a firm platform of profitable routes. All future efforts must centre around cutting costs and developing (strategically important) profitable routes.'

O'Leary listed the 'immediate and widespread cuts' that needed to be implemented. There had to be 'major people/salary reductions' in management and support staff. 'Use present "financial crisis" as basis for action,' he advised. The plush city-centre headquarters should be abandoned for 'Portacabin offices' in the executive jet terminal at Dublin Airport. This move would 'greatly improve costs/morale at airport'. A 'major overhaul' was required in the advertising and promotional budgets. 'Current "abuses" in system' had to be eliminated, including cash payments, company cars, hotels, free bars, family travel, free travel and taxis. All costings, including lease rates, fuel, spares and insurance, had to be reviewed and greater efforts made to use competitive tendering to reduce fees.

Beyond these specifics, O'Leary also called for a change of oversight in Ryanair, including a new 'system of strict financial control and discipline'. It would be essential to '*overemphasise* these controls' for the next six months. Ryanair had to have firmer leadership, with a 'stronger system of management from top down'. That meant management by decision, not drift. 'Management', he pointed out, 'are paid to lead the Company. Do so.'

Tony himself was asked to consider exactly what his commitment to the airline was. The Ryan family, O'Leary wrote, 'must consider this entire investment *now*.' An investment of £2 million would be required immediately just to fund the current deficit. Should the present management be given these funds? How should the company be directed? Was the family prepared to fund the additional development that would be required in 1989? What did the family wish to own in terms of Ryanair in three years' time? 'These decisions must be made now', O'Leary concluded, 'and subsequently followed through without distraction.'

O'Leary had cut to the heart of the matter for Tony. Did he want to keep putting his money into the airline, and did he trust O'Neill to spend it well? There was no question in Tony's mind about staying in. However, by the end of the summer of 1988 he had lost faith in his chief executive.

The tipping-point came in an incident involving Tony's middle son, Declan. At a meeting with Tony, instead of talking about the hole in Ryanair's finances, O'Neill made a presentation arguing for an investment in property in Portugal. Declan, as O'Neill's deputy, bit his tongue during the meeting, but afterwards he wrote him a coruscating note asking why they would be wasting money on property overseas when the company was running out of cash. O'Neill, assuming that Tony had seen the note, sent it to the entire Ryanair board in protest. In fact Tony hadn't seen this scathing assessment until the chairman of the board, Arthur Walls, forwarded it to him.

A tense meeting between Tony and O'Neill followed at the Westbury Hotel in Dublin. O'Neill protested that the note had been a challenge to his authority as chief executive. Tony asked him outright if Ryanair was running out of money. By the conclusion of the testy meeting it was clear to both men that they had reached the end of the road together. Shortly afterwards O'Neill was fired by the board. 'You were right to send him the memo,' Tony told Declan afterwards. 'In fact, you should have written it earlier.'

There were few doubts even among those close to O'Neill that he had deserved to go. 'Eugene had done a pretty good job of getting the airline up and running,' says Denis O'Brien, O'Neill's brother-in-law, 'but the cost side of the business was not in control, and that drove Tony mad.'

While O'Brien thought O'Neill could have few complaints about losing his job, the way in which he was sacked did not reflect well on Tony. 'It was absolutely awful,' O'Brien says, 'and Tony handled it really badly. It was very, very messy.' Even O'Leary, who argued strongly for the change of leadership, agrees that O'Neill was despatched without much grace. 'Ryanair was a complete mess,' he says, 'so it was "Right, out you go," boot him out and replace him. Then it all blew up.'

O'Neill was incandescent at both the fact and the manner of his dismissal. 'Eugene appeared to have lost the run of himself,' O'Leary suggests, 'reading all that "businessman of the month" stuff and believing his own BS that he was the next Tony Ryan or Michael Smurfit.' One minute he had been Mr Ryanair, the next he was out on the street. When O'Neill threatened to sue for unfair dismissal Tony told him in the bluntest language possible what he thought of that course of action. 'Eugene got very upset with Tony,' says O'Brien, 'and they had this row that went on for ever. Neither of them would give an inch. It was just a nightmare.' When the legal process began, O'Neill would swear an affidavit saying that Tony had promised to 'crush' him. Business, Tony was reputed to have told him, was made up of 'fuckers and fuckees, and in our relationship you are my fuckee.'

In the end an uneasy truce was worked out, with O'Neill settling and having his legal costs paid in return for surrendering his shares.

A separate case, in which O'Neill alleged that Aer Lingus and the GPA subsidiary TAI had conspired to thwart competition on airline routes, was thrown out by the High Court.

The settlement money didn't last long for O'Neill, who spiralled into financial meltdown and ill-health. His role in establishing Ryanair would often be minimised in the story of the airline, with the emphasis placed on the financial black hole rather than the achievements. In many ways O'Neill had done what Tony had asked of him, successfully launching a new airline with the kind of panache that quickly established the brand in the consciousness of Irish and British consumers. By 1988 the company needed to head in a different direction, and perhaps Tony could be blamed for failing to make O'Neill's departure more elegant. Yet brutality was the only language that Tony knew in business; he rarely offered praise or softened the blow. Silence was usually the best pat on the back anyone could expect. When O'Neill refused to go quietly, Tony simply went through him, because that was the only short-cut he ever knew.

O'Leary's judgement on O'Neill perfectly captures the ambiguity that Tony himself felt.

> Ryanair needed the flash and the representation to get it off the ground, and Eugene looked good, talked a good story and generated huge publicity. But you look back and it was a piece of shite. He sold it well, but the product was crap.

Tony now put Declan Ryan in to steady the ship while he was searching for a new CEO, finally appointing P. J. McGoldrick, who, as an experienced operations man, was the antithesis of O'Neill. His job was to stop money haemorrhaging out of the airline and to make it a viable business. 'I don't give a shite what you do,' Tony instructed him, 'just stop losing me money.'

Not that Tony was short of money that summer. A few weeks before sacking O'Neill he had stunned the Irish establishment and sent ripples throughout the international markets by acquiring a 5 per cent share in Bank of Ireland for more than £30 million. 'Tony Ryan and the bank enigma' was the *Irish Times* headline for a long article trying to work out what game he might be playing. 'Whatever Tony Ryan's motivation for taking a five per cent stake in Bank of Ireland,' it suggested, 'there are very few in either Dublin or London who believe that this is merely a long-term investment in a high-yielding stock by the GPA chairman.'

The acquisition of the shares had been done quietly and involved a certain amount of subterfuge even among Tony's staff. All correspondence on the matter at Kilboy was filed under 'Project B', with no direct references made to the target. In July 1988, shortly before declaring his acquisition to the Securities and Exchange Commission, Tony used a visit to GPA by a senior group from Bank of Ireland to break the news. 'At the end of the meeting', the bank's chief executive, Mark Hely Hutchinson, recalls, 'Tony asked me if I would go home with him for a cup of tea.' At Kilboy the two men chatted amicably about paintings and horses—as a young man Hely Hutchinson had ridden the legendary racehorse Arkle—before Tony showed him in to the office. There Tony announced that he was about to complete the purchase of shares in the bank. 'Can I pass that on?' Hely Hutchinson enquired. 'Yes, you can,' Tony replied simply.

Tony may have been a little put out that Hely Hutchinson's reaction was so bland, forgetting that Eton, Oxford and the Guards had made *sang froid* second nature to this younger son of Lord Donoughmore.

Tony would have been more pleased with the reaction back at head office. 'It was cat among the pigeons to some degree,' Hely Hutchinson says, 'with people scurrying to and fro, saying, "What does this mean?" In fact, even afterwards we never knew what it meant!'

The answer may well be contained in a briefing note drawn up the previous April at Kilboy outlining the pros and cons of buying into the bank. The recent history did not make pretty reading. Bank of Ireland was bedevilled by 'poor, conservative, unimaginative management'. It had a 'very high cost structure', was heavily 'unionised' and had 'no interdepartmental strategy'. Moreover, there were 'too many insiders' on the board, which needed to be revamped to change from a 'luncheon club' to a 'more dynamic commercial body'. All told, it was time for Bank of Ireland to 'join the twentieth century'.

Yet, for all these deficiencies, Bank of Ireland had represented an outstanding target for one reason, and one alone: 'impact'. There was no question that buying into the bank would generate 'huge publicity' for Tony. He would be able to use his 'contacts, reputation and selling skills' to improve the standing of the bank. His influence could bring in 'new, higher-profile directors'. There were exciting opportunities around the corner stemming from Dublin's new International Financial Services Centre as well as from deregulation in London. And for GPA there would now be 'major opportunities in aircraft finance'.

This assessment made a compelling case for buying into a bank. Perhaps the real surprise was that Tony chose Bank of Ireland rather than Allied Irish Bank. 'AIB would have been in tune with his style much more readily,' Hely Hutchinson judges. 'They were street-smart, whereas Bank of Ireland would be described as more thoughtful. AIB tended to take a decision almost on the spur of the moment, which would have suited his style, I think.' What Hely Hutchinson, with family wealth and a privileged upbringing, didn't fully understand was that Tony didn't want street-smarts: he wanted class.

Bank of Ireland was a historic part of the Irish establishment (nicely personified by Hely Hutchinson himself). For Tony to sit on the quaintly named Court of Directors was to become part of the traditions of a great Irish institution. At the same time as spending hundreds of thousands each year on art from the eighteenth century, Tony could now pride himself that he was a member of an institution that traced its origins from a royal charter in 1783.

'Talk about cultural differences,' says Laurence Crowley, who served on the Court of Directors during Tony's time as a shareholder.

'The Bank of Ireland in those days was a very distinguished pillar of old Irish society, something very distinct from GPA. Imagine the gulf for a new breed of Irish person.'

Any feeling of pride that Tony might have enjoyed lasted no longer than the opening five minutes of his first board meeting. 'From my limited experience,' he wrote to the governor of the bank, Louden Ryan, shortly afterwards, 'the Bank must be more commercial and the publicly perceived club atmosphere needs to be addressed and changed.' It was a criticism that would become more frustrated and strident over the next three years as Tony watched his multi-million investment spiral downwards.

Some of Tony's irritation was the result of perceived slights against him as a major shareholder. It was difficult not to be offended when, in 1989, David Kennedy, having just resigned as chief executive of Aer Lingus, was installed as deputy governor of the bank, overriding Tony's vehement opposition. Other frustrations were more deep seated and reflected Tony's growing awareness that his methods and those of Bank of Ireland were completely out of sync. 'Bank of Ireland is competitively mesmerised by Allied Irish Bank,' he wrote wearily in July 1989, a year after buying his 5 per cent of shares. 'My general frustration is that the Bank has enormous potential which is not, I am afraid, totally appreciated by the Board and some of its management.' It was a situation that was costing him money. 'Our share performance in relation to AIB is appalling,' he complained, with shareholders 'deprived . . . of hundreds of millions of value.' If matters did not improve, Tony warned, he would have to 'give serious consideration' to pulling out.

Frustrations were felt on both sides. Tony's relationship with the donnish Louden Ryan was always cordial, yet the two men never created any personal rapport. 'It was not that they disliked each other,' Crowley feels, 'but they just did not get on. They were so different—the academic professor from Trinity College, Dublin, and the gouger from Shannon.'

That compounded Tony's sense that his ideas and suggestions were not being taken seriously. Partly this was because, by character, he struggled with the role of non-executive director, which was essentially that of formalising, overseeing and advising. 'Meetings of the Court are ritual-driven,' he groused. 'I am still shocked at the waste of directors' time on pernickety minutiae.' In other ways it was also because the management team at Bank of Ireland saw him as a loose cannon.

Hely Hutchinson ventures that Tony, as a director,

> was fairly unprepared. I have the impression that he did not really read the papers he was sent. When you have somebody around the table and they're asking questions that have actually already been answered in the papers they were sent—you don't form a terribly positive impression of how well they read the papers. Maybe he only read the ones he wanted to read. He may have taken the view that we sent him too much paper and he would only read the bits that really interested him. But I would have the impression that he did not read them terribly well.

He was right: Tony was often under-prepared for meetings and hadn't read his papers properly, although not for the reason Hely Hutchinson imagined. In fact nothing captured Tony's continuing frustration at what he perceived as the bank's sloppy style more than its persistent failure to send him the paperwork in good time before the meeting. Time and again he complained about the matter to Louden Ryan. 'This late delivery is unacceptable,' he wrote when yet again his papers arrived only the night before a meeting of the Court of Directors. He wasn't expecting this kind of inefficiency and discourtesy, though board members from the early days of GPA might have reminded him that it was a trick he had pulled often enough himself.

The issue that brought matters to a head between Tony and Bank of Ireland was the disastrous purchase, agreed in April 1988, of First New Hampshire Bank in the United States for $370 million. It soon became apparent that it had been a calamitous investment. 'The revelations at the Court meeting on FNH were appalling,' a shocked Tony wrote on 14 July 1990. Projections had dropped from a planned profit of $10 million to a loss of $65 million. 'I have sat through too many Court meetings as a major shareholder being fobbed off with incorrect and protective answers,' Tony complained, letting the frustration of two years spill out of him. 'My commercial instincts warned me but I was frustrated by the traditional Court laissez-faire attitude. I intend to protect my major investment in Bank of Ireland. I need to see urgent radical change.'

It soon became clear what radical change he envisaged. At a meeting of the court in November, Tony called for the chief executive to be sacked. Hely Hutchinson didn't see the bullet coming.

> I was told that I needn't come back in to the meeting, and then half an hour later Louden came and told me, 'You can have a choice: you can resign, or we'll fire you.' We had a short discussion, and I said, 'Okay, let's not make a fuss about this. I will resign.' What Louden told me was that there were members of the court who no longer had confidence in my competence.

With good grace, Hely Hutchinson now says that, 'given the results, I couldn't fault the decision of the court to fire the chief executive.'

The dismissal of Hely Hutchinson gave Tony a 'head on a plate', but it didn't address the immediate problem that confronted him, namely 'a personal loss in excess of £23 million', by his own estimation. That figure represented the hard reality, 'soon realised, that the "club" atmosphere and traditional approach' in Bank of Ireland 'would not produce the rewards' he had expected. The realisation was a bitter disappointment for an investment he had taken on with 'potentially the most profitable company in Ireland'.

The following summer, in a decision that rocked the Irish financial world, Tony dumped his entire 5 per cent holding. 'Markets flabbergasted by Ryan's decision to sell' was the headline in the *Irish Times* on 11 July 1991.

> To say that the announcement of the sale of his entire Bank of Ireland shareholding by Dr Tony Ryan came as a bombshell to the market yesterday is no understatement. Brokers and analysts on both sides of the Irish Sea openly confessed to being flabbergasted, not just to the timing of the sale of the Ryan stake, but also the fact that Dr Ryan has apparently chosen to cut his losses on his untimely investment in Bank of Ireland.

The editorial in the same newspaper even went so far as to suggest that the sale 'cast doubt on the future of financial services in this State.'

In the weeks that followed, commentators and analysts speculated and hypothesised about the reasons for Tony's decision to divest from Bank of Ireland. In the end, however, the answer to that question was a simple one: he could afford it. As with the *Sunday Tribune,* Tony had tried applying his entrepreneurial brilliance in an alien business environment and soon tired of the frustrations involved. The initial decision had been as much about influence as about money. Michael O'Leary suggests that

> Tony was brave, but he was also an egomaniac. He had lots of money coming in, and he couldn't help it. It wasn't enough to run a successful company and make it bigger and better, like McDonald's. It was all about having political clout in Ireland when he shouldn't have given a shite.

Not that it seemed to matter to Tony at the time. There was some personal embarrassment in being seen to lose so much money, but he could live with that temporary dent to his reputation and wallet. And why not? Tony, after all, was still the man who had created a billion-dollar business in GPA. No-one doubted that Tony Ryan was still flying high; only in retrospect did it become obvious that he had got too close to the sun.

Chapter 10

ICARUS MELTING

Looking back, it is clear that by the early 1990s Tony Ryan was in serious danger of losing the run of himself. He may have been Ireland's most successful entrepreneur, having built GPA from nothing into a $4 billion company, but behind everything there now lurked a dangerous recklessness to match the brilliance.

By March 1992 GPA would have contracted commitments for new aircraft amounting to a staggering $9.4 billion—in effect a massive one-way bet on the continuing expansion of the commercial airline business in general and leasing in particular.

Over at Ryanair, Tony continued to pay out millions from his own pocket to finance an airline that even Declan Ryan and Michael O'Leary thought he should close down. The investment in Bank of Ireland had been a humiliation, bringing out all the begrudgers who were glad to see Tony humbled. 'One of our richest men', judged the financial journalist Shane Ross, 'has been exposed as frighteningly fallible in his strongest suit—making money.' Ross believed it was 'injured pride' that would cause Tony the most pain, because the lost investment would 'only hurt him a little'. In fact Ross was wrong: it was the money that would end up costing Tony more than anyone imagined.

While pumping millions into Ryanair, Tony had gone to Merrill Lynch to raise the necessary capital to invest in Bank of Ireland. In 1988 he had signed an initial facility agreement for $64.5 million, which was increased to $80 million the following year, with shares in GPA held as security. When Tony disposed of his investment in Bank of Ireland in 1991, realising $43.5 million, he was able to pay down some of the loan, reducing it to $35 million. Tony expected that the balance would be paid off by the conversion of his A ordinary shares in GPA, which were estimated to be worth $36.4 million. It was another gamble on the benevolence of the markets—one that would bring Tony close to personal destruction.

The risk involved in all these ventures illustrated the restlessness that many observed in Tony's character. He had made a vast fortune, enjoying success in the business world that his boyhood self had never imagined. His lifestyle was one of grand houses, elegant paintings, fine wines, domestic staff and fawning sycophants laughing at his every joke or enduring each brutal put-down. But it never seemed enough. There always existed a dissatisfaction—a desire to jump the next fence, do a bigger deal, conquer another sector. 'Where does that come from?' his friend Fergus Armstrong of McCann FitzGerald once asked him. 'I know where it comes from,' Tony replied enigmatically, 'but I'm not going to tell you.'

In truth, Tony probably didn't know. The restlessness was a trait that could generate unbelievable positive energy through an absolute refusal to allow himself or others to rest on their laurels. Playing the odds was essential to his character; conservative though Tony may have been in his private tastes, it was his restive nature that made him a risk-taker and even a chancer in business. He was a genuine radical in the sense of the eighteenth century he so adored: 'What is, must change.' But that inquietude also gave Tony a destructive quality that could lead him to put in danger the things that mattered most to him.

That was as true in his private life as in business. The year 1991 had seen Tony playing with fire with his personal debt and that of his businesses, but the first immolation came even closer to home. For close to seven years Tony had been in a relationship with Miranda Guinness—'the love of his life', judges Denis O'Brien. She had seemed to offer everything that Tony needed in terms of affection, status and private passions. Yet the inner agitation that had him always looking for change in business had a catastrophic effect on their relationship. 'It was a great weakness,' says Michael

O'Leary, 'because after Mairéad, his wife, who I didn't know, Miranda Guinness was the only woman he ever really loved.'

In the end it became too much for Miranda, who broke off the relationship and threw herself into the restoration of Wilbury Park. Miranda's departure removed an important emotional prop at exactly the moment when Tony would need it most. But in the end, Tony admitted afterwards to friends, he had only himself to blame, having treated their relationship too casually.

The split with Miranda and the financial decisions Tony was making at about the same time combined to create the impression that his judgement had gone off kilter by the early 1990s. Certainly many thought that this was the case with GPA. After years of dithering and hesitation the company was finally preparing to go public with the launch of an IPO. Yet while GPA had been considering such a move for years, in many ways the early 90s seemed the worst possible time to go public.

The global economy, which had improved every year since 1982, had finally started to go into sharp recession by 1990. Bad economic news dominated the headlines in 1991 and 1992, led by the United States, where unemployment jumped to 7.8 per cent by 1991—its highest rate in ten years. That had a direct impact in the airline business, where Pan Am and Eastern Airlines both went bust, putting 48,000 people out of work. Moreover, the so-called 'white-collar recession', with fewer business trips and family vacations taken, together with the war in the Persian Gulf, put further pressure on an already beleaguered industry.

The economic downturn led to some apocalyptic predictions, most notoriously an aviation-industry report by the Warburg Group that predicted an imminent 'airburst', with growth contracting to 1½ per cent from the previous pattern of between 5 and 9 per cent annually. Tony was enraged when he read the report, writing angrily in March 1991 to the chairman, Sir David Scholey, to protest about 'its strident tone (which sits uncomfortably with Warburg's reputation for objectivity).' Tony lambasted Scholey for 'conclusions which are significantly at odds with our own and those of the manufacturers and many airline managements.' He claimed that the report suffered from 'the shortcomings of desk study analysis removed from the field of action', contained 'basic flaws' and was 'unreasonably pessimistic'. Tony's conclusion was stark: 'Frankly, such treatment is dangerous as it contains the seeds of a self-fulfilling prophecy that unnecessarily damages the industry.'

Sir John Harvey-Jones, one of GPA's high-profile non-executive directors, later told Tony that Scholey admitted that 'they went OTT and is feeling the need to build bridges.' Yet the worry for GPA was that the Warburg analysis reflected nervousness in the City about the state of the industry in general. And of GPA in particular.

That spring Jim King interviewed specialist financial communications consultancies in London, asking their advice about a potential IPO. His report to Tony made bleak reading. 'There is a deep-seated suspicion, bordering on prejudice, towards GPA among British financial institutions and certain media.' It was based on a number of industry factors, including 'insular ignorance of the nature and global scale of aviation' and the 'perception that leasing is second class and a demonstrably dodgy activity'. But there was also 'a "Paddy" factor' based on 'scepticism about the combination of Irishness and success', which became 'disbelief when hundreds of aircraft, big money and a global operation were added to the proposition.' His unhappy conclusion was that 'GPA would be a difficult sell.'

Throughout 1991 the factors that made GPA an unattractive proposition increased dramatically. Underpinning the company's strategy for a global IPO was the assumption that Tokyo would help mop up any excess supply arising in other markets. That 'swing factor' was the primary reason for Nomura Bank being appointed global co-ordinator for the IPO, a decision that caused irritation in the City of London and on Wall Street.

Yet a series of financial scandals in Japan that year seriously undermined the credibility and standing of the country's leading security houses, including Nomura. Commentators everywhere were predicting a further deterioration in Japanese financial markets in 1992, taking with it the safety net for the IPO. That gloomy prognosis was compounded by continuing pessimism about the global recession, which had been more entrenched than many had forecast. In particular, the American economy stalled again in the fourth quarter of 1991, with no growth predicted until at least the third quarter of the following year.

Tony had demurred at launching an IPO during a period of boom, so it seemed inconceivable that he would push ahead now when confronted with such a negative set of circumstances. Yet there was one compelling factor that took precedence over all others: GPA was desperate for money. By the end of 1991 it urgently needed to raise equity. Their debt-to-equity ratio was spiralling out of control after a stalled profit performance in 1991—a shortfall of almost 10 per cent on the previous year—and a growing asset base, with further commitments to come. The $9.2 billion order for almost three hundred new aircraft was payable by March 1996, with staggered repayments of $2.2 billion in 1992, $2.6 billion in 1993 and $2.4 billion in 1994. That was already causing concern with the international rating agencies, which were expressing concern about GPA's poor off-balance-sheet financing obligations. Standard and Poor's had recently warned that GPA needed a sizeable equity injection soon and that unless this was achieved 'within a reasonable time frame' the company would be downgraded. Even the hint of further delays would likely see GPA put on 'credit watch'—itself calamitous for an IPO or private placement.

In December 1991 GPA's finance director, John Tierney, delivered a terrifying summary of the IPO storm ahead. 'Circumstances are no longer ideal,' he informed the GPA board. 'Financial markets are weak, airlines continue to incur huge losses and business confidence is at its lowest point in almost 20 years,' he wrote. 'However we do not have the luxury of waiting—we simply must raise equity within the next six months.' Failure to do so would send GPA 'into a spiral from which it might be difficult to recover.'

The context of the IPO was difficult enough, but the situation was made worse by poor strategy and tactics. To begin with,

GPA compounded the dangers already inherent in the launch by deciding against having the flotation underwritten, which would have guaranteed equity funding. This decision meant that GPA avoided the reality check that would have come from setting a fixed but inevitably lower initial share price.

Next there was how the IPO was being presented. The bankers on the IPO steering committee were vocal in expressing 'dissatisfaction' with the way in which Shandwick, the PR company chosen to front the IPO, had been performing, demanding that they be fired.

Finally there was the question of Nomura Bank taking the lead. It appeared a curious choice on every level. For a start, the bank seems not to have had much in the way of experience in leading a global IPO. Even the original rationale, which had been predicated on the Japanese market mopping up any excess shares, had disappeared. Nomura itself freely admitted this to GPA, advising that 'the Japanese market is still struggling to find direction.' At a meeting of the IPO steering committee in December 1991, John Howland-Jackson of Nomura pointed out that it was 'indicative of the difficulties being experienced' that up to sixteen IPOs scheduled for that month had already been withdrawn. His frank conclusion was that, while 'confidence would return to the market', he couldn't 'predict when in 1992 that would occur.'

The decision to stick with Nomura seems equally unfathomable when put in the context of GPA successfully raising $500 million that same month in a bond issue on the New York Stock Exchange. Given that representatives of Goldman Sachs, which had been involved in the bond issue, were on the IPO steering committee, it is surprising that so little consideration was given to making it the lead manager on the global IPO and to designating New York as the primary market—not least because the Nomura representative himself already seemed to have opened the door to the switch.

The combination of a non-underwritten flotation and the fact of being led by an apparently inexperienced bank in the wrong market, and communicated in an unsatisfactory fashion, looked like a death wish in such a volatile market. Yet as 1991 rolled into

1992 Tony remained bullish about the prospects for the flotation. In February he was able to announce anticipated record third-quarter profits of about $73 million.

That was an astonishing performance in a year that had been among the worst in airline history, with worldwide traffic collapsing and international carriers reporting massive losses or even going bust. Amid a deepening recession, GPA had placed 165 aircraft with fifty-seven airlines in thirty-two countries. So while at the half-way stage of the financial year 1991/2 net profits had been down by about 12 per cent, the third-quarter figures put GPA on target to beat the previous year's record profit of $262 million. 'The third quarter results', judged the *Independent* (London), 'suggest that GPA's financial performance is back to levels that existed before the onset of recession.'

Doubts remained, however, both inside and outside GPA. There were rows with the bankers at Nomura, Goldman Sachs and Schroders over the pricing of the forthcoming flotation, with Tony consistently pushing for a price that his advisers thought was overvalued by up to 30 per cent. Even on the day after the third-quarter results were announced the press were reporting that the flotation 'might only raise' $750 million—about half the amount previously expected. 'People who think this is a British Gas-sized float have got it wrong,' one of Tony's advisers unhelpfully briefed the media off the record.

Much of the rumpus surrounding the flotation concerned the position of Tony's own shares. As part of the IPO, Tony would be paid £21 million in cash to convert his A shares, which carried special dividends, to ordinary shares. It was a huge sum and one that revealed Tony's profit-sharing deal, which netted him just under 10 per cent of annual profits (£12½ million the previous year). All told, Tony's personal stake in GPA after the flotation was estimated at a quarter of a billion dollars. 'He built up the company from a worth of £50,000 to over £2 billion,' noted Gerry Grimstone of Schroders. 'I suspect shareholders think it's cheap at half the price.' In fact there was considerable anger about the move among shareholders, who protested that Tony, by insisting on a high share price, was putting personal gain above the interests of the company.

Relations were further marred by a series of public spats over the unpopular attempt by GPA to 'lock in' its shareholders for a set period after the flotation. One institutional investor, the Public Schools Employees' Retirement System of Pennsylvania, even threatened to withhold consent for the IPO unless concerns about Tony's own position were addressed.

Such PR misadventures, said the *Sunday Times* business correspondent, Alan Ruddock, allowed a 'cloud of doubt' to settle over the GPA flotation. From a potential share price closer to $30 earlier in the year, market analysts had by the spring downgraded it to about $22, with some even going as low as $18. There was a consensus that the combination of how GPA had handled the flotation and intrinsic problems with the company itself had knocked about 10 per cent off the share price. Added to a deep scepticism about leasing companies, particularly in London, where the markets had already been burnt by Atlantic Computers, this meant that GPA now found itself in danger of being perceived as an unwanted, unlucky stock.

At the end of April, as Moody's put the company on credit watch, Tony attempted to reverse the negative trend by wooing financial institutions and business correspondents at a series of dinners in London. It wasn't a job that suited him particularly well. For all his reputation as an outsized personality, Tony was in many ways an introverted character. He didn't often seek the limelight, he could appear stiff and uncomfortable when speaking at formal public occasions, and he detested dealing with the media.

This was partly the result of a certain self-consciousness about his lack of education, which he felt made him less dexterous in conversation than he might have wished (not least because he had to curtail the swearing that peppered his private conversation). Yet it was also the result of contempt. He appreciated the importance of public and media relations in theory. That, after all, was why he had employed the likes of Eugene O'Neill at Ryanair. But in his heart Tony despised the press, never really believing that he needed to explain himself to those he viewed as mediocrities who had never been tested in the entrepreneurial fires of business. Who were they to question him, a man who had built a business worth billions from nothing?

In their turn the British media seemed baffled by Tony. 'Mr Ryan is an intensely shy and private man,' concluded the *Times*, 'the opposite of the high-profile, garrulous Irish entrepreneur typified by . . . Tony O'Reilly and Michael Smurfit.' Appearing to make matters worse on these occasions was Maurice Foley, who was 'decidedly tetchy' when confronted with rumours about rows behind the scenes.

In May 1992, a month before the IPO was due to be launched, GPA issued an uncharacteristically gloomy pathfinder prospectus. It told the bleak story of a world slowdown in aviation, the over-supply of aircraft, the inevitable rise in unleased aircraft and even customers in financial difficulties. Moreover, there was no way of knowing how long the over-supply would last. All told, noted one analyst, it gave the impression of a company that had been 'dragged kicking and screaming to the market in one of the worst years on record for the industry.'

The effect on Tony was profound. 'It's not the way I would write up a business,' he complained bitterly as the prospectus was launched. Everything was 'very grey, very stark'. But in truth it seemed to reflect his own dark mood. Some of this was personal, especially because of the way the press had raked up old stories about Cathal's time as a pilot at Air Lanka, when he had been suspended for 'indulging in pugilistic activities while intoxicated'. Although Tony remained ultra-bullish in public, those close to him noted that he was increasingly down as the IPO approached. There were tirades about the mauling that GPA was getting among industry analysts and fund managers, especially in London. There was despair at the apparent near-collapse of demand in the key Japanese market. And Tony, under pressure from investors to consider his own role, even began to doubt whether he was the right man to lead GPA into a new era. Perhaps he had done as much as he could. Ryanair, for all its manifest faults, remained a labour of love. GPA was work, and, in fairness to himself, it felt like a job done.

'Coming up to the IPO, Tony said that he was getting tired and maybe it was time for someone else,' says Jim King. No doubt he would be 'president for life', or something similar, but in truth Tony was already unhappy at having to adapt his leadership style to be in line with the extra accountability that would be demanded of a public company. He had already separated out the roles of chairman and chief executive, handing over the latter to Maurice Foley. Now Tony began sounding out a number of prominent individuals about replacing him completely, including Bob Crandall at American Airlines, and some of these even met with members of the board. But as so often when this question had arisen before, no-one, least of all Tony himself, could quite bring themselves to make the final break. 'Tony's ambivalence about whether he was really ready to cut the umbilical cord led to that being dropped,' King says.

In fact Tony's ambivalence had more to do with not being able to convince his natural heir to take the job. Later he would confide to Gary Wendt of GECC that he had been determined to appoint 'a young Irishman (early 30s) who did not have a high profile. An accountant who is very bright and dynamic with a terrific track record, very tough—not dissimilar to you and Jack [Welch] and maybe tougher!' In the end, however, 'he was totally uninterested in joining GPA who he regarded as a bunch of softies.' Michael O'Leary was destined for Tony's second business, not his first.

A few days before the IPO, all the indicators seemed grim. Several of the biggest institutional investors that would normally be expected to buy in such a mega-flotation had indicated that on this occasion they would pass. Staggeringly, one of these was Schroder Investment Management, whose corporate finance arm was sponsoring the share issue in London. One leading investment manager was quoted as saying, 'I'm sure GPA is a fine company, but we will not touch this one with a hundred-foot barge-pole.' That was a judgement reflected in the business pages of the newspapers. 'Private investors beware,' summed up the *Daily Mail*. 'GPA's much vaunted growth shows only sluggish advances in recent years, and there are many potential sellers of the shares a year or so hence. *Avoid*.'

To compound matters, the beginning of the week in which GPA went public saw the global markets hit by turbulence, with sharp falls in the price of stocks. Tokyo's Nikkei index went into free-fall and would lose about 8 per cent of market capitalisation in the week. That had a knock-on effect in London and New York, which both saw markets fall. Moreover, in another stroke of bad luck, the last days before the GPA flotation heralded news of another price war among airlines in the United States. With three airlines having already issued predatory pricing suits against American Airlines and Delta Air Lines, it was no wonder that analysts were forecasting more difficult days ahead for the industry.

The most devastating news of all came from New York, where Wall Street investors passed on buying the stock. 'With only two days to go before the launch,' Tony testified afterwards, 'the American underwriters astonished [me] by cautioning less than satisfactory support in the United States.' In the event, 'despite a campaign which they deemed to have been an unqualified success,' the American firms had 'failed to bring in any American institutional support for the IPO.'

At a meeting at Nomura's London offices on Tuesday 16 June, GPA's advisers from Nomura, Schroders and Goldman Sachs gave Tony the bad news that the issue had closed at 6 p.m. heavily undersubscribed, with little hope of generating additional demand for the shares. 'I don't fucking accept that,' Tony roared back at them. 'Get out there and fix it!'

Over the next thirty-six hours sales personnel from all three banks began frantic phone calls to investors in whichever markets happened to be open. GPA had intended to issue 85 million shares, but Tony was prepared to accept 60 million. The subscription had closed at only 49 million, so there was now a scramble to find another 11 million. Attempts were made to track down the financier Sir James Goldsmith. Calls were put in to potential investors in the Middle East and Far East. Short-term deals were put on the table for consideration. Most humiliatingly of all, GPA's advisers went back to Hanson PLC, which had sold its 2 per cent share in GPA in March—a decision interpreted by the markets as bailing out on the company. In desperation, Nomura now pleaded with Hanson to come in on a conditional underwriting deal, with the flotation restructured and sold at a lower price than the $10 per share that had previously been indicated as the bottom line. Hanson considered the deal for several hours before declining. 'We were trying to breathe life back into a corpse,' one senior adviser reflected.

When the bankers reconvened on the evening of Wednesday 17 June, they all told the same story: no-one was buying. There had been some brief hope that Fidelity, the vast American fund manager, might invest, but this had come to nothing. Most enquiries had been met with more colloquially expressed versions of 'No chance'. Even more dispiritingly, a number of investors had performed 180° turns and walked away from verbal commitments. Goldman Sachs had barely managed to secure a single institutional investor. That astonished even the other bankers. 'I find it staggering,' an adviser noted. 'It defies credibility. One has to ask, "Were they trying?"'

In the early hours of Thursday 18 June 1992, confronted with a total rout, the representatives of the three banks took the decision that the GPA flotation had to be aborted. The failure would cost them $20 million in fees. John Howland-Jackson of Nomura was given the unenviable task of walking down the corridor to the boardroom where Tony was waiting. 'I'm afraid we all hid behind Howland-Jackson,' says one of his colleagues. 'We sent him off all by himself to give the bad news.' The consolation, they reflected, was that the lead co-ordinator was a big man, so 'at least if it came to blows' he could defend himself.

At first Tony refused to take the advice. 'Wait for Tokyo,' he instructed. An hour later, by which time it was clear that the Japanese market had failed to ignite, he was forced to admit defeat.

In the end Tony did so quietly and without rage. 'He probably thinks we're all rogues,' one financial adviser admitted.

Alone and uncharacteristically dishevelled after thirty-six hours without sleep, Tony finally left the Nomura Bank building about five in the morning, returning to Dukes Hotel in St James's. There he showered and changed, readying himself for the personal humiliation of announcing to the world that the GPA flotation was dead. What was going through his head as he walked the short distance from the hotel to GPA's offices in Pall Mall is anybody's guess. His reputation was in shreds. The IPO was a complete flop. There would be no personal share worth a quarter of a billion dollars. The cheque for $36.8 million to convert his A shares would not get written. Everything Tony had ever worked for had turned to ash in his mouth. Enemies and fair-weather friends would abound. After all, as one of Tony's GPA minions spitefully recorded, 'We can all spell "schadenfreude" now.'

Chapter 11

PROJECT REBOUND

The impact of GPA's failure to launch on 18 June 1992 was immediate and dramatic: both Tony and the company he founded now faced total ruin. Within hours the value of GPA crashed by more than 20 per cent. The next day even shares offered privately in Dublin at the equivalent of $8 per share attracted no interest. 'Anyone dealing today would need their head examining,' one broker advised.

That notional share price suggested a value for GPA of $1.8 billion, compared with a pre-IPO valuation of between $2.86 billion and $3.58 billion. Few believed that the now-toxic company was worth any of these figures. Instead the immediate focus was on whether the failure to raise new finance would force GPA to reschedule payments on the $11.9 billion worth of aircraft it had on order. Of those 331 aircraft, two-thirds were due to be delivered within three years. Stage payments of $2.9 billion had to be made within the current financial year. The credit ratings agencies Moody's and Standard and Poor's had indicated that GPA's rating was about to be reduced by two notches, making it more expensive for the company to borrow money. The whole situation was a gigantic mess.

There would be many complicated and long-winded analyses of why the GPA flotation had failed, but in the end the reasons were simple. GPA was seriously over-leveraged, with too many obligations to buyers at a time when the market was going through a severe downturn. Tony had needed to take GPA public to pay down the debt and bring in new equity for growing the company. Because the market had declined, he couldn't get the share price he wanted, so he had refused to take a deal in the days leading up to the flotation.

In human terms it is easy to understand why, with an expectation that one share was worth $10 (which was already lower than was hoped for), it would be hard to accept $7. What Tony didn't foresee, however, was that taking the lower value—indeed almost any value—was his only chance to avoid turning that value into nil. He seems not to have been well advised by his financial team, but in the end the call had been his. Had Tony raised the equity at a lower price he would almost certainly have ended up a billionaire. Instead he now stood to lose everything.

For many, Tony's reversal of fortune was a cause for celebration. The failure of the IPO, noted a *Sunday Independent* editorial, had been accompanied by 'more sniggers than tears'. After all, 'the inevitably noisy consequence' of being so 'phenomenally aggressive' was that Tony was not well loved. Under his leadership GPA 'didn't mind using its weight, it did not hesitate to shout and scream as long as it got its way.' Such an approach, the newspaper suggested, 'accumulates enemies'.

While many were happy to see Tony fail, there were others who stepped forward to help. Notable among these was the financier Dermot Desmond, who, only days after the IPO failure, wrote to Tony not just to express sympathy but also to give hard-headed advice. The sympathy was quick and to the point. 'None of us are masters of timing,' he wrote, 'other than commentators who have clairvoyance of hindsight.' His advice was simple. 'You should give very serious consideration to listing GPA shares now in New York and London/Dublin,' he urged. 'You should not seek to raise any money or to sell any shares—simply go for a listing.' All the documents were in place. Even though the initial price would be low, it would allow GPA to see future performance. 'Without the listing, nervousness will continue, even if performance is achieved,' Desmond warned. 'In the absence of a listing, the only long term exit for staff and shareholders would be the takeover of GPA by some large international group.' It turned out to be a shrewd warning.

Desmond's analysis was based on the assumption of 'normal performance over the next two years'. What he could not have known was just how parlous the financial situation at GPA now was. In July, Maurice Foley, as chief executive, attempted to reassure shareholders that 'our liquidity position remains good' and that 'resources are adequate to meet our projected commitments.' The upbeat assessment was part of the 'different storyline for investors' that had been discussed at a meeting in GPA for drawing up an action plan. That meeting had noted the 'loss of confidence in the company since the IPO deferral.' Particularly dangerous were the 'signs of uncertainty' being demonstrated by the company's creditors. If GPA was to have any hope at all of reducing the financial risk in its order books it would at the very least have to re-examine contracted financial commitments to aircraft manufacturers.

That approach seemed like a disciplined retreat in order to regroup and begin rebuilding the company. In fact it hid a situation that was far worse than Tony could have imagined. That same month he was shocked when he learnt just how apocalyptic GPA's future actually was.

'Maurice Foley phoned me three days prior to his going on vacation,' he wrote afterwards in a deposition, 'to warn that the company might run out of cash within ten days.'

Tony was flabbergasted. It had always been one of his greatest weaknesses that he never paid much attention to the figures; he concentrated on the big ideas while leaving others to sweat the numbers. But it was a weakness that to a certain degree he recognised in himself. It was why he employed Michael O'Leary to look after his personal affairs, and why he had sent him into Ryanair to clear up after Eugene O'Neill. And it was why Maurice Foley, who had been a stickler for the small details as a non-executive director, had subsequently been brought into the company as Tony's no. 2 and eventual successor as CEO. So to hear now that the company was only ten days from insolvency left Tony poleaxed (although Foley later vigorously disputed this recollection of events).

Tony shared the news with the other members of the board,

who were similarly 'shocked at the rapid deterioration and greatly concerned.' Second-quarter profits had plummeted by 20 per cent, and there was no obvious sign of new investment. Banks and manufacturers were now demanding what they were owed. GPA looked doomed.

Faced with the imminent collapse of everything he had built, Tony resolved to act. He elbowed Foley aside, once again taking up the reins as executive chairman of GPA. 'In the present challenging circumstances', he informed the staff, 'it is in GPA's best interest that there should be a single leadership focus and that duplication should be avoided.' That would allow the company to face 'the issues which we must address successfully, and quickly, so that we can resume our historic growth pattern.'

They were brave words, but in reality the situation was dire. Not only was GPA running out of money but its opportunities for generating revenue and equity were limited. It was stuck in a cycle of distrust and suspicion. Lack of confidence in the company had led to panic-selling of GPA bonds. That in turn had resulted in the company having no access to the bond market in order to raise capital. Similarly there were no buyers of GPA shares even at $8, and most banks were trying to sell their GPA debt.

This lack of finance, particularly bank finance, had a knock-on effect for GPA's assets and services. There was little or no demand for physical assets such as aircraft, which in turn was driving prices even lower as buyers anticipated a GPA 'fire sale'. When GPA's individual circumstances were coupled with a global airline business that was haemorrhaging money, the result was that the company's access to money was choked off.

This situation was calamitous, but in many ways it was one that suited Tony's temperament. At heart he remained a scrapper. The qualities that had seen him build GPA in the first place—hard work, aggression and unconventional thinking—were now required once again for what he optimistically called 'Project Rebound'.

His play was typically bold. Having identified the no. 1 priority as being 'to ensure liquidity,' Tony made the one phone call that he believed could resolve that issue. His relations with the American behemoth General Electric had not been easy when they were in business together, but his personal relationship with Jack Welch, the GE chairman, had been friendly enough. Now Tony went to him cap in hand. It was a gutsy, if humiliating, move but one that paid off. Despite the failure of the IPO, Welch still saw the potential of GPA in particular and airline leasing in general. If GPA and its fleet were there to be picked off, it made sense to establish a relationship now. After direct discussions between the two men in October, Welch agreed—'uniquely', Tony said—to a request to provide up to a billion dollars of liquidity on the basis of an aircraft sale.

Tony was ecstatic, believing that he had not only bought GPA time but also, in the longer term, found a potential buyer for a rejuvenated GPA. Therefore he was astonished when GPA's banks rejected the plan. 'This is a cherry-picking exercise,' they told him. 'That's incorrect,' Tony replied: 'aircraft can be replaced.'

Humiliatingly, Tony returned to Welch to explain that he was having trouble getting his banks to agree to the deal. Welch told him not to worry, that the offer was still on the table, and to stay in touch.

For the next five months Tony maintained that contact until, in March 1993, he again had the ground taken out from underneath him. Panicked GPA shareholders voted to approve a rights issue organised by Nomura Bank of $1 per share. Later, Tony would call it a naïve decision. At the time he was beyond livid. 'The company was now valued by its owners at $120 million,' he wrote starkly. It was no surprise when immediately afterwards 'Mr Welch called and withdrew his offer.'

Now GECC had a different offer to put on the table. By advancing $1.35 billion of financing to allow GPA to pay down some of its debt, they would take a four-year option to acquire majority ownership of the company for $200 million. Restructuring would see GPA split into two separate companies, with one owned by the existing GPA group and the other by a subsidiary of GECC. The company with the GPA name would be responsible for managing the vast debt that had been accumulated; the other would be responsible for managing the GPA fleet, along with the 450 aircraft already owned by GE.

In many ways it was an unsatisfactory deal, not least because GE had refused to take on GPA's debt. Yet, faced with the alternative of imminent 'examinership' (or 'administration'), it was no surprise when, after a summer of intense negotiations, an extraordinary general meeting of shareholders approved the deal on 18 October 1993.

Throughout the negotiations, Tony had been bedevilled by increasing rancour within GPA itself. Many had seen potential fortunes wiped out overnight. Maurice Foley had lost an estimated £9 million. For Jim King it was about £5 million. Colm Barrington had seen a potential £7½ million disappear and was left with a toxic loan of $1½ million, taken out to buy his GPA shares. Seán Donlon and other former public servants, including Niall Greene, Michael Lillis and Richard O'Toole, had also discovered how brutal the private sector could be. And many ordinary GPA staff members who had been banking on a windfall to keep them comfortable for life were left with nothing.

Tony was particularly frustrated by the constant backbiting and leaks to the press from the management team. 'The recent damaging reports of management division within GPA may have been fed by leakage from the company,' he had complained that summer. 'If this is so, it represents appalling disloyalty and disregard for GPA's well-being on the part of those concerned.'

Certainly there was festering antagonism among some at GPA. 'Not a whiff of acknowledgement of responsibility,' complained a senior vice-president, Christopher Brown, in his diary. 'Not a whisper of apology. Nothing. And there never has been. Yet again Tony and his directors present the situation as an achievement.' In fact, Brown thought, everything was 'Typical Tony—back to the old routine—criticism and kicks in the bollocks all delivered from the hip with his usual quiet intense asperity.'

Other criticism had been more targeted. On 2 April 1993, crucially while Tony was away in the United States, the senior managers

Patrick Blaney and Philip Bolger circulated a memorandum on 'survival-strategy issues' to all the executive and non-executive members of the GPA board. It offered a devastating critique of Tony's leadership of Project Rebound. 'This note is written because we are seriously concerned about GPA and its survival and because we see no evidence that GPA has either a viable plan for survival or the necessary management focus, and agreement thereon, to achieve it.' Morale in Shannon was 'at a level where the authors believe the core staff of GPA is on the brink of departing.' Attempts to move forward had been thwarted by backbiting and poor planning. The memo continued:

> Survival normally forces management to set aside their differences and focus on the essential talks in a co-ordinated and agreed manner. GPA on the other hand has been unable to do this . . . There has never been one management meeting, to the authors' knowledge, where the assumptions, issues and/or direction of Rebound have been raised and debated such that all involved can get to both understand them and agree what needs to be done.

The only way forward was to 'debate at some length these issues, develop and agree the *plan* going forward and how it will be implemented, *sell* it to the staff and our stakeholders, and then *do* it.' In conclusion, as well as offering their own resignations if required, they forecast that the 'agony of continuing the way we are cannot last much longer.'

Sending the memo was in many ways a brave act. 'It is the first time in eighteen years that anyone has stood up to Tony Ryan,' Jenny Brown, the manager of GPA's London office, was heard to remark. Yet if that was so it was because so few had learnt the lesson that Tony respected and even relished confrontation—he had, after all, employed those non-shrinking violets Denis O'Brien and Michael O'Leary as his assistants, neither of whom hesitated to challenge him in the most direct way.

Tony's reaction to the criticism from Blaney and Bolger—described breathlessly by workers at GPA as an attempted 'putsch'—was complex. His instinct was to fire both men on the spot. But almost immediately after doing so he reconsidered. Certainly he thought it would have been 'preferable and customary' for criticism to have been raised through 'established channels and procedures'. On reflection he put this down 'more to a consequence of inexperience and lack of awareness of the sensitivities between various constituencies than anything else.' However 'unfortunate' the approach to, and distribution of, the memo might have been, Tony recognised that it was indeed 'disturbing in its content'.

Back home, he called Blaney and Bolger into a meeting and subsequently asked them to address the GPA board. Afterwards, they were both promoted, with Blaney co-opted onto the board and appointed chief operating officer, with immediate effect. He was to report directly to Tony, and his mission was to develop and run Rebound 2. 'In this task', the message Tony circulated to all the staff read, 'he will have [my] full authority to draw the necessary resources from all sections of the company.'

It would be easy to conclude that Tony had caved in, not least if he had been put under pressure by his board. Yet as the unsympathetic Christopher Brown noted before the crucial meeting on the memo, 'the board is filled with Tony's sycophants and it will be like the morning meetings of olden days—Tony bullying his way through. It will be whatever Tony wants, I suspect.' Tony had the numbers to dispose of Blaney and Bolger if he wished. They remained because, through gritted teeth, Tony admired their courage and accepted their analysis that a new approach was needed. The fact that putting Blaney in to run Rebound 2 also sidelined Maurice Foley, with whom Tony had become increasingly frustrated, only added to the attraction.

For all the energy that Blaney brought to the task during the summer of 1993, Tony always believed that if the banks and the GPA board had grabbed the opportunity he had won from Welch in the autumn of 1992, the future of GPA would have been very different.

'The awful irony', he later wrote, was that the same process took place exactly a year afterwards 'but with all the advantages going to GECC at the expense of our shareholders.'

In a rare flash of public anger Tony complained that Welch had 'raped' GPA. 'What do you expect', Welch told him the next time the two men met, 'when you're walking around with no clothes on.'

If the downfall of GPA had been a humiliation, Tony—in his more reflective moments, at least—felt it had been an ordered retreat. He concluded that

> the deal with GE ultimately led to the consummation of various arrangements which underpinned the rescue and continuance of GPA, the preservation of the jobs of almost 200 people (and over 1,000 in ancillary companies) and the repayment of all bank debt together with interest as and when due. The company was thus enabled to continue to meet its debts (paying, for example, $1.4 billion to bondholders over the critical period) and [with] cash and available facilities in excess of $400 million.

The result was considerably better, Tony concluded, than the alternative of liquidation.

Others were less generous. 'Tony got away with murder,' the legendary PR guru P. J. Mara was overheard saying immediately before the emergency general meeting that approved the GE deal. In fact, as far as Tony was concerned, it was he himself who had been knifed.

The trouble had begun with the Public Schools Employees' Retirement System, the pension scheme in Pennsylvania. As a significant investor in GPA it had made it a condition of participation in the restructuring that Tony resign when the deal closed and that he waive any claims arising from his contract. That meant giving up, or at least putting into arbitration, a £1.8 million bonus paid over three years and share options independently valued at $28 million.

Tony believed that the 'irrational behaviour of PSERS' was nothing but 'bizarre' posturing. Others were more concerned. On 16 September, Maurice Foley, who despite being sidelined had remained as Tony's nominal no. 2, wrote to the non-executive director Sir John Harvey-Jones, advising that Tony should, in effect, be sacked. 'I believe TAR [Tony] will have to be formally pressed to resign without compensation,' he wrote. 'Obviously I regret that this may become necessary but we have to face up to the fact that it may be [the] only alternative to court protection.'

Foley also included a draft memorandum for Harvey-Jones to send to Tony. 'I regret that there is only one alternative solution now available to us and it is my painful duty to put it to you,' it stated. 'This is that you confirm to the Board in appropriate form that you will comply with the PSERS condition, i.e. resign and waive any claim to compensation as a result.'

It was a bullet Tony hadn't been expecting, but there was another to come that turned his life into a shooting gallery. He was angry about having been 'compelled as a condition precedent to the consummation of the GE Investment to resign my position and forfeit all rights, entitlements and claims against GPA.' He had already seen his personal-wealth potential from the IPO drop from a quarter of a billion dollars to nil. Now he had been fired. At the very least he might have been allowed to slip away to lick his wounds in private. But PSERS was not the only investor making demands.

GECC was setting it down as a condition of the deal that Tony remain in place to run GPA operations for a minimum twelve-month period. While his successors as chairman and overall chief executive would be given a four-year deal worth a combined $12 million, Tony became an employee of a GE subsidiary, GE Capital Aviation Services, on a salary of £300,000, with a bonus entitlement of less than half that amount. All this, he fumed, 'despite the fact that my responsibility [would] encompass the management and operation of a fleet of aircraft up to two times greater than originally owned by GPA and includes the entire GPA fleet.'

The demands from PSERS and GECC combined to make an intolerable situation for Tony. The pension company was insisting that the deal would not go through without his resignation; GE said he had to stay. The only way to make both happy was to resign and then return as an employee. At first Tony refused, but over the next few weeks he came under 'unbearable pressure which was placed upon me personally and was witnessed by a number of people who were present during these closing negotiations.'

One of those who saw the events close up was Michael O'Leary. His notes from the time record that Tony

> has been required as a *central* element to sacrifice his name, reputation and contractual rights by resigning from GPA and being compelled to work for GECAS. Intense pressure levied upon TAR during GE process to submit and comply with these onerous conditions but not limited to the repeated threat that if TAR did not agree to work for GECAS the entire deal will fall apart.

In the end, five minutes before the midnight deadline on 22 September laid down by GE, Tony signed the paperwork. Nigel Lawson, former Chancellor of the Exchequer and a non-executive director of GPA, acted as witness to his signature. It was not a casual choice. With Tony having previously come under such intense pressure to resign, Lawson had privately given him his own letter of resignation to use if he needed it. 'That was impressive,' says Declan Ryan, 'when so many guys were running for the hills. Tony appreciated that.'

Now Tony reflected disconsolately that he was 'saving GPA at the expense of my own personal financial position and reputation.' It was the culmination of a terrible period in his life, which had included a traffic accident in Ibiza that had tragically left a nineteen-year-old local man dead. 'It has been an awful year,' he wrote to Michael Smurfit, 'and the accident was the last straw.'

Working for GECAS would turn out to be a hugely frustrating experience. On so many levels it was a clash of cultures. To begin with, Tony was incensed by—and ignored—a crass email from the human resources department drawing his attention to a clause in the termination agreement that stipulated that he must return all company property, including his car and computer. It was an example of what Patrick Blaney called the 'normal GE subtlety'.

On a more philosophical level, Tony and GE were as much of a bad fit as they had been in the early 1980s. 'Does GE have any business being in airline leasing?' he asked Gary Wendt. 'I believe there is now clear evidence that the application and procedures that may suit other GE businesses does not suit GECAS. The company is floundering and is being choked by bureaucracy rather than being market driven.' There seemed to be more interest in 'meetings about meetings' than in any attempt to 'focus on the customer'. When Tony wrote that 'there is palpable frustration throughout the organisation' it was clear that he primarily meant himself. Even worse, despite being nominally in charge, Tony now found himself marginalised within GECAS. Board meetings were held without his knowledge and permission. That same board was appointed without any consultation. 'I first got sight of Directors names when I received the headed notepaper,' he complained.

The situation could not continue for long. On 11 April 1994 Tony resigned, concluding that there was little point carrying on, as 'I am virtually excluded from all elements of the operation.' It was not long before GECAS was pestering him again about returning the car and any remaining office equipment.

Tony had been staring at personal ruin as well as professional humiliation from the very moment the IPO failed in 1992. Without the $36 million he had expected from the conversion of his A shares to ordinary shares, he had been left with an outstanding $35 million loan from Merrill Lynch. After weeks of extensive talks in the early summer of 1992, Merrill Lynch declared Tony as in default at a meeting on 4 August. It demanded that he prepare a full and comprehensive asset and liability statement, and also asked for a list of assets sold or transferred over the previous five years. And, crucially, at a meeting on 24 November 1992, it raised for the first time the question of Ryanair and the family trust. That was the moment when Tony got ready for a legal fight, engaging the services of the elite law firm Herbert Smith. As one of Tony's creditors bluntly told him, things were going to 'get ugly'.

Tony had little choice but to hand over details of his personal assets, and it was revealing of his worth and lifestyle. His net salary was $200,000, with further fees of $100,000. His dividend income the previous year from GPA was $5.6 million. Interest on his deposit accounts generated a further million, all of which came to an annual personal income of $6.9 million. His expenditure was estimated at $150,000 a month, totalling $1.8 million per annum. Interest paid on bank loans totalled $1.5 million. Taken together, his incomings and outgoings left a discretionary surplus of $3.6 million. Post-IPO assets included properties in Spain and Mexico each worth $1 million. His art and antiques collections were valued at $10 million. He held $25 million in bank accounts and cash. GPA shares, which would turn out to be worthless, were nevertheless estimated at $234.1 million.

At a testy meeting on 5 February 1993, Merrill Lynch went through the entire history of all asset sales and transfers that Tony had conducted over the previous five years. At the end of the discussions, it reiterated its demand for information about the Ryan family assets, including those owned by the investment company Irelandia, others held personally by his children, and those owned by the CDS Trust (the Ryan family trust, so named after the initials of Cathal, Declan and Shane).

There now began an elaborate game of cat and mouse. Merrill Lynch went after the assets of Tony's children while their father fought tenaciously to protect the family. Formal letters were written to Tony's sons asking them to consider Merrill Lynch's request and to 'respond to same as a matter of urgency'. Peter Hagan, who ran negotiations for the bank, informed Michael O'Leary that 'their overall approach would be guided by the family's response.' O'Leary hedged, telling Hagan that 'we had written to the boys but did not expect their response quickly.'

Hagan followed up with a letter to Tony on 15 February in effect putting a deal on the table. Meetings with all the banks involved in Tony's loans had been 'positive'. However, before Merrill Lynch would refinance, O'Leary reported back, it was demanding that charges on the family assets 'be agreed by the boys'.

Tensions exploded to the surface in a nasty meeting in London on 22 February. Declan and Cathal had written to Merrill Lynch refusing to put up their own assets or those of the trust, including Kilboy, as security against the loan. A furious row now broke out when Hagan reiterated that Merrill Lynch could not go forward without undertakings from the CDS Trust. O'Leary launched into a blistering attack on Hagan, then became involved in a furious argument with other bank officials around the table. Tony had written to his sons, O'Leary bluntly told them, but, as they were separate legal entities, Cathal, Declan and Shane were perfectly entitled to say, 'Get lost.' Now tempers flared, with accusations thrown across the table from both sides. Ann Lane of Citibank was reported to have told Tony to 'can the crap'.

They were 'really gruesomely offensive to Tony at these meetings,' says O'Leary, 'but he remained remarkably stoic through it all, struggling through great personal humiliation with dignity.' On this occasion it was Tony who stepped in to try and calm matters down. The meeting continued in a more restrained fashion, but the damage had been done.

For almost a month there was 'total silence and unavailability of all Merrill Lynch people'. On Sunday 21 March it became apparent why: the story about Tony's debts had been leaked to the business editor of the *Independent on Sunday* in London. 'Tony Ryan in crisis talks on $35m loan', ran the headline. The article told of how 'Dr Ryan does not have sufficient security for the loan.' An unnamed spokesperson from Merrill Lynch was quoted as saying, 'We have had discussions between Dr Ryan and the group of banks to refinance the loan. Dr Ryan has put forward a variety of proposals and we have had discussions.' The story went on to contrast 'the man who describes himself as a simple Tipperary farmer' with the one who owned 'many thousand acres . . . a large country house . . . has homes in Spain, Monte Carlo and Mexico [and] a sizeable art collection.'

Tony was livid when he saw the newspaper. Early next morning he phoned Hagan to express his 'great concern' that Merrill Lynch had spoken to the journalist without his knowledge or approval. The fact that it had gone to the papers was 'damaging'. Moreover, it had started off a frenzy of press speculation in Ireland. Not only did that erode Tony's own position, it 'generates further nervousness amongst the banks and the bond markets' about GPA.

In fact, to Hagan's chagrin, he saw this himself that same morning at a meeting with Tony's other creditors (the timing of which coincided with the story in the *Independent on Sunday*). AIB Bank, which had previously been quite accommodating when working with Merrill Lynch on Tony's loans, now began 'causing problems' for Hagan. Soon afterwards, at a lunch meeting, Hagan would warn Tony that he had 'very few friends . . . in AIB.' Following the negative media coverage, AIB was telling everyone that Tony was still 'living like a lord', and therefore, Hagan judged, it was 'not inclined on emotive grounds to settle or assist.' Hagan explained that

> their main concern was the embarrassment in Ireland if for any reason you remain a wealthy person and have out-negotiated AIB. AIB, because of their banking relationship, are close to Aer Lingus, and are convinced that Ryanair was now very valuable and that after the settlement you would become chairman of the airline.

There now followed a tense poker game, with the banks demanding commitments on Ryanair and the CDS Trust, and Tony politely informing them that they were not his to give. 'As you will be aware from our previous correspondence,' he wrote in July 1993, 'Ryanair is not, and has never been within my ownership and/or control and therefore I am not in a position to give you the type of confirmations you seek. I have offered you all, repeat all, of my remaining assets, my shares, and my properties.'

Hagan continued to press the point. 'The banking group is not convinced that you have no control over Ryanair,' he countered, 'and further the banking group believes it can successfully challenge the transfer of money to the CDS Trust which is the capital base on which Ryanair operates.'

Still Tony refused to blink. 'It is a matter of fact, and indeed legal record that I have not, and nor have I ever exercised any ownership or indeed control over Ryanair,' he coolly responded. 'Ryanair is owned, operated and controlled by my sons. Whilst I was the source of much of the finance for it during its early years, these funds were settled by me upon CDS Trust some considerable time ago, and indeed with the full fore knowledge of both Merrill Lynch and the banking group.'

Relations were not always so glacially courteous. Tony's friend Ed Walsh, the founding president of the University of Limerick, recalls hearing how tense matters became.

> His world had collapsed, and they came in to take Kilboy and Ryanair from him. His key banker flew in from London to Kilboy in very dominant mode. The message was he was taking Ryanair as well as your personal possessions. So, anyway, Michael O'Leary and himself set upon this guy . . . and pursued him in such a way that he left having, according to Tony, not only wet his pants but the chair! So whatever Michael O'Leary and Tony said to this guy who came in to take everything from him, he went away and they retained Kilboy and Ryanair—and of course we know the story after that.

Thus it was that Merrill Lynch folded first. In the summer of 1993 Hagan indicated that he would be willing to consider a settlement at about 25 cents on the dollar—a repayment of $14 million. This represented a loss of more than $20 million for the bank, but Tony, who was famous for leaving nothing on the table during a negotiation, still wasn't done. He countered with an offer of $5 million, telling Hagan he could 'with some degree of confidence raise this figure from friends and other resources, and through the sale of the Mexican and Spanish properties.'

Another round of tortuous discussion and exchanges of letters followed throughout the rest of 1993 and into the new year, when Hagan finally confirmed that Merrill Lynch would 'positively respond' if Tony was to propose a settlement figure of $5 million and be in a position to make the payment quickly.

Tony agreed to 'do his best', but even now—having won—he couldn't resist having some fun with his beleaguered bankers. In March, with just weeks to go before the end of the financial year, on 5 April 1994, Tony returned to Merrill Lynch to say he was half a million dollars short. Glad to see the back of him, Hagan, 'after some toing and froing', accepted $4½ million subject to the transaction being done on or before 5 April. Tony left it to the last moment, but on the day itself he made the payment. The banks had taken a 'haircut' of $30.5 million. Six days later Tony also resigned as chief executive of GECAS. Finally he was free of the shackles that had bound him since 18 June 1992. As it turned out, Tony had 'got away with murder' after all.

To some degree Tony's ability to wriggle Houdini-like from the chains of debt was due to luck. Back in the mid-1980s he had set up the CDS Trust in a thinly veiled attempt to maintain the pretence that he—the chief executive of a company in which Aer Lingus was a major investor—was not setting up an airline to go into competition with the national carrier. No-one had believed him for a moment, but now the legalities of that arrangement had kept the CDS Trust and other family assets out of the grips of his creditors.

Pulling off the escape had required patience and unshakeable nerve. No amount of charm, threats, inducements, public humiliation or potential ruin had moved him. He was fortunate to have had O'Leary both as master of detail and as attack dog. In fact it was watching these attributes in action during the debt process that convinced Tony by the end of 1993 that O'Leary was the right man to put in charge of Ryanair.

Yet in the end it was Tony himself who had needed not to

buckle under the intense strain. Indeed, when he might have been expected to fall into depression, Tony had maintained his *sang froid* throughout. He joked with correspondents about reading *Leadership Secrets of Attila the Hun.* To others he quipped, 'I sleep like a baby—I wake up screaming every ten minutes.' In one conversation with Hagan he remarked laconically that he was speaking on a car phone 'and was passing Kilmainham Jail'. All told, it was a remarkable performance, whatever anxieties it masked.

That fortitude was a quality others admired. 'The story of GPA was like a Greek tragedy, with you as the tragic hero,' wrote Nigel Lawson. 'Nothing can alter the fact that you created a world-class company; and your conduct in the face of adversity which caused it all to be ousted from you was indeed heroic.'

Lawson's letter was one of many that buoyed Tony during the crisis. While he was often criticised behind his back and pulverised by the press, he also received a vast amount of correspondence offering support and consolation. Some was from those who had run across him at various times in his life, such as the old school friend who wrote to offer his 'utmost support at this time'.

Other correspondents were more elevated. Perhaps the letter that meant the most was from Jack Lynch, the former Taoiseach and a hurling legend of Tony's childhood. 'It is sad', Lynch wrote, 'when people like you who have the courage and initiative to take risks and achieve great success to the immense advantage of our country, find that unpredictable world events should operate against you.'

There was a sense of eulogy to most of these sentiments. Tony had played the game with great success, then lost spectacularly, before managing to pull himself back from the brink of personal ruin. Few thought that, in his late fifties, Tony Ryan had much more to give. In fact he was already planning how to win back his millions. AIB Bank, as it turned out, had been right: Tony had made fools of them all.

Chapter 12

RYAN REDUX

By the spring of 1994 Tony Ryan had emerged battered but intact from the rubble of GPA. Certainly he was left resentful and shell-shocked by the experience. 'People say I'm arrogant, and I am,' he told the *Irish Times*, 'but you should see those arrogant sons of bitches on Wall Street.' Yet while Tony had lost both his reputation and a vast fortune, he had at least wiped out his debts and held on to some of his assets. Now he began setting about regaining the wealth and esteem he had relinquished. His means for doing so was the airline that bore his name. Ryanair, so long an expensive drain on his resources, was going to make Tony rich again.

That prospect had seemed highly unlikely back in 1988, when the board had fired Eugene O'Neill, and Tony had despaired of ever making money out of the airline. Indeed his principal consideration had not been to make money but simply to stop losing it. Michael O'Leary, the PA who had been sent in to audit Ryanair, had reported back on a company that was haemorrhaging money, would continue to do so for the foreseeable future and required massive investment from the then still wealthy Tony. He had warned that the Ryan family had to consider the entire investment and asked whether Tony really wanted to continue funding the airline.

O'Leary and Declan Ryan, who became interim CEO until the appointment of P. J. McGoldrick, believed that the answer to that question should be no, and they advised him accordingly. 'It was lucky that Tony didn't agree with us,' Declan says, 'but he didn't like people telling him things he didn't want to hear. Thank God, he just told us to go run and jump.'

McGoldrick, O'Leary and Declan Ryan had set about addressing the structural chaos at the heart of Ryanair, but the most basic issue the puny airline had faced was that it was constantly out-punched by a heavyweight national carrier. When Ryanair began flying to the newly transformed Stansted Airport in London, Aer Lingus simply slashed prices and undercut its fledgling rival.

It was not a situation that could continue. Despite carrying more than 680,000 passengers and achieving an average load factor of 64 per cent, Ryanair had lost more than £3 million on revenues in excess of £33 million in the financial year 1988/9. Altogether the Ryan family had invested more than £20 million since the airline began.

By 1 March 1989 the new chief executive had concluded that there were only two options available to the company: 'immediate closure of the airline thereby stopping further losses, or the injection of the necessary capital to enable the airline to survive the next few years in anticipation that it will become profitable in due course.' Tony was determined to carry on, but he recognised that it would be a wasted investment unless Ryanair could secure from the Government a 'minimum level of protection' at Stansted and Luton Airports. 'It has been becoming increasingly obvious', McGoldrick noted after a meeting with Tony, 'that the company's long-term profitability can only be ensured if Ryanair is the exclusive Irish carrier to Luton and Stansted, while Aer Lingus retains its established monopoly to both Heathrow and Gatwick.'

That stark message was delivered in March 1989 to the Minister for Tourism and Transport, John Wilson of Fianna Fáil, without much success. However, Tony's luck changed on 12 July, when the first Fianna Fáil-PD coalition Government came to power. That saw Tony's friend Des O'Malley, leader of the PDs, return to office in a new Government with a more entrepreneurial, free-market spirit. O'Malley remembers Tony driving up from Tipperary to Rathmines after the election to urge him to join a coalition Government. 'I was suspicious that Haughey had sent him,' O'Malley says, 'but Tony had come up off his own bat, arguing that the country needed stable government and more competition.'

The new Minister for Tourism and Transport was Séamus Brennan, who earlier had come close to leaving Fianna Fáil for the PDs and was sympathetic to the new party's liberalising agenda. Urged on by O'Malley, Brennan met Tony and McGoldrick over the summer to talk about the Government's aviation policy. Brennan had already read a report by the TCD economist Sean Barrett that estimated Ryanair's impact on fares, time savings and increased tourism from Britain as generating £200 million for the Irish economy. Now Brennan heard Tony say that unless Ryanair was given room to compete with Aer Lingus through exclusivity on the Stansted and Luton routes he was going to close it down. 'They told me Ryanair was going into liquidation and the company would be closed on the following Friday week,' Brennan recalled. 'The losses were staggering.' However, if the Government agreed to a new 'two airline' policy Tony pledged to invest a further £20 million in Ryanair.

It was a high-risk strategy by Tony, but one that paid off. On 20 September, Brennan announced a new direction in policy to facilitate 'the strengthening of the Irish presence rather than having two Irish carriers actively pursuing traffic on identical routes.' Aer Lingus would maintain its exclusivity on the profitable Heathrow, Gatwick and Manchester routes; Ryanair got Stansted, Luton and Liverpool. New routes would be divided between carriers. 'This policy shift', noted Brennan's political adviser, Frank Lahiffe, 'gave Ryanair the opportunity to prove itself while also protecting Aer Lingus—the best of both worlds.'

Aer Lingus, despite keeping hold of 96 per cent of traffic to Britain, was predictably unhappy about the new arrangements. Union members even picketed Brennan's house and constituency office. Nasty rumours were circulated accusing Brennan, in effect, of taking a bung from Tony. Similar accusations were made to Brennan during an interview on the RTE Radio programme 'Morning Ireland', in which he was repeatedly asked if 'these concessions' were the result of a political donation to Fianna Fáil. Later the director-general of

RTE, Vincent Finn, controversially went on air to express 'regret that such a question was put to you which carried an implication for which no evidence was provided.'

Certainly Tony wasn't above making straightforward political contributions. In November 1995, for example, Fianna Fáil asked for and was given £50,000 to help clear party debts. In 1989 insiders at Ryanair speculated about whether money might have changed hands in a less formal way, not with Brennan but with the Taoiseach, Charles Haughey. 'Brennan was very pro-Ryanair, because he liked the idea of open skies and was very pro-that in meetings I had with him,' says Derek O'Brien, who was Ryanair's commercial director. 'But what went on behind the scenes I don't know, except that there was always this undercurrent of other conversations being held "sub rosa" with Charlie, so what Charlie got from those conversations God only can imagine.' Declan Ryan's reply to that question is unequivocal: 'He got nothing!'

In any event, the announcement was a huge boost for Ryanair. O'Brien says that Tony

> came up with the two-airline policy, and that's when Brennan began saying, 'Look, guys, there's space for everybody here, so let's not drive each other out of business.' I don't think there was anything Machiavellian about it. Brennan was very clear that if the suicidal competition continued we were going to end up with no second airline. The whole situation had been insane. His was the first bit of political sense that came into it.

The day after the announcement, Tony fulfilled his side of the bargain by announcing a new investment of £20 million in Ryanair. 'Only the most naïve would hold that the two developments might not be connected,' judged the *Irish Times*. 'The Ryan family can hardly be criticised for pressuring the government into giving them route advantages so as to render their airline profitable.' Even so, 'by any standards it is a considerable sum of money', and it was 'another stark reminder of Dr Ryan's determination to invest'.

The two-airline policy could not have been more helpful to Ryanair. The company would still make a loss that year of £5 million, but for the first time it was now competing on a level playing field, even if it still remained very much a Championship rather than a Premier League side.

The first task was still to stop the airline losing money—a job entrusted to P. J. McGoldrick, in conjunction with Declan Ryan and Michael O'Leary. 'I don't want to spend any more money,' Tony warned them. 'Cut the spending.' Every Saturday at 8:30 a.m. the three men would troop into Tony's office at Kilboy to give him an update. 'We used to be summoned down,' O'Leary recalls, 'and, to be fair, we still didn't know how bad the losses were, as the figure seemed to go up every six months: 3 million—no, 5 million—no, actually 7 million. Nobody knew how much the original thing had lost, because the bills just kept coming in—bills we didn't even know we had.'

The Ryans had brought in McGoldrick, says O'Leary, because he was 'brilliant operationally'. Slowly, over two years, the new chief executive began to restructure the airline, in particular rationalising the schedules. Ryanair went from about thirty routes to focusing on only four: Dublin to Stansted, Luton and Liverpool, and Knock to Stansted.

Meanwhile, O'Leary and Declan Ryan took a hatchet to expenditure, rationalising everything in sight. When Tony complained that the airline was starting to look just 'cheap' rather than 'cheap and cheerful', O'Leary told him, 'This is the way it has to be. You cut, you cut some more, then you cut more again.'

It was how the turnaround began, according to Gerry McEvoy of KPMG, who was Tony's personal taxation adviser. 'Michael and Declan started to drive the company forward in a significant way,' he recalls. 'The transfer of the company from loss to profitability was about Declan and Michael.'

They suggested to Tony that it was 'in the long term strategic interest' of the company to 'attract an international partner'. This was a tricky proposition, because Ryanair had to do so on its own terms in order to avoid getting picked off cheaply by a large international airline.

In the autumn of 1989, just weeks after Tony announced his £20 million investment, he was approached by Goldman Sachs with a proposal. At a meeting over lunch in London, it advised that it was working on behalf of a number of international airlines operating to and from Britain that would be interested in establishing links with Ryanair. It was a tempting suggestion, but the timing was wrong. Ryanair was going through its restructuring process, and the new rules of competition on the Dublin route, only just announced by Brennan, made immediate co-operation inappropriate. However, Ryanair would come back to them, Tony said, 'when the timing was better.'

Six months later Tony was ready to deal. Michael O'Leary and Declan Ryan met representatives of Goldman Sachs and told them to 'locate an international partner who might acquire a minority stake in the company.' Only after Tony had given the instruction did he inform McGoldrick. It was the kind of decision-making process that McGoldrick, who was unused to Tony's style, constantly struggled to comprehend. 'PJ was a very understated, nice person,' O'Leary remembers, 'so he really found it very hard to deal with Tony, because Tony was so mercurial.'

Tony personally oversaw the putting together of a 'suitable document' for Goldman Sachs to provide to their clients. However, he insisted that it 'will only be issued to those airlines who can bring substantial partnership benefits to the table in terms of the long term growth and development of Ryanair.' This was the beginning of an effort to turn Tony's ugly-duckling airline into something finer—hence the aspirational code-name Project Swan.

It soon became apparent that one of the airlines interested in Ryanair was British Airways, the recently privatised national carrier headed by Lord King. Throughout the summer and autumn of 1990 detailed discussion took place between the two sides to work out a deal. Negotiations centred on Ryanair taking over BA's Irish routes, including the entire sales operation. BA would become an equity partner in Ryanair and establish a new brand, Ryanair Express, to feed Heathrow.

Although the deal eventually fell through because of 'strategic and legal sensitivities' at the British end, the Ryanair team had noticed a real sense of fragility in BA's negotiating position and understood the reason behind it. 'BA's performance on the Irish routes continues to worsen monthly,' Declan Ryan had written to Tony in August. 'July's market share proves this point; this is the *first* time Ryanair has been higher than BA.'

On 10 December, BA informed Ryanair that a relationship would not be pursued. The explanation came a few weeks afterwards, when it stunned the market by announcing that it was pulling out of its Irish routes after forty-four years. 'This is the first time BA has ever moved off a route as a result of competition,' noted Michael Bishop, head of British Midland. Ryanair immediately moved to fill the gap by announcing extra services to Stansted.

British Airways had been an obvious potential investor for Ryanair. The other approach in 1990 was just as predictable in its own way. In the late summer, Ryanair's fiercest rival, Aer Lingus, entered into negotiations not to invest but to purchase the airline from the Ryan family. Tony put an initial price on the sale of £35 million plus. Negotiations with the Aer Lingus chief executive, Cathal Mullan, revealed just how bad the blood between the two airlines had become. In November, John Thornton of Goldman Sachs upbraided Aer Lingus for their 'slow speed' and pointed out that 'they weren't acting like people who were interested in a deal.' O'Leary reported that Aer Lingus 'held the view that this operation was of limited if little value, and therefore they didn't believe that they should pay a very significant price for it.' They also 'whinged about the price range, and insisted that if the Ryans were serious at this kind of price range, then there was no point in proceeding with the discussions.'

All told, it was unlikely ever to have worked out, not least, wrote O'Leary, because 'TAR was now getting involved in this . . . and the egos take over.' It seemed clear that Aer Lingus was only in talks because it wanted Ryanair 'to go away, either by acquiring them or by shutting them down'—frankly, they 'didn't care which'.

When Tony got a report on such attitudes he was predictably 'upset'. Aer Lingus took 'three months to get to this stage,' he complained. That had left him 'appearing very weak' for putting up with such a slow pace. 'Tell them now to do a deal or feck off,' he barked. Declan Ryan believes that the sale of Ryanair to Aer Lingus 'could have been done in five minutes if they had really wanted it, because Cathal Mullan was capable of being a deal-maker.'

Formal negotiations were quickly broken off. Ryanair instead focused its efforts on keeping the show going on a stand-alone basis. But the negotiations hadn't been worthless. Ryanair had learnt important lessons about their principal rival. 'Aer Lingus were now convinced that Ryanair would stay in business,' concluded an internal memo for Tony, and they were 'a bunch of old ladies'.

That accusation was not one that could be made against the management at Ryanair, with its mantra of 'Cut, cut, cut.' This policy brought Ryanair a certain amount of unpopularity, not least because the cut-backs involved redundancies and salary cuts.

There was also a clash of cultures within the airline, which saw the departure of many of the 'old guard' that Tony had brought in to run it in the early days. 'Some of them were good in their day,' says O'Leary, 'but their whole thing was "You can't get rid of the meals, nobody will fly with us." When they said, "I'm going to Tony," I said, "Fine, go to Tony, but you know he's going to tell you the same thing." So they couldn't really hack it.'

Many of these exits were unhappy, especially that of Christy Ryan, who had been an original partner in Ryanair. When Christy had asked to go back to Waterford, Cathal Ryan suggested that Tony, as a gesture towards long years of friendship, should buy out Christy's shares even though in the early 1990s they seemed next to worthless. Years later, Christy would be devastated to miss out on the bonanza that Ryanair became. 'Christy made a big deal out of the share value and essentially accused Tony of ripping him off,' recalls Graham Boyd, who had worked with them both from the earliest days of GPA. 'By that time Christy had fallen on hard times. He could always have come back and got another job with Tony, but he couldn't face it after he had made all the accusations about the shares.'

Tony did his best to patch things up publicly with his old friend. 'I remember they ran into each other at a party,' says Boyd. 'Tony and Christy went for a walk together to try to talk things out, but it didn't really resolve anything. It was such a shame, because they had been really tremendous friends.'

'What guys like that didn't know,' counters Declan Ryan, 'was that Tony had been seeing Christy all right with regular financial contributions for years and continued to do so for the rest of his life. He was generous to Christy financially and emotionally, not that he ever got much thanks for it.'

At the end of 1991 P. J. McGoldrick announced his intention to resign as chief executive. He had stemmed the losses in Ryanair and rationalised its operations. By the time of his departure he had turned an annual deficit of millions into a small operating profit of £300,000. The figure itself didn't seem much and had in fact been supplemented by Ryanair's disposal of a travel subsidiary. Yet, in the context of what he had inherited, McGoldrick's had been a herculean effort, not least in the forbearance this mild-mannered character had demonstrated during the dressing-downs he had endured at Kilboy each Saturday. At his last meeting he was able to report that, while Ryanair was not financially secure, it was at least stable, for which Tony typically gave little beyond a grimace in the way of thanks.

The question for Tony was who should run the airline after McGoldrick. Initially there was speculation that Declan Ryan, who was already deputy chief executive, would be put into the post. However, for all the progress that had been made, the odds against Ryanair surviving were still not much better than evens. Tony's eldest son, Cathal, had endured a miserable time in running the failed offshoot London European Airways. It would be bad enough, in the event of the failure of Ryanair, having 'Ryan' in the name of the airline; Tony wasn't going to make matters worse by having one of his sons at the helm. Declan accepted the decision with more grace than Tony himself would have done.

Other observers expected O'Leary to be installed at the airline, unaware that Tony already had plans for him as a possible successor at GPA. Instead, Tony made the surprising choice of Paddy Murphy, a former CEO of Irish Ferries. 'He was a good guy,' says O'Leary, 'but he didn't seem to understand we had no money.' Murphy barely lasted a month in the post.

The next appointment was more propitious. Conor Hayes, as a trained accountant (from KPMG, like O'Leary), was the ideal man to push on with the 'cuts' strategy. He quickly introduced further restructuring and launched a new, popular, easy-to-understand fare structure, including the Ryanair signature £29.99 'Happy Days' flights to London. Market share jumped from 15 to 26 per cent in a year, and the airline returned another small profit.

Part of Hayes's restructuring effort was to keep stripping away any luxuries in the Ryanair service. Frequently this included the flight itself: if not enough seats had been sold, a flight would be combined with a later one, with little care for the inconvenience that decision might cause passengers. These kinds of measures irritated Tony when he heard about them and were the beginning of a growing disenchantment with the airline that would last for the rest of his life.

'It was getting cheaper and nastier,' admits O'Leary, 'and Tony didn't like cheap and nasty. He would get complaints from his pals that a flight was late, so he would be on the phone complaining to Conor that this was unacceptable.' When Tony asked for friends to be given the VIP treatment, Hayes was left to explain that there was no VIP treatment to give on Ryanair. It was a point that Hayes and O'Leary reiterated at their weekly audiences at Kilboy when 'we were getting called out about not making enough money.'

In the end Tony couldn't do much more than grouse, because the strategy was clearly working. By the end of 1992 Ryanair was able to announce a trading profit for the year of £850,000. In fact the profit was closer to £3½ million.

At this stage, however, Tony had good reason to hide the profitability of his airline: the collapse of GPA had left him with vast personal debts. Already his bankers were eyeing the family airline as a way to recoup some of their losses. It was no harm at all for Ryanair to look like a struggling business. By the time Tony had evaded the clutches of the bank in 1994, his PA had stepped into the role of chief executive at the airline. 'I had learnt enough about the ops side from McGoldrick and the finance side from Conor, so I was ready to shove myself out there,' says O'Leary. It was the beginning of a new period in the history of the airline—and in Tony's life.

One of the remarkable aspects of what happened to Tony when he lost his fortune was the extent to which it seemed to galvanise rather than depress him. Certainly there was genuine regret that his downfall had affected others. Figures such as Jim King, who had been loyal throughout and had staked their own fortunes on Tony's success, had been left with nothing from GPA. Tony was only too aware of sensitivities and possible resentment towards him. 'Most of these guys must hate me,' he observed when attending a party in 1995 to mark GPA's thirtieth anniversary.

Yet, in truth, that seemed not to be the case. Indeed it was striking how loyal those close to Tony remained even when they had lost everything. 'I was like a zombie for the first year,' reflects King, 'but most of us survived, and there weren't too many cry-babies.'

Tony was careful to respect those sensitivities. He might have railed against the bankers whom he felt had shafted GPA, but in the end he accepted that the responsibility was his. 'I remember Gay Byrne interviewed him on RTE,' says Gerry Power, who worked at GPA and became a good friend in the period after the IPO. 'It was a very honest Tony you heard, saying the buck stops with him and taking full responsibility. That was good, because there would be a number of people that would have said, "Tony, you're right: you *were* responsible for the IPO failing".'

For all the public self-flagellation that Tony was prepared to display, those who observed him behind closed doors every day saw a different character. 'It was amazing, but he never got knocked back by it,' says Derek Doyle, Tony's driver. 'Even at the height of everything going bad with GPA he never showed any sense of disgrace. He was still exactly the same with me. I knew he was going through a lot of personal bother and was concerned about the company, but he never showed it. He was a gutsy person.'

By temperament Tony was never a 'sharer', so it would have been surprising if he had chosen to unburden himself on his driver, however trusted. Yet unless he possessed superhuman qualities of self-control, the most likely explanation for Tony not displaying any sense of disgrace is that he didn't feel it. Accepting that you might fail is an essential aspect of the entrepreneurial character. When Tony got knocked down, his principal consideration was not to lament finding himself on the floor but immediately to consider how to get back up.

'Most people would have gone away and hidden themselves,' says his friend Ed Walsh. 'But he was at his best when things were really going against him.' In Ireland a humiliation such as Tony had endured meant that 'you're a failure—rejected.' But, says Walsh, Tony understood the lessons of the great American entrepreneurs who 'fail and fail again, but they pick themselves up and are wiser as a result of failing.'

Walsh had seen this kind of persistence up close at the height of the GPA crisis. Shortly beforehand he had invited Tony to chair a development committee for finding a permanent home in Limerick for the John Hunt Collection, one of the great art bequests to Ireland of modern times, ranking alongside those of Chester Beatty and Sir Alfred Beit. It was a project that appealed to Tony's growing interest and expertise in art, and he embraced it enthusiastically. In 1990 Hunt had arrived at Tony's office in Dublin with a bag filled to the brim with stuffed stockings. 'To my astonishment,' Tony later recalled, 'he produced out of it the Leonardo Horse and other treasures from his family's collection, which he placed on my desk.'

From that moment Tony was 'determined to do what I could' to create a Hunt Museum.

By January 1992 a beautiful site had been identified at the dilapidated eighteenth-century Custom House in Limerick. The question then became one of funding. Serious lobbying began just after the failure of the IPO for GPA. When Tony might have been expected to back off or drop out, instead he threw himself into the political hurly-burly with vigour. He solicited help from such famous Limerickmen as Terry Wogan and Richard Harris. ('The answer is definitely yes, I would love to do it,' Harris wrote graciously.)

Tony's friend Des O'Malley was a local TD, and he remembers Tony asking him in September 1992 to intercede with the Taoiseach, Charles Haughey, and the Minister for Finance, Bertie Ahern. After a meeting with Haughey, Tony got the Taoiseach's agreement to give a speech in Limerick to announce that the state would give the old Custom House to the Hunt Collection.

All the last-minute negotiations centred on getting one extra word—'*restored* Custom House'—into his speech. It was a word worth an extra £3 million. As the hours ticked down, Walsh and Tony cornered the Taoiseach at a lunch in Dublin on the day of the speech and then followed him back down to Limerick by helicopter to see him make the commitment. 'Tony, of course, was at the centre of this,' says Walsh, 'and the fact that he was chairing the Hunt committee had got Charlie Haughey's attention.' That Tony had done so in the middle of the worst crisis of his business life was another example of his resilience, his chutzpah and, says Declan Ryan, 'his love of everything Irish'.

That approach characterised Tony's whole mindset after the failed IPO. It explains why he fought the bankers so tenaciously to keep them away from Ryanair. Denis O'Brien, Tony's former PA, remembers calling in to Kilboy at about this time and being amazed to find his old boss talking so enthusiastically about building up Ryanair. 'I heard what he thought,' recalls O'Brien, who took to heart the lesson in how to keep the entrepreneurial fires burning.

'This is how to build a huge business,' Tony told him. 'If it doesn't work, revise the strategy. If it still doesn't work, revise the strategy again.'

'Tony had that view, that if he kept going he would eventually get it right,' says O'Brien. 'That's how Ryanair happened. When the business became successful, people forgot that Tony deserved the credit not just for setting up Ryanair, but for sticking with it.'

Gerry Power agrees. 'Michael O'Leary used to tell Tony to close it down, and Tony kept on putting money in and believed in it,' he says. 'He was steering Michael in the right direction, so when GPA went, Tony had it to fall back on, and that made his second fortune.'

O'Leary had been keen to shut down Ryanair throughout the late 1980s and into the early 90s for reasons that were both professional and personal. One look at the books had convinced him that not even Tony's multi-millions could make a silk purse out of this particular sow's ear. That was bad news for O'Leary, who was on a profit-sharing deal to take 5 per cent of any money he made for Tony. Rather than Tony sending money into the abyss that was Ryanair, O'Leary would have preferred to see the money being spent on more obviously profitable ventures. 'I just thought, This thing can't make any money,' O'Leary says. 'It's impossible.'

O'Leary's calculations changed after the failed IPO. With Tony's millions gone, Ryanair became the way in which both master and protégé could hope to make money. Before the GPA flotation, O'Leary had stepped away from Ryanair, leaving Conor Hayes to run the airline. O'Leary 'grew tired of Conor,' Declan Ryan recalls, 'so he moved into Irelandia's offices.' Only in 1994 did O'Leary return to Ryanair, taking over from the departing Hayes, as chief executive. After years of trying to tie him down, Tony at last had his man.

Tony motivated O'Leary by making him a *de facto* partner in the airline. That deal would become the stuff of legend: O'Leary would get 25 per cent of any profits that Ryanair made over £2 million. The two other executive directors, Cathal and Declan Ryan, would also share 25 per cent of profits. The arrangement would be formalised as the Executive Directors Performance Incentive Bonus Programme. They had 'learnt it from him,' O'Leary recalls of the deal, 'because profit-sharing was how he had made all his money in GPA.'

Over the next few years, as Ryanair went from strength to strength, Tony would try to bargain his CEO down on the 25 per cent. 'It happened every year with Tony,' O'Leary wryly recalls. 'I would say, "You owe me 25 per cent," but he wouldn't pay me. So I would send in my letter of resignation to the board and then he paid me. The more I did that, the more I became irreplaceable.' Tony understood that too. He looked forward to the annual game about profits but never for a moment considered calling O'Leary's bluff by accepting his resignation. To his friends he always said the deal with O'Leary was the best bit of business he ever did.

Having secured O'Leary as chief executive, Tony also gave him a strategy. Back in the 1970s, when Tony was clocking up millions of air miles travelling around the world to drum up business for GPA, his eye had been caught by the start-up airline operated by Herb Kelleher in Dallas. Southwest Airlines was run along very simple lines: it was a no-frills airline that concentrated on minimal expenditure and maximum profit, combined with a philosophy to 'LUV' its staff and passengers. Whenever Tony had run across Kelleher, the two men had got along famously, drinking Wild Turkey bourbon together late into the night. The original Ryanair had been an attempt to introduce the low-cost model into the Irish market, but only latterly had it embraced the 'no frills' concept that was so vital to Kelleher's success. Tony had decided that his own 'cheap and cheerful' airline could learn more from the Southwest model. 'Get down there and take a look,' he told O'Leary.

When O'Leary wrote to Kelleher asking to visit he received a polite rebuff. 'I tremendously appreciate your interest in Southwest,' Kelleher responded. 'Unfortunately neither my schedule nor the schedules of our Revenue and Yield Management folks will accommodate even the briefest of meetings in the foreseeable future.' Tony picked up the phone to call Herb personally. 'I had got to know Tony fairly well and liked him a lot,' Kelleher remembered.

'He called me and asked me in essence whether I would be willing to sit down and talk to Michael. So I said, "Yes, I would be delighted".'

O'Leary left for Dallas still feeling sceptical. 'Tony knew about Southwest,' he recalls, 'but the problem was that I was still struggling in Ryanair, thinking there's no real future in it.' The introduction to Kelleher changed that assessment overnight. In some regards this was about stepping out of Tony's shadow. 'I went off on my own,' O'Leary recalls, 'so I didn't have Tony going on in my ear.' But what he found when he got to Dallas was a man who in many ways resembled the one he had left behind at Kilboy. 'Kelleher was a genius and all ego, like Tony,' he says, 'so I knew how to handle that. But when I saw what Southwest did, it was like a Formula 1 operation. It took me fifteen minutes to see that we could replicate this in Europe.' As Kelleher himself remarked, O'Leary now assumed 'leadership of our European Fan Club!'

Towards the end of 1994, in his first year as chief executive, O'Leary put what he had learnt down on paper in 'The challenge of replicating Southwest Airlines in Europe'. It offered a blueprint for Ryanair. 'The future of the international airline business, or more importantly its salvation, has arrived,' he wrote. 'In the US it is called Southwest Airlines.' Their model came from 'a constant focus upon challenging every received wisdom in the airline industry, and constantly innovating new procedures and systems with the sole purpose of increasing efficiency, heightening productivity, eliminating unnecessary frills, and above all reducing costs.'

Moreover, there was a style that went with the Southwest model. 'Kelleher has imbued his people and Southwest with a "can do", service oriented culture,' he enthused. 'The ethos of Southwest is to provide a service to the passenger which will amuse, surprise and entertain.' That was now the aim for Ryanair.

> We must reeducate our people. This is the airline business—this is a fun business . . . If we are having fun, the passenger is having fun. To requote Kelleher, we must amuse, surprise and entertain. To those who believe it will never happen here, in

> Europe, to you I say just one word: 'McDonalds'. Just as surely as the Big Mac has revolutionised the fast food industry, so will Southwest and its replicas change the way we view air travel and manage the airline business.

Tony had galvanised O'Leary in the most profound way possible by sending him to Southwest. His PA-turned-CEO would become (in the phrase made popular by Malcolm Gladwell, about the joint founder of Apple, Steve Jobs) the most brilliant 'tweaker' in the history of the modern commercial airline industry. Where Tony was a 'visionary' and an 'inventor', O'Leary's genius was in taking someone else's idea and endlessly refining it, bringing energy and vision again and again to the same narrow territory he had marked out for Ryanair. That would eventually bring the airline the kind of success that not even O'Leary himself envisaged. 'I do not propose that Ryanair will in ten years' time threaten every major airline in Europe,' he predicted in 1994. 'It will not.' In fact, the model would succeed beyond his or even Tony's most fanciful dreams.

Tony and his chief executive agreed that Southwest was the model for Ryanair to pursue. 'In Ryanair, you are king,' Tony would tell Kelleher later. Quite what the Southwest model meant, however, opened up a fissure between the two Ryanair men. Even as O'Leary was outlining his blueprint in the autumn of 1994, there were some sharp exchanges about how to interpret what Southwest represented for the Irish airline. 'Ryanair is not a "quality" product,' O'Leary wrote to Tony in September. They would 'get no return for style or elegance. We are the Woolworths of the industry.' Tony disagreed. 'I do not fully accept your reference that Ryanair is not a quality product,' he countered. 'More importantly I believe that Ryanair should become a quality product while offering the lowest possible fares.'

Over the years, this debate about the direction of Ryanair would become more embittered. For Tony, the Southwest example of 'amuse, surprise and entertain' dovetailed perfectly with his initial vision of the airline as offering low fares alongside 'a smiling face to the public'. O'Leary, on the other hand, quickly abandoned this ideal. 'I've driven way beyond the Southwest model,' he concedes, 'and it's much more efficient, much more aggressive on costs, much more aggressive with passengers, so what we've done every year since then is keep improving the model. While we were doing that, I would run into fights with Tony.' In essence, the battle was between whether Ryanair should be cheap and cheerful or just cheap.

These debates would simmer away as Tony began to emerge from the shadows at Ryanair. On a personal level, the year 1994 ended in great sorrow for him, with the death just before Christmas of his mother. The two had always remained close. Lily was a regular guest at Kilboy and often travelled around the world to join Tony at his various houses in the sunshine, particularly in Ibiza. At the height of her son's power and wealth at GPA, she had been one of the few people still able to give out to him. Tony had learnt the hard way, through a dressing-down in front of his driver, that sending a car to the airport to collect her was not the same thing as coming himself. It was not a mistake he would make twice. Tony would always bitterly regret that his mother had to witness his downfall at GPA without seeing him rebound through Ryanair.

Lily's funeral was itself a sad reminder of Tony's dramatic reversal of fortune. Ann Reihill, publisher of *Irish Arts Review*, attended the service with John Meagher and was shocked at how few people bothered to turn out. Only one GPA director showed up. Otherwise it was just family, including Mairéad, and friends. 'It was not a big funeral as he might have expected a year earlier,' she reflects. 'It was after the IPO and before Ryanair took off. He really seemed all alone.' Afterwards, she expressed her concerns to Meagher. 'No, he'll be all right,' he reassured her.

Meagher's judgement was right. Lily Ryan's funeral in many ways drew a line under a troubled and unhappy phase in Tony's life. As 1994 turned into 1995 he emerged once again into the public gaze with his spirit and confidence renewed. Since the foundation of Ryanair, Tony had always denied that he had any connection with the airline other than having provided capital for his sons. The formalities of that arrangement had saved him from losing the airline to his creditors. The reality, of course, had been different. It was no wonder that AIB Bank had been the most vociferous in protesting that Ryanair should be used to pay off Tony's personal debts, because there wasn't a person in Ireland who didn't know that he controlled the airline. Every Saturday when Tony was in the country, the key management team would traipse down to Kilboy to be grilled about the state of the company. He may not have been involved in its day-to-day operations, but the direction of strategy and appointment of personnel had been determined by him alone.

Now that his GPA fortune had been lost, Tony moved to formalise his role within the airline he had founded. In the past, Ryanair had been an expensive hobby. But now that he was no longer the all-powerful head of GPA it provided him with a certain status and an arena in which to expound his ideas.

Tony enjoyed the formalities of the board room and everything that went with it—but only when he was in charge. Committees he had joined in such organisations as Bank of Ireland and the National Gallery had only frustrated him. Those he chaired, such as GPA and the Hunt Museum, gave him considerable pleasure. He loved circulating memos in advance of meetings, correcting minutes, phoning round beforehand. Nothing irritated him more than when the formalities of a meeting were transgressed. Tardiness in giving notice of a meeting or in preparing paperwork was not tolerated. Being late for a meeting would often see the offender barred from the room. Management who failed to keep the board informed were given a dressing-down. All told, chairmanship was a sacerdotal function for Tony, not least at meetings of the board itself, when he would hear confession, give penance and, very occasionally, offer absolution.

The GPA failure meant that he no longer had any outlet for these pleasures. Therefore it came as no surprise when, in February 1995, Ryanair announced that he would be joining the board. Furthermore, Tony was appointed 'chairman-designate' and would take over from the outgoing chairman, the former Minister for Finance, Ray MacSharry, on 1 January 1996. In reality, he was already at the helm. In a nice touch that demonstrated the convoluted ownership arrangements of the airline, it was Declan Ryan who wrote to his father confirming the terms of his appointment as a non-executive director of Ryanair.

Inevitably the nature of Tony's relationship with the company dominated the media coverage that followed. 'Dr Ryan', reported the *Irish Times*, 'has always denied having any direct connection with Ryanair.' The airline itself stuck vigorously to that line. 'Dr Ryan has no equity in the company, and he has no intention of taking equity,' a spokesperson stated. His involvement had come about simply because 'he has more time on his hands' following the restructuring of GPA. Tony himself was also keen to point out that he would not be adopting any kind of 'hands-on approach'. Instead, he told the RTE Radio 1 evening news, 'the implementation of strategy will be for the management.'

Expectations that Tony would be running Ryanair were rife not only in the media: they were shared within the airline itself, not least by the chief executive. It was no coincidence that about this time Declan Ryan began to emerge as Tony's closest business confidant. In part his job was to keep an eye on O'Leary and clip his wings if he lost the run of himself. 'Overall, the airline's recent performance has been very good and I certainly am not throwing cold water on our results,' Declan warned everyone as Tony joined the board in April 1995, 'but it is quite easy for us to get somewhat "euphoric" about our position.'

In advance of Tony's appointment as incoming chairman, O'Leary had angered him with a memo setting out the chairman's role as he saw it. 'In your capacity as chairman, you have the potential to substantially improve, or equally substantially damage the larger controllable items here,' he warned, returning to his principal concern about Tony's vision for the airline. On cost reduction the 'mission is ruthless': 'low cost—no frills . . . at [the] expense of style, charm & elegance if necessary.' Tony had a role to play in reinforcing that line with the public through 'dealings with the press, speeches, appearances' in order to 'get [the] message across'. Obviously he also had a role in helping to 'determine medium term strategy.' Nevertheless, O'Leary warned, it was essential that there should be 'no distractions, no "coups".' The chairman had to have 'tunnel vision [in] pursuit of making money (profits and cash)'. O'Leary may have signed off with a jocular 'Over to you Mr Chairman!' but the real message had come earlier in the memo: 'Stick to the knitting.'

That was never going to be Tony's style. Instead he immediately embarked on an ambitious, eye-catching project that O'Leary thought was mad: a new commercial airport at Baldonnel, the site of a military airfield south-west of Dublin. On one very basic level the proposal was symptomatic of the geographical tie that Tony always retained to his native county: Baldonnel is beside the N7, the road to Tipperary. More importantly, it was about creating a new home for Ryanair away from Dublin Airport, which was dominated by the airline's rival, Aer Lingus, and run by what Tony saw as its creature, Aer Rianta.

The idea for developing Baldonnel was not new. In 1986 Fine Gael's spokesperson on transport and tourism, Gay Mitchell, had put forward a similar proposal as a means to 'relieve congestion' at Dublin Airport and help redevelop 'an unemployment black spot'. Although Fine Gael had been in office at the time, the idea failed to gain any momentum within the coalition Government. Subsequently a decision was made to expand capacity at Dublin Airport by building a second terminal.

By the time Tony took up the idea, in 1995, he hoped that circumstances might be more propitious. The Minister for Transport, Michael Lowry, was a fellow-Tipp man, and, although they weren't particularly close, Tony was essentially taking a Fine Gael idea to him. On 18 May, Tony received the pamphlet 'Dublin City Airport' and immediately despatched one to Lowry's house in Tipperary.

The concept was launched on Pat Kenny's show on RTE two days later and marked the beginning of a round of media interviews to drum up support for the idea. That fact alone demonstrated Tony's commitment to the project. Although he would very occasionally venture out onto the RTE News or give the odd interview to a journalist, Tony didn't like or seek the media spotlight. This meant he was often not the best advocate for his own ideas or projects, as had been seen during the run-up to the IPO in 1992, when journalists had observed how he bridled under questioning about the health of GPA. That Tony was now prepared to appear on a 'magazine' talk show with Kenny, who was bound to ask questions about how he had been affected by the GPA collapse, signalled to those who knew him well that Baldonnel, like Ryanair, was a project involving the heart as well as the head.

Tony handled the inevitable GPA questions with a lightness of touch that he rarely displayed when dealing with the media. He told how, after the failed flotation, he had gone to Spain to recover and had spent his time running up and down the beach to lose weight. 'Some asked later how much I lost,' he now joked, 'and I said, "Three hundred million dollars, and twenty pounds".'

Press reaction to the Baldonnel scheme was overwhelmingly positive. So too was opinion in the Baldonnel area. Tony commissioned Lansdowne Market Research to poll local people on the issue, and it showed that 80 per cent of those asked believed that the airport would bring new jobs into the area. Only 14 per cent opposed the idea, on the grounds of additional noise and traffic.

Tony bombarded ministers and TDs with brochures and personal letters. The Minister for Finance, Ruairí Quinn, replied encouragingly, 'I spoke to Declan [Ryan] about this', adding that he would 'be in touch with you soon'. A meeting with the minister followed in the Department of Finance in June. Hugh Coveney, the soon-to-be-demoted Minister for Defence, with oversight of the airfield, also confirmed that 'in principle, I think it's an excellent concept.'

Similarly, many in the business world sensed an opportunity. Michael Smurfit wrote to say that the project was 'very imaginative and one which I would support 100 per cent.' He promised to raise the matter 'when I meet with the ministers.' Tony was also able to tell the minister himself that he had been 'approached by a major Irish developer [Tom Roche, Snr, of CRH] who wished to invest in the project.'

Lowry suggested that Tony should meet Derek Keogh, chief executive of Aer Rianta, 'to endeavour to find a possible working relationship.' At that meeting Tony outlined how 'the Ryanair Group and its investors would build a larger passenger terminal at Baldonnel' than the proposed new terminal at Dublin Airport. The development would represent an estimated saving for the state of £300–400 million. There would be no disruption to Dublin Airport. The aim of the new venture would be to 'allow Ryanair to continue to offer low fares both to the UK and in the near future to the continent.'

Ryanair had long endured a testy relationship with Aer Rianta, but the meeting was surprisingly amicable, and Tony and Keogh agreed jointly to commission a British company familiar with airport development to carry out a feasibility study.

On 21 July, following a meeting at the Department of Transport, Lowry told Tony to investigate the physical and aeronautical feasibility of the project. His own department would 'address the fundamental issues . . . which the Baldonnel concept throws up', not least 'whether a second commercial airport for the Dublin area is necessary or desirable now or at any time in the future.'

Six months later the minister gave his answer by fax. After 'consulting my cabinet colleagues,' he wrote on 24 January, 'my conclusion is that the project would not be in the interests of the aviation sector and the economy generally.' He also enclosed his press release, which contended that Dublin Airport 'has the capacity to cater for traffic demand for several decades' and that 'views which have been expressed about an alleged high cost base at Dublin Airport are not borne out by recent independent studies.' Privately Tony was informed that the Department of Finance didn't want competition for Baldonnel.

Tony was incensed, retorting that

> Ryanair's concern is cost, and Dublin continues to be Ryanair's most expensive airport. Having an Aer Rianta monopoly at Irish airports is bad for aviation and tourism development. Ryanair must now fundamentally review its future to recognise that its growth will be restrained by this monopoly.

To Mary Harney, leader of the PDs and a supporter of the Baldonnel project, he wrote that 'the spurious arguments put up by the Government press office and in particular Aer Rianta are most irritating.' Harney issued her own press release warning that 'Ireland is in danger of losing Ryanair'. That was never going to be the case. Nevertheless, the decision would be part of a process that would see Ryanair move the base of its operations from Dublin to Stansted Airport, which soon provided the airline with its own new state-of-the-art terminal.

Tony never liked to let an idea rest and would return to the Baldonnel project again. 'I am beginning to believe the writings of Machiavelli,' he wrote, half amused, to one correspondent, as if he had ever doubted the Italian. Yet, for now, it was enough that he was back to his old self, on the charge once more after an unhappy period in embattled retreat. A profile in the *Irish Times* had noted that 'Mr Ryan seems mellower' after the experience of GPA. The *Sunday Tribune* got closer to the mark. Tony's Baldonnel project, it suggested that January, 'has grand sweep and is based on strong forecasts for airline passenger growth larded with a large helping of public relations.' That was 'typical of the man', it concluded. 'The grand vision explains the epic scale of his successes and his failures.'

Chapter 13 ~

IN THE LION'S DOMAIN

Dublin Airport, 2 February 1996

It must have been quite some sight. As early morning commuters rushed hither and thither inside the airport terminal, there at the Ryanair desk, check-in staff in Moorish attire greeted passengers for what was clearly not an ordinary flight. Irish consumers had become so used to Ryanair's witty advertising gimmicks that most commuters doubtless assumed that these elaborate costumes were part of yet another attention-grabbing stunt. Others might have noticed that all the passengers seemed to know each other, so perhaps it was some kind of corporate junket. In a way, they were right, for these gathering passengers were all members of a very particular club: the friends of Tony Ryan. And they were off to Marrakesh to celebrate his sixtieth birthday.

The themed events continued on board, as belly dancers emerged from the galley of the Ryanair jet to shimmy their way down the aisle. At the controls was Tony's son Cathal, who, once they were airborne, announced over the intercom that the flight had been diverted to Lagos due to bad weather. The destination was a joke, although the weather was not: thick fog around Marrakesh Airport made landing extremely difficult. Just as they were coming in, Cathal came back on to announce that Tony was now at the controls and that they should all start praying.

Marrakesh itself stubbornly refused to join in the celebratory mood. 'We had been told to bring our summer gear, because there will be swimming and so on, but when we got to Marrakesh it was more like Knock,' Ed Walsh recalls. 'So we had lunch in miserable rain and then got back on another three-and-a-half-hour flight back.'

Ann Reihill was another guest on the trip. 'It rained the whole time we were there,' she wryly concludes, 'so we might as well have been in Dublin at the Burlington Hotel.'

The weather may have been a disappointment, but the birthday trip to Marrakesh was in so many ways a return to form for Tony. This festive event was the kind of occasion the 'old', pre-IPO Tony might have put on—extravagant, brash and tongue-in-cheek. It was a sign to his friends and the wider world that the chutzpah was back, as well as being an indicator of what was financing it. Ryanair was Tony's airline; it was the key to the restoration of his fortunes. Now he didn't care who knew it.

If Tony's sixtieth birthday celebrations demonstrated that the exuberance had returned, that self-confidence also found an outlet in one of the most ambitious projects of his life. Over the years, initially encouraged by Miranda Guinness, Tony had taken a growing interest in architecture and the decorative arts. By the mid-1990s he had developed not only great enthusiasm but also considerable expertise, particularly in the eighteenth-century style.

'He had the most extraordinary eye,' says his friend the architect John Meagher, who noticed how these aspects had over the years come to matter the most to Tony. This was particularly the case during the unhappy period working for General Electric after the failed share offering for GPA. 'He adored the whole business of aircraft,' says Meagher, 'but he was just bored with pushing paper and money around the table. It is almost as if he felt . . . he wanted to build something. In many ways he was a frustrated architect, so he started looking for something to put his energy into in order to satisfy that.'

Another friend, Ken Rohan, who was on the board of the National Gallery, agrees with that assessment. 'It was part of Tony's bold character to use his wealth to engage in a huge project to restore a great house to how it would have been.'

The project that Tony settled on in 1996 was Lyons Demesne (predictably near the N7 road to Tipperary), the eighteenth-century residence of Lord Cloncurry, on the Dublin-Kildare border. The original house had been designed by Oliver Grace in the 1790s and was then considerably remodelled by Richard Morrison in the early nineteenth century. Among the glories of the house were the frescoes by the Italian painter Gaspare Gabrielli, whose landscapes formed part of what were generally considered to be the finest interiors of any residence in Ireland. The house was set in a glorious estate of about 600 acres, with formal gardens and rich, fertile land. The north-west of the estate was bounded by the Grand Canal. From the house, elegant lawns swept down to the spring-fed lake set against the imposing background of Lyons Hill. In the middle of the twentieth century this beautiful pastoral setting would inspire the English poet Sir John Betjeman to write an ode to the lake after staying at the house.

However, by the time the Ryan family bought the Lyons estate it had fallen into serious disrepair. For most of the previous thirty years it had been an outpost of the Faculty of Agriculture at University College, Dublin, whose farm was nearby. Laboratories had been set up in the grand reception rooms. Partitions had gone into the bedrooms. The grounds were overgrown. The most grievous wound was to the Gabrielli frescoes, which were covered with wallpaper paste and lining paper. 'When I bought Lyons Demesne in 1996, parts of it were in close to ruinous condition,' Tony wrote, 'yet it seemed to possess an indomitable spirit that challenged restoration or retreat. I chose the former.'

Tony now threw himself fearlessly into the mammoth project of reconstruction. He was involved in every stage of the meticulous process of restoration that took place, and he had a constant presence in the house as the work was being done. 'We encountered many surprises along the way,' Tony recalled, 'a myriad terrifying examples of decay or neglect, every now and again wonderfully relieved by discoveries such as that of the beautiful ceiling in the Family Room.' In addition to re-roofing and the replication of floors, window sashes and plasterwork, the restoration attempted to adapt the original structure to twentieth-century living. No detail was too small for attention: the rear elevation, remodelled in keeping with the period detail on the front façade, was constructed using the same mellow granite quarried from the original source near Blessington in Co. Wicklow. Tony was even said to have recruited the head gardener from Versailles to restore the grounds, much to the astonishment of his friend Seán Donlon, who had arranged a visit to France simply for Tony to look at the gardens.

Perhaps the greatest thrill of all for Tony came in furnishing the house. 'He was always engrossed in plans or a stack of catalogues from the leading auctioneers around the world,' remembers John Meagher. 'He would go through them meticulously and would mark what he thought the value was for the things he was interested in.' Tony's idea was to buy Irish furniture that had been sold over the years and had gone abroad. He brought items back and stored them in warehouses. Meagher recalls that

> the day he was going to move into Lyons, I remember him standing on the steps with a clipboard with about fifty pages on it. When something came out of a truck he'd say, 'What number is that? Okay, that's a gilt chair, and it goes on the right-hand side of the bed in the third bedroom on the second floor.' He knew every single thing. He knew where everything was going and had planned it all. It was amazing.

When the restoration was completed, Hugh Montgomery-Massingbird, the renowned expert on the 'Great House', judged that Tony had 'accomplished the largest, most ambitious and exhaustive programme of restoration ever undertaken in a private capacity in the history of the Irish state.'

Lyons Demesne would give pleasure to Tony for the rest of his life. Later he would redevelop the nearby village of Lyons, which had been burnt by English soldiers in 1641, with new houses, shops and restaurants. The small, ruined parish church dedicated to the

Blessed Virgin Mary was also redeveloped and in the end would be Tony's final resting place—a symbol of how much Lyons truly had become 'home'.

—

There would be one other major restoration project for Tony, although of a very different kind. Shortly after finishing Lyons Demesne he bought Castleton Farm in Lexington, Kentucky, amid the rolling savannas known as the Bluegrass. It was one of the world's great centres for the breeding of thoroughbred horses and in its own way was steeped in as much tradition as Lyons Demesne. Tony renamed the 1,200-acre estate Castleton Lyons to make the connection with the one in Co. Kildare.

He planted two thousand trees and renovated the many dilapidated outbuildings. A bridge was built across the lake, and nineteenth-century English ironwork gates set in Kentucky limestone were installed at the farm entrance. The Greek Revival mansion, built in 1841, was restored to its former elegance, with mahogany floors restained and plasterwork restored to the ceilings. Paintings and furnishings from Tony's collection in Ireland were brought to the United States, which combined to give the house a remarkable similarity to the interior of Lyons.

The interior of both houses had been designed by Tiggy Butler, with whom Tony had at one stage been romantically involved.

One of the most striking aspects of Tony's relationships was the way in which, more often than not, he was able to break them off without any bad feeling on either side. Occasionally friends would hear stories about a messy exit, but most of the time Tony managed to retain a friendship with those he loved. After Tony's funeral, in 2007, Denis O'Brien recalls hosting a dinner for Martine Head, Tony's partner when he died, and his 'exes' Miranda Guinness and Louise Kennedy. 'They were telling mad stories, because it had all been in Tony's character,' he says. 'Of course he had been very difficult, but somehow he managed to leave them all still loving him anyway.'

Meshing these relationships into family life could sometimes be tricky, particularly with the feelings of Tony's estranged wife, Mairéad, to be considered. Yet, for much of the time, life simply went on, and everyone seems to have muddled along. Cathal Ryan's son, Cillian, for example, remembers happy times at Christmas as a child down in Kilboy, opening presents alongside the children of Miranda Guinness. Ireland itself was going through a quiet social revolution, and the realities of second relationships applied as much behind the walls of Kilboy and Lyons as they did anywhere else in the country.

Friends noticed that those realities, particularly when Tony was between relationships, could at times leave him lonely and prone to bouts of depression. 'When he started living at Lyons,' says Seán Donlon, 'if I was driving back from Dublin I'd phone him and say, "Tony, I'll be passing near Lyons in half an hour." And sometimes he was there and sometimes not, but a lot of the time—and people should never underestimate this—he was lonely.'

Michael O'Leary has a different view. 'Tony was very mercurial,' he says, 'and people like that, who are geniuses, they must have long nights of the soul. But Tony was never a depressive: he was a fighter. The easiest thing at this stage in his life would have been to roll over and die, but he never, ever did that.'

Certainly as Tony got older he found it increasingly difficult to sleep, and he started taking medication. His friend and legal adviser, Fergus Armstrong, remembers going to Lyons on one occasion only to find Tony half exasperated, half amused. He hadn't slept at all the previous night. Having been advised to put up extra security gates not long beforehand, he had found himself locked behind a barrier and unable to get out to the car in which he had left a briefcase that contained his sleeping tablets. It was the ultimate image, Armstrong reflected, of a great tycoon trapped in his elaborate palace.

Donlon believes that it was always Tony's relationship with his sons that helped keep his head above water. 'He was close to his three boys all the time. They were his lifelong friends.'

Certainly it was true that when Tony's children, particularly Cathal and Declan, had been younger the family had not been his priority. He had been flying hundreds of thousands of miles every year in order to build up his business, and often the family was based on different continents. Amid such instability Tony's priority for his children had been to provide them with an outstanding education at Clongowes and to root them firmly in Ireland.

Yet, for all the separation this involved, outsiders like Donlon were often struck by the incredibly close relationship that Tony enjoyed with all three boys in adulthood. According to Gerry Power,

> you could argue that while Tony was at GPA and travelling all over the world . . . perhaps he neglected his family somewhat, because he was away all the time. But when he left Kilboy to go to Lyons, from then on he spent so much time with the three lads—a lot more, in fact, than when they were younger. They all got on really well together.

On one level Tony's loneliness and isolation might well have been exacerbated by the move to Co. Kildare, where he didn't have the deep roots and associations of Tipperary. Yet the crucial element for him was that his children had homes in Kildare and its neighbouring counties.

Friends noticed how each of the boys, in their different characters, seemed to reflect aspects of their father's own character. 'I overheard Tony say that once,' Power recalls. 'Somebody asked him about his children, and he said, "Well, Cathal is the playboy and real fun, Declan is the serious one with a magnificent heart, and Shane is the innocent".'

Where Tony had been tough as a father when they were younger, in later life he seemed genuinely happy to help establish his children in whatever fulfilled them. The CDS Trust would make each of them independently wealthy, but Tony's initial impetus in setting up that arrangement had been at least in part to give his boys something to build up and run themselves.

Declan inherited his father's entrepreneurial streak. They worked closely together on Ryanair, and Declan would eventually run Irelandia, the private investment vehicle of the Ryan family. When Cathal and Shane pursued other interests, Tony seemed unconcerned and instead set them up in following their passion for horses. Cathal managed Swordlestown stud farm in Co. Kildare, and Shane would run Castleton Lyons. It was made clear to all three brothers that their relationship with each other and with their father mattered more to him than almost anything else. 'He instilled in all of us the importance of family and how important good relations were,' Declan says. 'In the end he got very close to all of us.'

Another great bonus of the move to Lyons was that it was only ten miles or so from Clongowes Wood, where many of his grandchildren were studying. Tony seemed to take a genuine pleasure in his grandchildren and was uncharacteristically soft on them. 'I remember giving out to my son when he was ten or so,' remembers Declan, 'and Tony said to me, "You're being very harsh on him," and I thought to myself, Talk about the pot calling the kettle black!'

For that reason Tony's grandchildren adored him. Cathal's son, Cillian, says that he was

> far from a 'Werther's Original' granddad, but he knew the stuff that was important to you at five years old, or fifteen, or twenty-five. He grew with you. Sometimes, two months down the line, he would ask me about something I'd said and I would think, You have all this other stuff on your plate and yet you know what's important to me. It was touching, and that was how he built relationships with all of us. He knew what was going on in your life and was able to relate to it.

Cillian's sister, Danielle, agrees. 'He was always doing something, but he always found time to indulge us.'

Often those treats also gave Tony's grandchildren a real insight into his character. In March 1999 he helped the sixteen-year-old Cillian mitch from school to fly to New York to watch a world heavyweight title fight between Evander Holyfield and Lennox Lewis. They flew first class across the Atlantic and arrived at Madison Square Garden in good time, only to be told that their tickets were fake. Cillian recalls that he had

> never seen granddad in any kind of business meeting, but I got a glimpse of it when the guy said to get out of the line. Granddad just turned round to this huge monster of a man and said, 'Young man, I have flown all the way from Dublin to be here with my grandson—the last thing I would have done is buy a dodgy ticket. You have two choices: you can let me in, or I can make you let me in. Which is it going to be?' He stood his ground and, amazingly, the guy apologised and let us in.
>
> There was just such an assurance about him—so much confidence in the way that he did it. That always stuck in my mind, because he wasn't going to be intimidated by size or location or the matter in hand. It was a man who was saying, 'This is going to happen my way.' I was really impressed by that, and of course we then had a ball and always had that connection between us afterwards.

Conor Ryan, Declan's eldest son, has similar memories and recalls being struck by the informality that Tony cultivated with his grandchildren.

> Staying with him was great, because you did all the things you wouldn't be allowed to do at home. There were no boring, posh restaurants: it was staying in and eating in front of the sport on the television. If we went out it was to Harry Ramsden's. He used to challenge us all to see if we could eat a whole 'big meal', which was absolutely huge.

As with Cillian, sport was the bond across the generations, and again the experience was telling for Conor.

> I'd have gone to the hurling with him. That was when you saw the real man—there was so much passion. If you're from Tipperary, then hurling is in your blood. But it was more than that: it was about the importance of remembering who you are and where you came from.

As Tony himself said, 'Hurling is a game that demands soul!' Declan Ryan believes that Tony was generous with the grand-children because he appreciated having a second chance. 'He'd not had enough time to spend with his own kids, but when the grandkids came along he had more time,' Declan says. 'So he really learnt that lesson.'

It might have been the moral for Tony's post-IPO life: the second time round he was going to stop and smell the roses.

Chapter 14

'RYANAIR IS TERRIFIC'

By the mid-1990s, having freed himself from the nightmare of personal debt that followed GPA's failed IPO, Tony Ryan was relishing spending more time with his family and indulging his passion for architecture and the decorative arts. But the desire to remake his mark—and money—in the world of business remained intense. His accession to the board of Ryanair as incoming chairman in 1995 was a signal that he was back in the game. The chairmanship may have been a non-executive role, but to Tony that simply meant a focus on strategy, without the aggravation of day-to-day operations. Intellectually and emotionally, as the majority owner, he was more committed than ever to making a success of the airline.

To announce his presence on the new board, Tony convened a gathering at Kilboy with Declan Ryan, Cathal Ryan and Michael O'Leary, and circulated an *aide-mémoire* to fellow-directors in advance of his first meeting in March 1995. 'Ryanair is terrific' ran the subject line. It was a blueprint—or a command—for how he expected the airline to conduct itself. 'I set out hereunder random thoughts as to how to raise the profile of Ryanair and convince the public that the airline offers true quality travel and value,' it began. 'After many years of negative rumours—old aircraft, Romanian pilots, poor punctuality, unacceptable service, bad manners from handling agents together with serious questions on its financial viability—Ryanair needs to address its branding and project the airline as it is managed today.' Obviously, 'cost cutting is of paramount importance'. However, 'a lean, well organised company' also had to 'command respect and gain the confidence of the traveller'. That meant such priorities as 'safety, value, cleanliness, friendliness, punctuality'. Ryanair had to get itself 'a smart image'. This would require 'a concentrated effort by everyone' at the airline. 'I believe Ryanair is terrific,' he concluded, but 'we must make the public believe that Ryanair is terrific.' One way to do that was to become the airline that 'again carries a little humour'. For Tony that was a return to the theme that had been present from the outset: Ryanair had to show its customers a smiling, cheerful face.

As well as striving to impress customers, Tony was hopeful that the airline might now attract a suitor. In 1990 the senior management team had engaged in talks with British Airways about a possible investment, and when the issue came up once again, in an informal conversation between Tony and the new BA chairman, Lord Marshall, the process began again.

Declan Ryan was frankly sceptical about BA's intentions. 'Unfortunately I believe BA will show interest', he warned in April 1995, 'but will not take any action.'

Nevertheless, talks began in earnest that month, with Tony indicating that the Ryan family 'would be open to accepting an offer from BA', adding that there was 'the real possibility of taking the airline [Ryanair] public in a year or two.'

After nine months of negotiation, BA announced that it had reached a 'firm view' to invest. Then, as Declan Ryan had predicted, the deal began to unravel. Tony reported that BA's chief executive, Bob Ayling, frankly admitted at a one-on-one meeting that he was 'nervous' of Tony's 'negotiation reputation'. It was the prelude to a messy tussle, inevitably about money. Tony wrote to Ayling on 2 May: 'Unfortunately our teams have still not concluded all the commercial points but more vitally we still have not agreed on price.'

At the start of the negotiations, Tony had 'tentatively concurred' to sell 25 per cent of Ryanair to BA for £26 million, adding that 'the vendors would retain all cash as of date of completion.' That represented significant cash in hand for Tony and his family at a time when his personal reserves had been depleted by the failed

GPA flotation. However, as negotiations dragged on, Tony began to accuse BA of attempting to erode Ryanair's position, in effect of devaluing its worth. Tony told Ayling he had 'deliberately but reluctantly stayed clear of the negotiations and minutiae of contracts' but was 'unhappy to note your negotiating team's efforts to downstate all our profits going forward.' In all, he believed that BA had reduced the value of the business by £40–50 million. 'Quite simply,' Declan Ryan told the BA negotiators, 'we are not prepared to concede any further in this area.'

On 26 May, Tony wrote to Ayling to bring discussions to an end, noting that 'our position was being further eroded as the negotiations progressed.' At the end of the day, Ryanair negotiators had found BA peremptory and arrogant in its belief that Ryanair was to be seen as a dodgy upstart that needed to be subsumed into the BA global empire. As Declan told their negotiators, 'perhaps our fundamental understandings of the deal were different from the outset.'

If the mutual misunderstanding needed a symbol it was surely the glossary of terms BA felt it necessary to provide on its flights across the Atlantic for passengers watching *The Commitments,* set in working-class Dublin. Tony kept it in his briefcase thereafter.

Tony was disappointed when the BA deal collapsed, not only because it would have netted him a large cash payment but also because of the lost brand and credibility. Nevertheless he was undeterred in his strategy. Ryanair's position 'has not fundamentally changed', he wrote after talks with BA concluded. 'Our preferred option is to divest of a significant portion of equity and align the airline with a strategic partner.'

Indeed that strategy was already under way. While Tony had been negotiating with BA, he was simultaneously engaged in talks with its biggest competitor, Virgin. At the end of 1995 David Bonderman, a founding partner of Texas Pacific Group and a legend on Wall Street, met Declan Ryan to propose a 51 per cent takeover of Ryanair. 'We would contemplate that the new controlling shareholders would be a group led by Richard Branson [of Virgin] and ourselves,' Bonderman confirmed afterwards to Tony. 'The game plan going forward would be to change the name of the airline to use the Virgin brand and expand into continental Europe while retaining as much of the existing cost structure, method of operations and management as possible.'

In January 1996, as talks rambled on with BA, Michael O'Leary met representatives of the TPG consortium to discuss 'Project Virgo'. At the end of the meeting Jeremy Ferris of TPG sought to 'establish a schedule of action from here'. His idea was that they should 'do a selling job' on Virgin to 'get [them] comfortable' with the idea of dealing with Ryanair. The fly in the ointment, O'Leary reported back to Tony, was that, while Bonderman 'wants to do this deal', Branson and Virgin were 'highly distrustful of TAR'. There was 'still a nervousness towards the *Ryan factor*' after the GPA debacle. O'Leary's strategy was to 'play down the Ryan involvement quite heavily at the meeting, explaining that the airline was run by the management with no interference from the family for the past five years, and emphasising that the family had been fully supportive of the low-cost, no-frills policy at every stage over the past five years.'

It was a clever, if patently misleading, tack, but the exchange sowed the seed in O'Leary's mind that Tony's reputation was irreparably damaged in Britain. That sense was confirmed when the talks with Virgin, like those with BA, collapsed amid a general sense that Tony and Ryanair were too tricky as potential partners. 'Even more,' Declan Ryan suggests, 'they just didn't believe Ryanair could be a success.'

The tenor of the cross-channel relationship was neatly captured the following year in a fax O'Leary received from Branson taking him to task for saying his airline Virgin Express was losing money. 'Dear Michael,' it said. 'Bollocks! Kind Regards, Richard.' When Tony saw the fax, he immediately fired one back in kind. 'Dear Richard, The correct spelling is *Bollix*. Warmest regards, Tony.' The fax was accompanied by a cutting from the *Times* (London) reporting on a new dictionary of Irish slang in which the word 'bollix' had been highlighted. It was yet one more example of Anglo-Irish misunderstanding.

That sense of cultural dissonance had forcefully struck Bonderman, one of the principal actors in the failed Ryanair-Virgin talks.

> I suppose we should have known the thousand years of history. The British and the Irish sides did not get along swimmingly in the context of this deal. I never discussed their actual thoughts, but it was clear that the British thought the Irish were a bunch of hayseeds and the Irish thought the British were a bunch of snobs, so they were not going to get along together in any respect. Branson and the Irish seemed not to stand each other. The whole deal fell apart and nothing happened.

Declan Ryan remembers that at the first Ryanair board meeting with the TPG directors Bonderman 'asked us about the different use of the word "bollocks". We told him there were at least six different uses, with the most positive being "the dog's bollocks". The Americans were in stitches of laughter with that definition!'

While Branson may not have seemed to like Tony and Ryanair, Bonderman certainly did—and not just for the humour.

> We thought it was an interesting business model. It was small and it was rapidly growing, which is the right time to buy into something, when it's just starting. So when Tony called me up and said, 'There's a new game plan. Would you be interested in a minority investment?' I said I would be interested in that under certain circumstances.

Those circumstances were that 'we had to have some influence over what happened.'

In effect, the conversation with Bonderman was the moment Tony let go of Ryanair. 'Because of GPA, the airline could not go public with Tony,' Bonderman recalls. 'As a result, the deal was that I would become chairman and would take the company public.'

Afterwards, rumours circulated that Tony was ousted from the Ryanair chairmanship against his will. Bonderman flatly contradicts that assessment.

> Tony was a shrewd, smart guy. He absolutely understood that he couldn't be seen to be in control of the shareholding and be chairman if Ryanair was going public. That's why he was interested in doing this deal. He called me up and said, 'You become chairman and the public face of the company going public.'

Any resentment Tony felt seems to have been directed not against Bonderman but against O'Leary. Tony had initiated the move to step away from the chairmanship. However, he didn't take kindly to O'Leary's suggestion that he should leave the board altogether. 'We needed to get rid of the Ryans,' O'Leary says, 'or at least downplay Tony and the rest of the Ryan influence, if we were going to seriously float the company on the London Stock Exchange. It was only a few years from the GPA mess, so Tony can't float it. You have to take the Ryans down.'

Declan Ryan remembers events differently, pointing out that, aside from the family being majority shareholders, Tony had full support from the new chairman. Bonderman says the spat between Tony and O'Leary was just like a 'father-and-son situation, where the father is still in charge and the son is trying to come out on his own.' Ultimately Bonderman thought Ryanair needed both men, because even if 'they fought like cats and dogs' the pair remained 'a great combination'.

Tony stayed on the board, but friends knew he had been personally wounded by O'Leary's attempt to oust him. 'Tony was quite hurt,' judges Denis O'Brien, 'but he put it to one side, which was very unusual for him.'

Only occasionally did friends get a hint of what lay beneath. There had been 'traumatic times when your support was critical for one's sanity,' Tony wrote at about this time to Gerry McEvoy, his friend and personal accountant. 'There have also been dark and awkward moments in the life of Ryanair.'

In retrospect, O'Leary regrets the tension that developed between him and Tony. Echoing Bonderman, he says:

> We were fighting like cats and dogs, and, to be fair to him, I would say I was an odious little jerk, because I wanted to get rich. Tony was older—more mature—and wanted to give me my head a lot of the time, because I was delivering the goods. But he wished I would tone it down a bit, and he was probably right in that respect too.

O'Leary also understands something of the personal cost for Tony at about this time.

> It was tough for him, because he deserved a lot of the credit for Ryanair. It wouldn't have been there if he had followed my advice and shut it down. But he wasn't going to get any of the credit for it—the great success, the comeback and the rest. He had to bite his lip. As it turned out, he was happy to take the money.

The first part of that process of 'taking the money' came in August 1996, when a complex deal was signed with Bonderman, bringing in his colleagues Rick Schifter and Jeff Shaw. It saw their Irish Air LP consortium take a 20 per cent holding in Ryanair. The sale valued the privately owned airline at £56 million. The Ryan family were left with 62 per cent ownership and more than £50 million in cash. O'Leary had an 18 per cent holding.

Informal talks with bankers in London, New York, Los Angeles and Dublin drew a 'positive' response to Tony's decision to divest himself of 20 per cent of his shareholding. That mood was further enhanced when, at a board meeting three months later, Tony enacted the deal he had struck with Bonderman. 'In light of the decision to proceed with the IPO,' the minutes recorded, Tony felt 'the timing was now appropriate for him to resign his position as Chairman.' He also indicated that he intended 'to continue as a director of Ryanair and would continue to contribute to the development of Ryanair.' To emphasise the sense of an elegant handover, Declan Ryan formally proposed Bonderman as the new non-executive chairman of Ryanair.

'I have made my contribution,' Tony told the press afterwards, 'and I think it right, at the age of sixty, to draw a line beneath it and hand over to another generation.'

From the moment Bonderman and TPG joined the board, the strategic focus shifted to bringing Ryanair successfully to the market. A significant aspect of that process, as papers presented to the board freely conceded, was to determine 'what is to be our public stance on the extent of the Ryan family involvement in the airline.' Certainly it was true that a difficult legacy remained, particularly in London, from Tony's part in the GPA debacle.

In talks with potential investors, Bonderman was quite open about the negative factors surrounding Tony's previous failure with a share offering, noting the 'hangover' from GPA. However, the remedy was not as simple as locking Tony away. As the 'Preparation for Flotation' briefing note for the board pointed out, 'it is important that the Ryan family remain closely associated with the project. At present, it is clear that the family is giving substantial support and it would be highly desirable that this profile be maintained up to and post the initial launch.' The reasoning for this approach was straightforward: 'There could be suggestions that the public launch is to provide an exit mechanism for the exiting shareholders in the short term. In summary, the Ryan family should remain identified with the project for the foreseeable future.'

Such was the delicacy of the 'Tony question' for the flotation that an entire PR brief was drawn up to deal with the inevitable questions from the press. The emphasis would be put on how the family had a 'strong commitment to remain private and low key'. With a 'new strong independent management team now in place... the family's position is predominantly that of shareholders.' In that function they remained 'dedicated and supportive'. There would also be an emphasis on the fact that 'the family has invested up to £20m from 1985 into the group.'

Perhaps the most significant piece of information in the 'strictly confidential' brief was that the family's shareholding in Ryanair 'will be reduced to under 50% and may continue to decrease over time.' Tony was now on the brink of giving up ownership of the airline he had founded just over a decade earlier.

In the end, too, it was Tony who gave Ryanair the answer to overcoming any negatives surrounding his own public image. To stop potential investors and the media thinking about Tony, he advised the board, they had to focus on someone else. 'Going into the IPO, the company needs a "Mr Ryanair",' he said, going on to identify O'Leary as the man for the task. Bonderman agreed. Thus it was that the hitherto publicity-shy chief executive of Ryanair was thrust out in front of the cameras. It was, says O'Leary, the start of 'all the cheap PR stunts'.

In many ways O'Leary was the perfect fit for Bonderman's strategy for taking Ryanair public in the spring of 1997. His idea, critical for the roadshows, was to promote Ryanair as the Southwest Airlines of Europe: a low-cost, no-frills carrier on the verge of doing for European aviation what Herb Kelleher's outfit had done in the United States. 'Come and join the party while it's still so cheap,' was Bonderman's basic message to investors. Given that O'Leary was a 'true believer' in the Southwest gospel, he conveyed utter sincerity in his appearances in front of the media and investors at roadshows throughout Britain, Europe and the United States.

Tony understood that he had to remain in the background throughout the flotation process for Ryanair. Yet, however hard he and those around him tried to keep him off stage, he inevitably found his name and reputation thrust back into the limelight.

On at least one level this attention was the result of jaw-droppingly bad timing. In February 1997, as news emerged that Ryanair had appointed the giant American investment bank Morgan Stanley to lead the Ryanair flotation, the Ryan family found themselves engulfed by public scandal. Michelle Rocca, the mother of Cathal's daughter Claudia, took Cathal to court over an alleged assault. Tony was visibly distressed by the circumstances of the case, which Rocca won, not least because he had always been so tenacious in guarding the privacy of his family.

Yet he had been no less determined when it came to keeping prying eyes away from the Ryan family's airline. As a private company, there had been very little obligation to make much more than basic information available to the public; but as a company about to float, a bright light was now shone into every corner of Ryanair. The result was a commotion that, in its own way, was every bit as intense as the Rocca scandal.

When the company's pathfinder prospectus was launched in May 1997, media attention instantly honed in on pay and bonuses. Tony had stuck to the deal he had negotiated when O'Leary became chief executive. The prospectus revealed that the Executive Directors Performance Incentive Bonus Programme had paid O'Leary, for example, approximately £17 million in the previous three years.

Reaction even among business correspondents was one of astonishment. 'O'Leary is living proof that nothing motivates the human spirit more than naked greed,' judged the *Sunday Times*. 'The greed that permeates the Ryanair boardroom is in danger of giving capitalism a bad name.'

To many the prospectus seemed to point to exactly the kind of excess that had been at the heart of the GPA collapse five years earlier. Furthermore, the revelation of profits showed that the company had been far better off than it had told its staff, whose salaries had been cut by an average of about 25 per cent since 1993. That new information brought with it the threat of industrial action. 'There will be a feeling that Ryanair's best days are behind it,' the *Sunday Times* gloomily predicted. This seemed exactly 'the type of negative publicity that punctured Tony Ryan's attempted £1 billion flotation of GPA in 1992. Investors who decide to catch this flight should keep their seat belts tightened.'

To make matters even worse, that May also saw investors spooked by the rattling of a skeleton in the Ryanair cupboard. The former chief executive Eugene O'Neill had already settled his claim for wrongful dismissal in 1993. His case was that Tony had used his influence to prevent Ryanair filing a complaint with the European Commission against Aer Lingus for abusing its dominant position in the Irish aviation market. The failure to file the complaint, O'Neill said, had cost Ryanair and its shareholders £23 million. O'Neill believed he had been made a scapegoat for the financial difficulties that followed for Ryanair. Now he chose the eve of the flotation to reopen his claim, in which he tried to institute proceedings against Ryanair and Tony personally. In the end the claim would go nowhere, but at the time, as one correspondent noted, it meant that 'potential investors were further unnerved'.

The inopportune coming together of scandal, past resentments and claims of greed had all the hallmarks of a looming disaster of the kind that had taken GPA down in 1992—a point the press were only too happy to repeat time and again. That hostile environment more than confirmed the wisdom of Tony's decision to step back from the flotation by handing the chairmanship to David Bonderman. Tony would have found it almost impossible to present a case that separated Ryanair from GPA. Bonderman had no such trouble. Indeed, from the olympian position he held among investors on Wall Street, his simple pitch to them was, in effect, 'Trust me.'

It was a coolly executed play. Bonderman used his good working relationship with Morgan Stanley to have the bank underwrite the IPO, which in turn convinced the Investment Bank of Ireland to sign on. When it became clear that journalists and advisers in London had been unable to move beyond the GPA 'hangover', Bonderman simply bypassed them by not listing on the FTSE at all. The City of London, he said disdainfully, lacked sufficient understanding of the low-cost, no-frills philosophy of the airline. The IPO was instead listed in Dublin and New York.

'Ryanair is right,' judged the *Observer*. 'London is clearly not prepared to take a leap of faith ... What they really cannot get over, of course, is the fact that Ryanair is part-owned by Tony Ryan, whose planned flotation of his leasing business, Guinness Peat Aviation, was aborted so spectacularly.'

In the end Tony had no need to worry. There would be no repeat of history. On 30 May 1997 Ryanair was simultaneously launched on the Dublin Stock Exchange and the NASDAQ in New York. The result was a triumph. Shares in the airline were more than eighteen times oversubscribed at 195 p. Even before the IPO was launched, dealers were quoting a 'grey market' price of 300 p for shares. That latter price valued the company at IR£477 million. In the United States the *New York Times* reported that shares in Ryanair 'soared in their first day of United States trading as investors clamored for a piece of the company, an Irish no-frills airline.' By the end of business in New York, shares had closed at $25.50, sharply higher than the offering price of $14.734.

For Tony and his three sons it meant that they had made more than £40 million from the launch price while retaining a 35 per cent shareholding in a company now estimated to be worth £166 million—and that figure would turn out to be a conservative valuation.

Tony was exultant in the aftermath of the flotation. Before heading out to a party with the Ryanair staff at the Coachman's Inn, near Dublin Airport, he faxed his congratulations to O'Leary. 'A remarkable triumph!' Tony proclaimed, with all lingering irritation now put to one side. 'I send my congratulations and thanks.' In response to a warm note of congratulation from Dermot Desmond, Tony said he was 'chuffed with the market reaction'. To P. J. McGoldrick, the former Ryanair chief executive who had done so much to pull the company back from the brink, he reported that 'as you will have guessed, all of us are overjoyed at the result.'

Yet even amid the triumph there were still lingering thoughts about the previous failure—what Tony described to Richard O'Toole, a former GPA company secretary, as his 'dog hell days'. Despite having gained a new fortune, Tony believed that 'Goldman Sachs treatment of GPA was criminal', and he could neither forgive nor forget it.

Of all the correspondence that poured into Lyons following the flotation, none was more poignant than the fax of a handwritten note that Tony received from Christy Ryan. 'Congratulations on the outstanding introduction of Ryan Air to the stock markets.'

Christy had been Tony's oldest pal. Now Tony was on his way to vast riches once again, while Christy, beset with personal demons, was left with almost nothing, save the regular generosity of his friend. It was a brutal reminder, if one were needed, that in the Darwinian world of business the line between success and failure is a fine one—and that for every Tony Ryan there were Christy Ryans at ten a penny.

Chapter 15

A PLACE BETTER THAN LYONS

In the days after the successful flotation of Ryanair there was a palpable sense of redemption, not to mention *schadenfreude*, for Tony Ryan. 'It isn't often that you have to feel sorry for American investment banks,' pointed out the *Sunday Times*, 'but there must be a few Merrill Lynch bankers who are unable to read the newspapers just now without their blood boiling.' Tony had never been shy in expressing his contempt for Wall Street. He blamed bankers for the failure of the GPA flotation that had almost ruined him. Merrill Lynch had attempted to grab Ryanair to recoup a $35 million debt. In the end it had given up, accepting a loss of more than $30 million. How must Merrill Lynch feel, asked the newspaper, now that it was 'left with a written-off loan and Ryan's family can keep their millions'?

At the age of sixty-one, Tony had regained a fortune and restored his reputation for having the Midas touch. Yet even amid the celebrations and congratulations, he experienced an odd sense of anti-climax. For the first time in almost a quarter of a century Tony was no longer the Top Man. From the mid-1970s onwards he had been the undisputed boss of GPA, and even when that company fell apart he still had Ryanair. He might have taken a back seat in the day-to-day running of that company, but its strategy and direction had been controlled from his office. Even in the year leading up to the flotation, when he had taken a tactical step back into the shadows, he remained the majority shareholder and owner of Ryanair. That changed in May 1997 when the company floated. Although the Ryan family was still the largest single shareholder, it no longer held a majority. The airline still bore Tony's name; but he could no longer call Ryanair his own.

Playing second fiddle on a board was never a role that suited Tony, and there was no reason why Ryanair should be the exception, not least because he had been concertmaster for so long. In particular the sense of irritation that had been growing with his former protégé Michael O'Leary, the Ryanair chief executive, now threatened to spin out of control.

Just weeks after the flotation, Tony wrote to the Ryanair chairman, David Bonderman, attempting to insert himself in the policy and strategy-making process. He complained bitterly about the 'dearth of Ryanair board meetings' and suggested 'a review of the company and discussion of the airline's short term strategy game plan.' He was particularly concerned about the fact that passengers were not being given enough respect.

'Currently we are treating our customers poorly,' Tony complained to Bonderman and O'Leary. 'Fine in a good market but very dangerous as our competition strengthens. More importantly, a positive change of attitude to our passengers does not necessarily cost money. We are playing Russian roulette at times with our cavalier attitude with our image.' Then, in an attack on O'Leary, he charged that the airline needed a public face, one able to 'create a less aggressive and more caring image.' It was the start of a rift with O'Leary that would last for the remainder of Tony's involvement with Ryanair. 'We would fight like cats and dogs,' says O'Leary again, 'because I kept pushing to be more aggressive—more PR stunts and all that. Tony wouldn't like that.'

The sense of frustration that the Ryans felt about O'Leary's 'aggressive' strategy for Ryanair was captured in a memorandum by Declan Ryan in 1998. He expressed himself 'disappointed but not surprised' that the most recent strategic document produced by O'Leary 'did not cover the areas of customer service.' He pointed to the bad press that Ryanair had been getting on the topic. This included a phone-in on 'The Last Word' on Today FM, which, it was reported in the press, heard 'a litany of complaints about the service provided by Ryanair and the attitude displayed by members of Ryanair towards customers.' It was 'indicative of how many people feel about Ryanair . . . being tough, uncompromising and unsympathetic, which is not that far from reality.'

'Let's try to avoid another heated debate on this issue,' Declan pleaded with O'Leary. 'As in previous discussion don't dismiss this note as a proposal to increase costs. It is in fact stating that we have gone too far and too cheap.'

He may as well have been talking to a brick wall. 'As is often the case,' Tony complained, 'Michael said yes and then did his own thing.'

Shortly afterwards the Ryans announced that they were reducing their holdings in Ryanair by a third, leaving them with a 17 per cent stake. It was the beginning of a gradual goodbye. Declan Ryan would eventually resign as a director of Ryanair in 2004. 'His considered decision does not surprise me,' Tony told Bonderman, 'but the ramifications are disturbing.' Later, Declan would simply say that 'the buzz from Ryanair was gone.'

Declan Ryan's resignation was the first of many steps that would lead to the Ryan family's withdrawal from Ryanair. Throughout 2003 and into early 2004 Tony continued to express 'concerns in relation to the airline'. He offered Lyons Demesne as a venue for a 'tiny group of directors' to thrash out the issues. In particular, Tony remained vexed by O'Leary. 'I am becoming more and more convinced that Michael's utterances are very negative for the company,' he complained to Bonderman in the summer of 2004. The note was accompanied by 'a recent expletive-full article on Michael in Ryanair (*Sunday Times*).'

Bonderman was not unsympathetic to these concerns, especially to that of convincing Declan Ryan to stay on the board. 'As to Michael, I am in agreement,' he admitted. 'I am working on it, but you know Michael!'

Looking back, Bonderman believes it was an irreconcilable difference of approach.

> Michael was and is concerned about costs, almost to the exclusion of anything else. Tony was much more concerned with image—the company's and his own. Michael didn't care about customer complaints. He dealt with them, but I think Tony thought you should run the business so well there shouldn't be complaints. Michael was happy with the 'cheap and cheerful' slogan of Ryanair. But if it was just cheap and not so cheerful, he didn't mind.

Matters came to a head in the autumn of 2004. After another vociferous complaint from Tony about O'Leary's behaviour, Bonderman sent an email saying he had spoken directly to O'Leary about the matter. 'David was a good referee,' concedes O'Leary, who had not taken kindly to being upbraided.

Bonderman had urged restraint. 'While Michael certainly is a man of strong viewpoints,' he reported back to Tony, 'I believe he did listen to us on a number of points, specifically including his use of language. Accordingly, I think we should press on and see how it goes.'

That approach was not good enough for Tony, who now had the bit between his teeth. 'I am really not sure if there is an improvement,' he replied. 'The fact that I write directly to you probably says it all. Michael does not want to listen.' Then he added ominously, 'I must therefore give my own position further thought.'

Tony wrote to Bonderman again on 1 October 2004. 'I have given my position further thought and have decided that I will resign with immediate effect. This decision I deeply regret as I am extraordinarily proud of the company and its management. I know it is the correct action for the Board.' In a gracious touch, Tony added a line of personal thanks. 'David, you have been a great friend of Ryanair and have steered the company in a most sophisticated manner. My family and I are indebted to you.'

Bonderman might have been glad to see an end to the fighting between the founder and the chief executive of Ryanair. Yet he fought hard to convince Tony to stay. He immediately phoned Lyons for a long conversation with Tony and at least stalled the decision by asking him not to do anything precipitate. As a gesture of good will, Tony agreed to take a week to think about it. 'Your phone call last evening is much appreciated,' he wrote to Bonderman by email.

A week later Tony went back to Bonderman to say he was resolved to go. O'Leary's behaviour had become unendurable. 'As per your request, I have given the question of my resignation considerable thought over the last few days,' he wrote on 7 October. 'The Chief Executive's lack of interest in Directors' views leaves me no alternative but to resign.' The email was copied to O'Leary.

Bonderman tried again to persuade Tony to stay, eventually convincing him on the grounds that his resignation would inevitably be presented as a lack of faith in the company.

'I am now concerned that my resignation may be misconstrued,' Tony conceded. In fact he would remain on the board until his death, in 2007, but in 2004 he effected his withdrawal in another, more concrete way. Earlier in the year Declan and Shane had disposed of shares worth €44 million, representing 0.8 per cent of the company. In the autumn Tony followed suit, selling half his remaining shareholding in the airline, raising €25 million in the process. That left him holding only 0.75 per cent of Ryanair, following an earlier sale in June 2002 that had raised €20 million. In total, Tony and his three sons had made about €500 million from Ryanair shares. They retained an interest estimated at a further €300 million, but the largest individual shareholder was now Michael O'Leary.

Tony's gradual withdrawal from Ryanair had been more profitable and elegant, and less traumatic, than his exit from GPA. Nevertheless it was an extended farewell that brought to an end the second of the two great entrepreneurial projects to which he had dedicated most of his business life.

This time round he had been left with multi-millions that would allow him to live out his retirement in luxury. He purchased a stake in the famous Bordeaux vineyard Château Lascombes and enjoyed beautiful properties at home and abroad, including

Castleton Lyons in Kentucky, a house in Ibiza, a fine apartment in Cadogan Square in London, and, primarily for the purposes of tax residency, another apartment in the luxury La Rocamar building in Monte Carlo. (In December 1997 he was lucky to escape an attack by intruders at his property in London. The incident only served to confirm his habitual dislike of city living.)

Indeed, in these years, friends often thought that he should have made even more of enjoying his great wealth. Denis O'Brien suggests that Tony was

> full of contradictions. He would pay a thousand euro for dinner, but then he would take a Ryanair flight down to Ibiza instead of using a private jet. I remember talking to J. P. McManus about it, and he said, 'Don't even think about what the jet costs, because you'll be in a box quick enough.' Tony didn't have that attitude.

Whatever Tony's riches, friends also noticed that his characteristic restlessness seemed undiminished. He remained fascinated by the aviation business and was always on the lookout for new opportunities. He tried to buy Milovice Airport in Prague to establish a low-cost hub in the centre of Europe. The deal eventually faltered when the Czech government refused to give him indemnities over the land. As a former military airport it might, for example, have been contaminated with radioactive material.

More profitable was an investment made in Singapore. In 2003 the family's investment vehicle, Irelandia, had taken a 14 per cent holding in Tiger Airways, a new no-frills airline offering low-cost fares to destinations including Malaysia, Indonesia, India, Thailand and Vietnam. Charlie Clifton, who had worked for Ryanair since the early days, when he was taken on as a sixteen-year-old, was put into Tiger Airways to set up the operation and find a chief executive. His new job also allowed him to get in a few jibes on Irelandia's behalf. Tiger Airways, Clifton informed the press, would certainly attempt to replicate the Ryanair model, but it would be very different in style from the operation run by O'Leary. 'Michael has a very personal way of doing business that might work down here, or people might be highly insulted by it,' he observed. 'If a potential candidate comes in cursing, roaring and shouting, that doesn't mean that they will get the job.'

Clifton had also worked on Tony's failed attempt to get a second airport for Dublin, at Baldonnel, so he was also able to dispense a cuff round the ear on that score too. The Singapore government would be building a new low-cost carrier terminal for €22 million in order to cope with the additional passengers it expected. The *Irish Times*, after a briefing from Clifton, reported that 'the Singapore government was surprised at the lack of such facilities in the Republic.' Soon enough the *Irish Times* was writing headlines about how 'Asia listens to roar of Ryan's Tiger Airways'. When Tiger Airways floated in 2010, Irelandia netted an estimated €40 million from the investment, repeating the trick of Ryanair in 1997.

Another start-up investment was even closer to Tony's heart. In 2006 he established a venture called RyanMex, which took a 49 per cent holding in a new Mexican low-cost airline, VivaAerobus. It was one of a long series of investments that Tony had made in Mexico. In the 1980s GPA had facilitated the privatisation of the national carrier, Aeroméxico, and leased aircraft to most of Mexico's airlines. GPA also had interest in a leisure company with holdings in major tourist hot spots. But Tony's commitment to the country went beyond business. 'People had very little idea how many pals he had down there,' Tony's friend John Meagher says. 'He absolutely adored Mexico.'

Years earlier Tony had bought a beautiful house, nicknamed 'Casa Paddy', in Careyes, on the Pacific coast, to which he would frequently bring friends and family on holiday, often for New Year. The billionaire financier Sir James Goldsmith lived next-door. In 1990 Tony's interest had even extended to accepting an invitation from the Mexican government to become Honorary Consul in Ireland. This led to one of his more bizarre encounters.

After a couple of years struggling to learn Spanish, Tony had taken himself off to an immersion school in Mexico to get to grips with the language. He arrived only to be confronted by Eamon Casey, the recently disgraced Bishop of Galway, who was learning Spanish in advance of being sent on a mission to Ecuador. Seán Donlon, who had been the Irish ambassador to Mexico, collected Tony afterwards. 'I greeted him warmly in the Camino Real Hotel and started to speak to him in Spanish,' Donlon recalls. 'And he said, "For feck's sake, shut up. I've been speaking English for two weeks with Eamon Casey!" Neither of them had learnt a word.'

Donlon was more impressed by Tony's knowledge and connections in Mexico than by his language skills. When he was secretary-general of the Department of Foreign Affairs, Donlon had worked closely with Tony on the case of the former president of Mexico, Carlos Salinas, who was dogged by allegations of corruption. Donlon recalls that Salinas

> had moved to the United States, but the Americans said we would be doing them a favour if we gave him asylum, because they didn't want him in the States, or the embarrassment of a messy extradition case. So Tony was involved, and it was all done very gently. It showed that his contacts in Mexico were superb. I had been ambassador to Mexico, but Tony in fact had far more high-level contacts in Mexico than I had.

In 2004 the Mexican government awarded Tony the Order of the Aztec Eagle—the highest decoration that could be presented to a foreigner—for his outstanding service in strengthening ties between Mexico and Ireland.

As well as exploring investment opportunities with start-up businesses, Tony was also prodded to think, reluctantly at first, about his legacy and the future of entrepreneurship in Ireland. Early 21st-century Ireland was still riding the Celtic Tiger hard. Money was being made hand over fist, driven by easy credit and a property bubble. Where previous generations had aspired to be writers and poets, or to have the safety and respectability of employment in public service, a new generation now wanted to be entrepreneurs and property developers. Universities and colleges were happy to cash in on the trend, creating courses that taught young tigers how to make their fortune. Tony, however, thought that the whole notion was BS until his sons and an old friend changed his mind.

It was Declan Ryan who had phoned Ed Walsh of the University of Limerick to say, 'Shane, Cathal and myself want to do something in education to recognise Tony.' Walsh soon approached Tony and told him he was heading over to the Massachusetts Institute of Technology, one of the finest colleges in the world. Would Tony like to join him to have a look? Tony agreed to go, apparently looking forward to mischief-making at an institution he knew would be hoping to extract an endowment. Sure enough, as soon as Tony arrived he started behaving badly. 'Come on, let's leave this fecking place,' he told Walsh after the first dinner. 'We'll go to Israel, where they know something about entrepreneurship.'

Ken Morse, head of the MIT Entrepreneurship Center, was having none of it. 'Ryan, you're an old-fashioned entrepreneur,' he told him, playfully grabbing Tony's lapels. 'You're badly educated, and if you were trying to start now, you wouldn't succeed. Be here for the breakfast meeting at 8 a.m. and you'll see why.' It was a risky strategy but one better suited to Tony's instinctive dislike of sycophancy.

When Tony turned up next morning, he found himself at a table with a group of twenty-somethings who had come to do an intensive one-week course on venture capitalism. Walsh recalls that they

> all looked as if they had just done their Leaving Cert, so Tony said, 'What are you lads?' expecting that he'd pick them off. By the time he got round the table he discovered that all of them had already launched successful companies and had such wealth

that they wanted to know what to do with it. So Tony started paying attention. He really liked them, because they were his kind of people.

What Tony soon discovered was that his new friends were MIT graduates who, whatever their principal subject might have been, had all taken modules in entrepreneurship. By the time Tony was half way through listening to his first lecture, Walsh remembers, 'he was writing things down!'

The climax of the day came in a back-and-forth exchange with Morse in front of four hundred MIT students. Tony was entranced by the whole experience. As he came away he turned to Walsh and said, with all the conviction of a convert, 'I want a Ryan Academy!'

Tony threw himself into the new venture with characteristic gusto. He persuaded Walsh to act as pioneer. Tony and the family would donate €7 million to establishing the academy in the new digital park at Citywest, under the auspices of Dublin City University. When the DCU Ryan Academy of Entrepreneurship was established, in 2005, Tony committed another €10 million as a seed fund for start-ups developed by students.

His involvement was more than financial. In particular he took a great interest in the architectural aspects of the scheme. John Meagher was engaged to oversee the project, although that turned out to be a mixed blessing for him. 'He drove me completely mad over the Ryan Academy,' Meagher recalls. The 10,000 square foot glass-and-titanium building was very contemporary in design, with plans for an impressive granite entrance. Tony, however, wanted something more traditional, including a classical portico at the front. Meagher refused point blank.

At a meeting with the DCU advisory board in the Orangery at Lyons, Tony attempted to browbeat his friend into submission. 'Don't worry, John will change it,' he told the university president, Ferdinand von Prondzynski. Meagher refused to give ground, saying, 'We've discussed this—the answer is no.' When Tony came back at him again, Meagher simply stood up and left the meeting. 'I was upset with myself for having a go at him in front of all the board, and I was upset because he was winding me up,' Meagher recalls.

Tony knew immediately that he had overstepped the mark. As Meagher arrived at the ancient wooden front door of Lyons he felt a hand on his shoulder. 'I'm sorry, okay?' Tony said. 'Just do it the way you want.' Without waiting for a response, Tony turned and went back to the meeting. It was a rare example of him climbing down in front of others and a testament to the depth of feeling he had for the friendship.

Although Tony had taken some persuading about the Ryan Academy, it was in many ways an obvious project for him. His next scheme, however, caught everyone off guard. With its long tradition of emigration to the United States, Ireland had been deeply affected by the terrorist attacks in New York in 2001. There was even a national day of mourning held, with schools, offices and shops closing throughout the country. Tony was horrified by images of the planes he loved so much being used to wreak death and destruction. Though he had travelled throughout the world, he realised he knew little about Islam. Always an avid reader, he began to immerse himself in its history and culture. His friends and family were used to these spurts of interest in whatever captured his imagination at any given moment. Sometimes, as with his passion for architecture and the decorative arts, they went somewhere. At other times, such as when he bought the house from the film *Ryan's Daughter,* they were nothing more than whims.

But on this occasion Tony surpassed himself in audacity. In the middle of 2005, with controversy still raging over the war in Iraq, he phoned his friend Seán Donlon with a bold suggestion: he wanted to create a foundation to help build bridges between Islam and Christianity. Astonishingly he was willing to donate Lyons Demesne, then worth more than €100 million, to house the foundation. And he wanted the former US president Bill Clinton and the sitting British Prime Minister, Tony Blair, to head it.

Donlon reflects that it was

> in some ways the most unexpected project, because it had no commercial interest. But Tony was always a big thinker. He never thought in terms of little things—he always had grand ideas. He was probably the most international of Irish people that I ever worked with, including those like Garret FitzGerald, Tony O'Reilly and Michael Smurfit, all of whom were very internationally focused. But Tony was not only internationally focused: he saw a big picture always. Now, towards the end of his life, he wanted to leave some sort of contribution to peace.

Just as Walsh had been the right choice to steer through the Ryan Academy, Donlon was the best man to spearhead the faith foundation. Once he had got over his surprise at this 'most improbable turn', Donlon turned his mind and his years of experience to the task in hand.

His first act was to express scepticism about whether Blair, who had taken Britain to war in Afghanistan and Iraq, was the right person to involve in a foundation designed to reconcile Muslims and Christians. However, Tony, who greatly admired Blair for his work on Northern Ireland, insisted on his choice.

When Donlon put out feelers in London, he received encouragement. 'It was clear to me that the Blair people were definitely interested,' he says, 'because they saw not only the possibility of getting a fine headquarters for the foundation, but I think they also saw the possibility of getting big money from Tony Ryan.'

A meeting was put together involving Jonathan Powell, Blair's chief of staff, and Tim Phillips, special adviser to Clinton. Donlon also tapped up Irish diplomatic luminaries such as Noel Dorr, who had once chaired the UN Security Council. With Blair set to retire as Prime Minister in 2007, everything looked set for the establishment of a faith foundation at Lyons.

Fatefully, it was not to be. In October 2006, shortly after Blair announced that he would soon be stepping down, Tony Ryan received a devastating medical diagnosis: he had pancreatic cancer. In many ways the shock of the news was compounded by the nature of the disease itself. His own father, Martin, had died in his mid-fifties of a heart attack, and Tony fully expected that his genetic inheritance would see him go the same way. He had intermittently worried about this fact, taking steps to lighten the load or to consider retirement. There were periodic efforts at weight loss and at giving up the cigars he habitually smoked after dinner. And he walked and walked, sometimes going out five times a day, much to the amusement of his grandchildren, who would take turns to accompany him during the school holidays. The urge to take on new challenges had always pushed Tony back into the front line, but the thought that one day he might simply drop down dead of a heart attack was often with him. These thoughts had been exacerbated at the turn of the century by open-heart surgery, which, he joked to friends, made him a member of the 'zipper club'.

Cancer was not something Tony had expected. Neither did it promise the kind of death that suited his temperament. Active until the end and felled by a heart attack, like his father—that was the kind of ending (as much as any) that Tony had half-wanted and expected. Yet over the next year, as it became clear that there would be no remission, friends and family were struck by how positive and upbeat he remained in fighting to the very end.

Tony's courage was on display from the outset. He received his diagnosis on Friday 13 October 2006. The next morning he went ahead with an interview already scheduled with Marian Finucane on RTE Radio 1. 'It was an incredibly brave interview, because he had just been given a death sentence,' remembers Tony's friend Gerry Power. 'The day after that interview he flew to the United States and started treatment immediately.'

Over the next twelve months Tony would endure painful treatments at the Markey Cancer Center in Kentucky and at the Blackrock Clinic and St Vincent's Hospital in Dublin. Despite the severe physical discomfort, friends noticed a new mellowness in Tony that replaced his characteristic restlessness. He was very happy in his personal life with Martine Head, who lived with him at Lyons and cared for him with great tenderness through his last illness. He also took great pleasure during these last months from the Village at Lyons, which he had developed beside the Grand Canal. Work was continuing in restoring the ruined mill village, with new restaurants already opened.

Tony now enjoyed nothing more each day than pottering down to the village, helped by the steadfast Derek Doyle. He would talk to craftspeople about decorative ceilings and wall plasterwork, painting and detailing, french polishing, and every aspect of colours, materials and tones. Auction catalogues would be scoured for just the right artefacts. Designers and architects would be summoned.

'We'd go trundling around,' John Meagher says, 'and he'd be saying, I'm going to do this here and going to do that there. He was still going over everything a hundred times.' Particular care was taken with the chapel, which, Meagher was astonished to find, was being shored up with vast quantities of reinforced concrete. 'You know that's enough to hold up the QE2,' Meagher told him. Tony blandly replied that it was needed because of all the water nearby. It was only later that Meagher realised that Tony had been making preparations for his final resting place.

By the autumn of 2007, as it became obvious that the end was near, friends and family were called in for what Tony called the 'exit interview'. That humour was characteristic of his mood during those final days. At the last gathering of all the family together, as they departed from Lyons, Tony appeared on the balcony of his bedroom to bestow a papal-like blessing on the crowd below, before dissolving into helpless laughter.

When Jack Ryan, Declan's eleven-year-old son, came in to see his grandfather for the last time, he was offered words of comfort. 'You know I'm going to a better place,' Tony told him.

Jack walked to the window and looked out over the grounds, puzzlement on his face. 'Really?' he said, as his grandfather roared with laughter. 'A better place than Lyons?'

——

Tony Ryan died at home on Wednesday 3 October 2007 at three o'clock in the afternoon. He was seventy-one. In the days that followed, tributes poured in from Ireland and around the world. The Taoiseach, Bertie Ahern, described Tony's contribution as 'immense', and he hailed 'one of the greatest Irish economic success stories.' Michael O'Leary said his former boss was one of the twentieth century's 'greatest Irishmen'. The Ryanair chairman, David Bonderman, praised his 'extraordinary vision'. Tony O'Reilly spoke of how Tony had 'changed the skies of Europe, not just for Irish people, but for all Europeans.' The former Taoiseach Garret FitzGerald noted that 'it was Tony Ryan who showed us how to transcend Ireland's geographical isolation.'

Newspapers around the world reported Tony's death, with widespread coverage particularly in the United States and Britain. American newspapers focused on the story of how the 'son of a train driver' became one of 'Ireland's richest people'. In Britain the emphasis was on the importance of Ryanair. 'Founder of Ryanair whose independent and forceful approach transformed European air travel,' summed up the *Times* obituary. The *Daily Mail*—house newspaper of the English middle classes—put it more pithily: Tony Ryan was the 'maverick who gave us the world'.

In the weeks and months that followed, vast coverage continued in Ireland about every aspect of Tony's life and legacy. Friends and former colleagues filled the opinion pages with vivid recollections. Colour sections and diary pages told stories of passion and great luxury. Business pages drew lessons from his entrepreneurial ups and downs. Politicians and pundits told us what his story meant for Ireland in a globalised world. Yet behind all the stories and pages of analysis there ran a lingering bafflement about how the hell Tony had done it all.

Many years earlier Michael Dargan, former chief executive of Aer Lingus and a Tipperary man, had neatly expressed that sense of bewilderment. 'The magnitude of Tony Ryan's success is baffling. The historian may record it, but he can hardly explain it.'

On one level the task of explaining Tony Ryan might seem

deceptively straightforward. After all, his life appeared to conform to one of the most attractive narratives in human existence: the working-class boy made good. Tony came from a happy home, but his family didn't have much in the way of money or entrepreneurial ambition. When he got a job in Aer Lingus shortly before his father died, his parents were delighted, because a public-service job in the Ireland of the 1950s brought both security and respectability. For a long time Tony seemed happy with those qualities, until a slow epiphany drew him towards the entrepreneurial life and unimagined riches. The story didn't have to turn out that way—the example of his friend and namesake Christy Ryan, who started out in Aer Lingus at the same time and pursued his own entrepreneurial dreams, without much success, was stark proof that it was Tony who made his own life and that it could have turned out entirely other than it did.

By any standard the rise to riches of this train driver's son was an astonishing story. Nevertheless, as Malcolm Gladwell points out in his influential book *Outliers,* even the most brilliant of self-made men come from somewhere. 'People don't rise from nothing,' he writes. 'It makes a difference where and when we grew up.'

That was certainly the case for Tony. It was no coincidence that the transformational figures in the business life of modern Ireland—Tony Ryan, Michael Smurfit and Tony O'Reilly—were all born in the same year, 1936. Ireland might then have seemed the bleakest ground in which to plant entrepreneurial seeds; but in fact the timing was perfect. By the time they were starting out, Ireland was emerging from an era of self-imposed, crippling economic isolation. In the 1950s the forward thinking of politicians like Seán Lemass and public servants such as Ken Whitaker and Todd Andrews began to transform a relatively barren landscape into one cultivated for competition and entrepreneurial activity.

Membership of the European Community from 1973 further extended the drive towards competition and opened up a vast marketplace. Because the free market was a new frontier in Ireland, it presented opportunities for 'change agents', without as many of the rules and constraints that would later develop, and no preceding generation that had already made off with all the best new ideas. Like a young second lieutenant in a war who suddenly finds that all the officers above him have been killed, Tony and his generation unexpectedly found themselves in charge. That was the environment that enabled Smurfit to grow his small business into the world's largest paper-packaging company, and O'Reilly to create a media empire while transforming the global fortunes of the famous but languishing Heinz. Tony was the third great member of that business generation, creating a brand-new industry in airline leasing and initiating a revolution in European air travel. It was quite some legacy for the class of '36.

Timing was also a specific factor for Tony in the arena where he chose to fight his battles. In the 1950s and 60s he had pottered along in the airline industry, just like everyone else in Aer Lingus. When he was asked in the early 70s to get rid of two Jumbo Jets that Aer Lingus had sitting idly on the runway in Dublin, it sparked an idea inside him that perfectly exploited the revolution waiting to happen.

Deregulation of the skies, first in the United States and then in the European Union, transformed the airline industry. Tony was an 'outlier' in that process, first by inventing, alongside his rival Steve Udvar-Házy, the new industry of aircraft leasing and then by forcing competition on the routes across the Irish Sea, and then Europe, with Ryanair. In both these endeavours Tony showed vision, bravery and tenacity, but neither idea could have succeeded a generation earlier.

So too, Tony's background, modest though it was, contributed in a profound way to his brilliance and his success. At the most obvious level it is easy to see how the thrill of fast travel was in his blood. There was a glamour to rail travel in the 1930s; his father's job was one to be admired. What boy would not thrill at the excitement of standing on the footplate of the engine, with the fire blazing and the countryside rushing past in a blur of speed? Trains offered drama and escape in Tony's otherwise drab life.

Aeroplanes simply transformed that experience into one on a global scale.

Tony also learnt about ambition and sacrifice from his father. The family had enjoyed a comfortable life in Limerick Junction, but Martin, in his ambition to be an engine driver, was prepared to uproot his family to miserable accommodation in Thurles. It was the kind of single-mindedness that Tony would apply in his own career, often to the detriment of family life.

Location too was an important factor in Tony's success. Co. Tipperary from the 1930s onwards may not have been an obvious place for ideas of global entrepreneurship to be germinated. But that is to underestimate the impact of Shannon Airport, Co. Clare on the young Tony Ryan. Not only did it offer the chance of a decent job during times of profound economic hardship but it also had an intense effect on his imagination. If riding on trains with his father told him that all of Ireland was his to discover, Shannon said, 'Go see the world.' The transatlantic flights that came in and out of Shannon after 1945 promised a different world from that of 'cosy homesteads' and the 'romping of sturdy children'. The very existence of Shannon Airport seemed to imply that there could be *another* Ireland to dream of.

What did make Tony exceptional was that he turned the dreams he shared with his generation into reality. That came about not because he wanted to make a fortune— although he was happy when he did—but because he had the vision to see where the market was imperfect, the courage to stake his claim, and the tenacity to see the job through. In that regard Tony was the epitome of what it meant to be an entrepreneur.

Research by the global financial services firm Ernst and Young has identified three behavioural characteristics that successful entrepreneurs seem to share: an opportunistic mindset, acceptance of risk and potential failure, and independence and control. These are all attributes that Tony displayed in abundance.

Both GPA and Ryanair were the result of an opportunistic mindset. Someone was always going to create an airline-leasing business; deregulation was always going to lead to competition in the skies. Tony didn't just happen to get there first: he barged his way to the front to stake his claim. Once there, he didn't allow anyone or anything to get in his way until the business succeeded.

Once Tony discovered his entrepreneurial streak, in his thirties, the acceptance of risk and failure became second nature. Critics would point to his accepting too much risk, most notoriously in GPA. Yet it is the failure of GPA as much as its earlier success, together with the later triumph of Ryanair, that marks Tony out as a true entrepreneur. He only knew how to play for high risk. Sometimes he came up 'snake eyes', with disastrous consequences for himself and others. Yet the alternative was safety and caution—a job at Cork Airport instead of at JFK, sticking with Aer Lingus instead of striking out with GPA, closing Ryanair when it was losing millions. That would have made Tony a good manager, not an entrepreneur. Unpredictability and even foolhardiness have always been the prerogatives of the creative genius—'Tony getting all mercurial,' as Michael O'Leary says.

The third characteristic, the determination to control your own life, is in many ways the strangest conundrum. For all his childhood and the early part of his adulthood, Tony was utterly conventional, even passive. There were no stand-out moments of brilliant individuality or commercial activity. Even more unusually, he was not rebellious by nature as a child. Tony was a friendly lad of middling ability who didn't make much impact on the world around him. He married the pretty girl around the corner, got a decent job at Aer Lingus and looked set for an utterly conventional life. In many ways it was Aer Lingus that gave him his real schooling, and eventually it became the establishment against which he rebelled. Tony's entire career from the early 1970s onwards can be seen as an act of rebellion against his parent company. The fact that by the time of Tony's death Ryanair had supplanted Aer Lingus as Ireland's biggest airline seemed to him an inevitable and proper outcome of the process.

Over more than thirty years Tony had scaled the heights and plumbed the depths of the entrepreneurial life. He had built up two businesses that transformed international aviation. Even the one that eventually failed created a new leasing industry that superseded GPA itself in importance. The company's legacy is that Ireland remains the centre for half the world's aircraft-leasing and aircraft-financing business. As to Ryanair, few would doubt that it transformed the lives of millions of ordinary people. For the first time, air travel became the right of the many instead of the privilege of the few. As the *Sun,* Britain's best-selling newspaper, put it the day after Tony's death:

> Little did we know way back in the 1980s that we would soon be flying abroad for next to nothing. Tony Ryan helped ensure this by setting up Ryanair in 1985 and driving down air fares. He died yesterday but his spirit lives on in the sky.

A NOTE ON SOURCES

This book was written primarily from the papers of Tony Ryan held at Lyons Demesne in Co. Kildare. The papers were well maintained during Tony's lifetime, using for the most part a system of subject and name files. There was also a separate system that recorded daily telephone calls, including personal messages. Because the papers are privately held I have not included references in the text, as these would serve no useful purpose for historians or general readers.

In addition to consulting the archives, a number of Tony's family, friends and former colleagues generously made themselves available for interview. These included Declan Ryan, the late Simon Ryan, Kell Ryan, Cillian Ryan, Conor Ryan, Ed Walsh, John Meagher, Des O'Malley, Ann Reihill, Margaret Downes, Ken Rohan, Olive Braiden, James Meyler, Derek Doyle, Arthur Finan, Phyllis Finan, Gerry Power, Tom Ryan, David Kennedy, Neil Gleeson, Robert Greenspon, Niall Weldon, Bronwyn Conroy, Mick O'Carroll, Peter Ledbetter, Jim King, Seán Braiden, Margaret Clandillon, Mairead Mason, Seán Donlon, Graham Boyd, Joe Clarkin, Derek O'Brien, Fergus Armstrong, Laurence Crowley, Gerry McEvoy, Pat O'Brien, Mark Hely Hutchinson, David Bonderman, Denis O'Brien and Michael O'Leary. A number of other interviewees spoke off the record.

Tony appeared frequently in the news, so contemporary newspapers have been an invaluable resource, particularly the *Irish Times* and the *Irish Independent.*

In addition, the following books and articles have been especially useful: **Chapter 1:** Michael Hallinan (ed.), *Tipperary County: People and Places* (1993); William J. Hayes, *Thurles: A Guide to the Cathedral Town* (1999); Albert Maher, *Signalman's*

Memories: Railway Life in Rural Ireland (1998). **Chapter 2:** On the development of Shannon and the transatlantic route: Mike Cronin, *Doesn't Time Fly?: Aer Lingus: Its History* (2011). On the early days in the airport and the life of a traffic assistant: Valerie Sweeney, *Shannon Airport: A Unique Story of Survival* (2004). **Chapter 3:** On the state of the airline industry in the 1970s: Bernard Share, *Flight of the Iolar: Aer Lingus Experience, 1936–86* (1986); Bartholomew Elias, *Airport and Aviation Security: US Policy and Strategy in the Age of Global Terrorism* (2009); Mark T. Berger, *The Battle for Asia: From Decolonization to Globalization* (2004). Competing claims on the GPA start-up are covered in Siobhán Creaton's excellent history *Ryanair* (2007 edition). **Chapter 4:** Tony Ryan commissioned a short history of GPA in the mid-1980s, and I am grateful to its author for permission to consult that unpublished text. **Chapter 5:** On Kilboy: Mike Bunn, *Four Farms.* On Irelandia: Alan Ruddock, *Michael O'Leary: A Life in Full Flight* (2008 edition). On the deregulation of the airline industry: T. A. Heppenheimer, *Turbulent Skies: The History of Commercial Aviation* (1995); Sean Barrett, *Deregulation and the Airline Business in Europe: Selected Readings* (2009); Stephen Breyer, 'Airline deregulation revisited', *Business Week*, 20 January 2011. **Chapter 6:** On the *Sunday Tribune*: John Horgan, *Irish Media: A Critical History since 1922*; David Kenny and Nóirín Hegarty (eds.), *The Trib: Highlights from the 'Sunday Tribune'* (2011). On the aircraft-leasing industry: Edward Cahill's indispensable *Corporate Financial Crisis in Ireland* (1997). **Chapter 7:** On the Air Transport Bill (1984), and the deregulation of the Irish airline industry more generally, I follow Barrett, *Deregulation and the Airline Business in Europe.* Barrett's fine book has the advantage of being written not only by a leading analyst of the airline industry but also by one of the foremost advocates of deregulation at the time. On Ryanair: Ruddock, *Michael O'Leary*; Creaton, *Ryanair.* **Chapter 8:** On Tony Ryan's personal life: Emily Hourican, 'Beauty and bounty at Renaissance prince Tony Ryan's court', *Sunday Independent,* 10 July 2011; Lucinda O'Sullivan, 'We'll greatly miss grace and beauty of Miranda', *Sunday Independent,*

2 January 2011. On Japanese negotiations: 'A History of GPA'. On ILFC: Cahill, *Corporate Financial Crisis in Ireland*. **Chapter 10:** Financial figures for GPA in 1992 are drawn from Cahill, *Corporate Financial Crisis in Ireland*. **Chapter 11:** The collapse of the IPO is subjected to characteristically forensic analysis by Cahill in *Corporate Financial Crisis in Ireland*; 'Crash landing', *Sunday Times*, 21 June 1992; Christopher Brown, *Crash Landing: An Inside Account of the Fall of GPA* (2009). **Chapter 12:** On the two-airline policy: Frank Lahiffe, *Séamus Brennan: A Life in Government*; Creaton, *Ryanair*; Ruddock, *Michael O'Leary*. On Southwest Airlines: Matthew Brelis, 'Herb's way', *Boston Globe*, 5 November 2000. **Chapter 13:** On the history and restoration of the Lyons estate: *Lyons Demesne: A Georgian Treasure Restored to the Nation*; 'Lyons Demesne: Works from the collection of the late Dr Tony Ryan' (Christie's, 14 July 2011); Bunn, *Four Farms*; 'Kentucky blue blood', *Architectural Digest*, June 2006. **Chapter 14:** Creaton, *Ryanair*; Ruddock, *Michael O'Leary*. **Chapter 15:** Malcolm Gladwell, *Outliers: The Story of Success* (2008); Anthony J. Mayo et al., *Entrepreneurs, Managers and Leaders: What the Airline Industry Can Teach Us about Leadership* (2009); John Byrne, *World Changers: 25 Entrepreneurs Who Changed Business as We Knew It* (2012); Cahill, *Corporate Financial Crisis in Ireland*; 'Entrepreneurs', *Economist*, 14 January 2012.

ACKNOWLEDGEMENTS

For help in a variety of ways, I wish to thank the following: the late Michael Adams, Bertie Ahern, Simon Ball, Kate Breslin, Maurice Bric, Robert Brigham, Anthony Carragher, Karina Daly, Ronan Fanning, Claire Joyce, Jim King, Marion McGowan, Denis O'Brien, Michael O'Leary, Fintan O'Toole, Michael Staunton, Peter Strafford, Harry White; the President, faculty and students at Bard College, particularly Deirdre d'Albertis, Michèle Dominy, Peter Gadsby, Stephen Graham, Mark Lytle, Wyatt Mason and Karen Sullivan; archivist of the Ryan papers, Áine Mc Hugh; Kathryn Aldous, Brian Murphy and my outstanding researcher Niamh Puirséil for reading the first draft; Michael Gill, Fergal Tobin, Deirdre Rennison Kunz, Teresa Daly, Jen Patton and the team at Gill & Macmillan; Georgina Capel at Capel and Land; and Kathryn Aldous, Elizabeth Aldous and my mother and late father for their constant support and encouragement. Finally I would like to thank Declan Ryan for asking me to write this biography and giving me the freedom to get on with the job—a testament to his confidence that Tony Ryan's legacy will endure.

Richard Aldous
Annandale-on-Hudson, New York

INDEX